NATURAL
DRILLS IN EXPRESSION

WITH

SELECTIONS

A SERIES OF EXERCISES COLLOQUIAL AND CLASSICAL,
BASED UPON THE PRINCIPLES OF REFERENCE TO
EXPERIENCE AND COMPARISON, AND CHOSEN FOR
THEIR PRACTICAL WORTH IN DEVELOPING POWER
AND NATURALNESS IN READING AND SPEAKING,
WITH ILLUSTRATIVE SELECTIONS FOR PRACTISE

BY

ARTHUR EDWARD PHILLIPS

Author of "Effective Speaking;" Director, Department of Public Speaking, the Theological Seminary of the Evangelical Lutheran Church at Chicago;
Principal, Phillips School of Oratory, Chicago

———————

CHICAGO
THE NEWTON COMPANY
1913

COPYRIGHT, 1909

BY

ARTHUR EDWARD PHILLIPS

All rights reserved

CONTENTS.

PART I—DRILLS

PART II—ILLUSTRATIVE SELECTIONS

CONTENTS

CONTENTS

CONTENTS   vii

EXPRESSION AND THE GENERAL ENDS—

CLEARNESS—

IMPRESSIVENESS—

BELIEF—

ACTION—

ENTERTAINMENT—

INDEX OF DOMINANT TONES, PROMINENCE AND PAUSE

INTRODUCTION

THE VALUE OF THE TONE DRILLS

The reading aloud of poetry and prose is a process different from that of ordinary conversation. In natural conversation everything is spontaneous. There are real objective and subjective causes, and in all likelihood we are unconscious of delivery. But when reading aloud we have not these real causes and are conscious of our processes. And even in speaking extempore it is the exception to find the speaker free from this consciousness and not artificial.

Exactly here we find the office of the teacher of expression. It is to so assist the reader or speaker that he will be able to express the thoughts and feelings as effectively as in spontaneous conversation; in fact, more so.

How is Vocal Expression to attain this? How is the teacher to proceed? What would common sense tell us? What does the best pedagogics say? What does psychology say? We must proceed from the simple to the complex, from the easy to the hard. In expression what is entitled to be called simple? It surely will be those things that we do and do constantly. Those things that we know, those things with which we are familiar; those things that are within our experience.

We set before the student these lines from Tennyson and ask him to read them:

Ah, blessed vision! blood of God!
My spirit beats her mortal bars,
As down dark tides the glory slides,
. And star-like mingles with the stars.

What a miserable failure he makes! Why? Because he
is asked to give spontaneous expression to the thoughts and
feelings of another, couched in words, style and arrangement
foreign to his own experience. In the case of the average
person who for the first time tries to read such language as
this, the words and their arrangement, the strangeness of it
all, the marked difference between the phraseology and that
in daily use—all these erect a barrier which, without assistance, it seems impossible to surmount. A student looks at
Tennyson's lines and says to himself, consciously or unconsciously, "I never said 'blessed vision,' I never said 'Blood
of God,' I never said 'my spirit beats her mortal bars,' and
I never heard any one else speak them—these sensations and
this phraseology are all outside of my experience!" Hence
he flounders through it in a manner that would make Tennyson weep.

What then must be done? The student has told us that
it all seems outside of his experience. Then, if that is so,
before we can attain true naturalness we must show him that
this phraseology and these sensations are not so foreign as
they seem. How can this be done? Very simply. And
therein is to be found the core of the true method of instruction. We can get the student to tell these thoughts and
feelings well only *by likening them to something in his own
experience*. They must be likened to something that the
student has himself said or done or felt, or heard, or seen.
The complex must be reduced to the simple, the unknown
must be translated into the known, the unfamiliar must be
shown to be based on the familiar. *The primary problem,*

then, is the recalling and the making vivid to the pupil his own experiences and showing their resemblance, in essence, to literature. The accomplishment of these ends is the main purpose of this book.

For over ten years the author has used in class and in private instruction the major portion of the drills in expression set forth in the following pages. During that time he has found nothing so effective in attaining satisfactory results in speaking and reading as these Tone Drills.

The interest with which a class seizes upon these Tone Drills, the fact that the colloquial examples come within ordinary experience, that the Drills enable even a large class to be given personal recitation and criticism at every session, that they permit of chorus drill with the retention of each pupil's individuality, that they make vivid to the pupil the objectivity of utterance, that the colloquial and the classical are placed in constant relation—all these things combine to make the Tone Drills the most valuable of exercises for truth and naturalness in expression.

The value of the Tone Drills might be summarized thus:

The Tone Drills help to *rid the pupil of artificiality and secure naturalness.* They do so by coming vividly into the pupil's experience and by showing him that the classical in literature has its similarities and equivalents in his own sensations, and vice versa. He sees that the colloquial "what a magnificent sunset!" (See Tone Drill 1c) and the classical "what a piece of work is man!" (see Tone Drill 1d) have an underlying relationship of feeling.

The Tone Drills *develop spontaneity.* They enable a student to respond more quickly and more vividly to a given sentiment. In the phrase "O, look at those lovely roses, look at them!" (see Tone Drill 1a) the student finds the thought, the feeling and the phraseology a part of his own vivid experience, and almost all difficulty of responsiveness vanishes. *He discovers himself expressionally.*

The Tone Drills enable the teacher to give each pupil of a class *individual drill and individual criticism at every session.* Many of the Drills take no longer than twenty to thirty seconds for oral expression, and yet each Drill offers a field, *complete in itself,* for criticism upon the expression of the feeling, and also, if desired, for criticisms of articulation, use of voice, attitude, facial expression, gesture, emphasis and pause. It is surprising how much can be driven home by a capable teacher with these half minute drills.

The Tone Drills impress upon the pupil the *infinite variety in expression.* By the constant transition of feeling demanded by the various Tones, the pupil sees the utter falseness of monotony, and becomes a severe critic of himself. A student cannot pass from Amazement to Anger, from Anger to Awe, from Awe to Annoyance without vividly appreciating the variety of utterance.

The Tone Drills furnish an *excellent drill for the voice.* In a ten to fifteen-minute practice of the Drills the voice can be given definite and valuable exercise. If vocal attack is needed, the pupils can be given drills under the feelings that demand attack such as Command, Authority, Assertion, Denial, and the like; if volume of voice is needed, the pupil may be given drills calling for emotions of breadth such as those under Sublimity, Defiance, and so on; if musical quality, drills under Solemnity, Sadness, and similar feelings; if brightness, drills under Gayety, Mirth, and the like, and so on through every phase of voice culture. (See suggestions at end of Tone Drills.)

The Tone Drills win the *instant interest of the pupil.* Coming vividly into his life, associated with real experience, he feels the zest of true states, and has the enjoyment of creative work. Instead of wishing the teacher would pass him by he is eager to be called upon. There is aroused the *desire to do.*

The Tone Drills *realize the best psychology in respect to instruction.* The principles set forth by Herbert Spencer and insisted upon by William James in their respective works on psychology and education are realized in these Tone Drills. The process of reaching the complex through the simple, development by the law of comparison and inference, the law of the association of ideas and the law of habit, all are recognized in the Tone Drills.

The Tone Drills *economize time* by permitting *chorus drills in class without ill effects.* Each example, not exceeding a minute, and dealing with one phase of feeling, enables the pupil to give *his own rendering,* and the chorus effect is *unity with variety.* One pupil is more intense than another, one's solemnity differs a little from another's, because of different personality, yet *each has felt the specific feeling desired* and each has made his *own expressional effort.*

The Tone Drills *reveal the expressional faults of the pupil* not only to the teacher but to the *pupil himself.* Criticism, therefore, comes with the force of confirmation, and is double in its power.

The Tone Drills help to secure *the true expression of feeling* in both speech and literature. Practice upon the expression of the feelings as they are found in our every day life gives the student, in time, a sure grasp of emotional states, he can distinguish the false from the true, and, also, he can determine accurately the *degree* of feeling.

The Tone Drills help to *train the imagination.* They impel the student not only to recall past experiences, but to reconstruct and combine them. The student is impelled to see "the lovely roses," "the magnificent sunset," to hear "the beautiful music" with its "purity" and "sweetness." He finds himself picturing "mountains behind mountains." Now he is defying soldiers, now at a convention, now comparing costumes or constructing a street episode. In the Classical examples he is building in his mind "the cloud capped towers, the gorgeous palaces," or sympathizing with the faithful Adam in "As You Like It," or he is on the field of battle with Richard III. Constantly there is a brief but pointed call for the exercise of the imagination, both representative and constructive.

The Tone Drills *rid the pupil of self consciousness.* The Drills come so vividly into his experience, bring him into states in which he has been so essentially objective that he *forgets self* in the *desire to tell.* This realizes one of the most important requisites in the pedagogics of expression.

The Tone Drills *develop a love for the best literature* and develop it in a *natural way.* Distaste frequently arises from the perception of difficulty; when a thing looks hard to attain we shun it, but when it is seen that there is comparatively little obstruction, that a slight exercise of the reason and the imagination will lead the student into the expressional joys of the great writers and poets—will make them see what they saw, feel what they felt—then there arises in the student a genuine appreciation of the best literature. The Tone Drills accomplish this desirable end by showing the student that *the complex is nothing but the simple refined or combined,* that underneath the strange phraseology lie experiences and ideas that much resemble his own, and experiences and ideas that give pleasure.

The Tone Drills develop an *appreciation of the technique of expression.* They attain this end by ridding expression of all stiffness, formality and complexity. The pupil finds the avenues of expression replete with pleasing experiences, and not, as he thought, a long lane with almost insurmountable obstacles.

The Tone Drills aid in the *development of the power of*

written expression. A ready responsiveness to the ideas of the printed page means an increased artistic sensitiveness. The Tone Drills have associated conception with expression, and the effect of this is not only to create a desire to set down our ideas in writing but to increase the power to express an idea freely and faithfully. *Feeling is the basis of style.*

The Tone Drills help to *develop personal power.* They engender that animation and enthusiasm that attracts and wins. People are drawn to us and influenced by life, energy, the manifestation of vitality, and these are materially quickened and strengthened by the practice of the Tone Drills.

The Tone Drills impel the pupil to a *more thorough and accurate analysis of literature.* Constantly realizing by actual practice on the Drills, that underneath all phraseology lies not only thought but also feeling, the pupil finds himself seeking the complete emotional conception of all he seeks to interpret or to read. He is alert for all those delicate shades and distinctions of tone which reveal the picture or situation in its completeness and tell us of the artist. He knows, through the Tone Drills, that not only every phrase but every word in literature has its true tone, and he will not be satisfied until he has seen and felt the full significance of all.

The Tone Drills achieve the *coördination of the entire expressional organism.* Coming into the experience of the pupil vividly and arousing objective desire, the pupil finds himself putting the whole man into the expression. The eye, the face, the body, the tone, the attitude all work together, and the result is a coördinate interpretation.

It will be seen from the foregoing details how wide is the scope of usefulness of the Tone Drills, and the author can only reiterate that he has found them the most valuable of all methods for the development of the fundamentals of expressional power.

THE TONE DRILLS.

1. *In all Spoken Language there are not only Thoughts but Feelings.*—In "John, go right home this moment," there is the thought that John is to go right home, and there is the feeling with which it is said. We can say "the soldier smote the man," so as to show pity for the smitten, or anger at the smiter, or indifference; can, in fact, always say the same words always telling the same thought (that the soldier smote the man), but showing a different feeling.

2. *The Great Failure in Reading and Speaking is the Inability to Rightly Render the Feeling.*—For one who fails to effectively express thought there are a thousand who fail to effectively express feeling. It is the common remark of the artistic reader that he has never fully satisfied himself in the portrayal of the emotions that his selections demand.

3. *Feeling is the Soul of Utterance.*—Without the true rendering of feeling there will be monotony. Feeling gives life, energy, variety, interest.

4. *The Symbol that Conveys Feeling to the Listener is Tone.*—Listening outside a room we hear voices and though we can not distinguish the words, we are very positive in regard to the feeling of the speakers. We say one is angry, another is laughing, and so on. As by our premises we do not hear the words, but catch only vocal sounds, we can make our conclusions only from these sounds. The something in these sounds which proclaims the feeling we call tone.

5. *The Best Way to Develop the Power to Portray Feeling (Oral Responsiveness) is to Practice the Rendering of Familiar Phrases, Sentences, and Selections that at once Appeal to the Students' Experience, thus Presenting the Feeling or Tone very Vividly to Him.*—Common sense will readily admit that the more simply, the more clearly, the

more strikingly a task is put before a student the more likely will that task be effectively performed.

6. *The Best Way to Lead the Student into the Correct Interpretation of the Higher Literature is to Show Him Its Relationship to the Experiences of Daily Life.*—When it is perceived that underlying the language of the classic authors are found emotions and thoughts similar to those of every day experience, at once, the difficulty of interpretation is largely overcome. This perception of relationship is attained by placing together the colloquial and the classical.

THE MANNER OF USE OF THE TONE DRILLS

In the use of the Tone Drills seek for Naturalness, Vividness, Completeness, Ease and Grace, and the Perception of the Relationship of the Colloquial to the Classical.

NATURALNESS. Aim to secure a rendering of each example that would be *identified instantly as manifesting the feeling demanded.* This is attained best by having the student tell the example to a listener, either a fellow student, the teacher or the class as a whole. Naturalness is also secured by drill in *chorus.* In this simultaneous work the self-conscious student loses his self-consciousness. Here as in individual drill each student should be objective and speak the example to some particular person or persons. A further aid to naturalness is to have the student compose for himself a colloquial drill of not more than a dozen words for each tone, and have him orally express it.

VIVIDNESS. Aim to secure *degrees of intensity,* as, angry, angrier, angriest. This is attained by spurring the student to stronger endeavor. Vividness is also attained by having the student search for examples of the more intense degrees of the various tones.

COMPLETENESS. Aim to secure a rendering that is *complete,* that brings into play all the organs of expression that legitimately can aid in the interpretation. This is attained by having the student express the example silently, using only facial expression, gesture and attitude; this to be followed by expression aloud, all the organs of utterance coöperating; finally secure expression with regard not only to the feeling but to the pause, emphasis and articulation.

EASE AND GRACE. Aim to secure a rendering of each example that attains the *maximum of effectiveness with the minimum of effort,* and which, at same time, so coördinates as to make a harmonic whole; in other words, aim to secure a rendering that is *artistic.* This is attained by frequency of rendering, by seeking for variety of render-ing, and by criticism in respect to things overdone, or not adequately done, or left undone.

PERCEPTION OF RELATIONSHIP OF THE COLLOQUIAL TO THE CLASSICAL. Aim to develop in the student a vivid appre-ciation of the underlying kinship between the colloquial and the classical. Let him see that the strange, complex or exalted, is after all, the familiar, the simple and the normal, differently clothed, refined or combined. This end is attained by drill on the Colloquial, followed by alternate renderings of the Classical and Colloquial, Colloquial and Classical. Also by having the student make a *tonal analysis* of selections as explained and illustrated under Interpretation (pages 75 to 83).

Always the teacher must cause the student to realize that his aim in speaking and reading is *objective*—to convey the thought and feeling to some particular person or persons.

NOTE.—Practice the most those exercises which are executed least effectively. Thus, a student may be excellent in the expression of indignation and kindred emotions, but poor in the expression of admiration, love and the like. Let him give special attention to the latter group and so on with all the feeling in which he is expressionally weak.

THE TONE DRILLS

EXAMPLES ILLUSTRATING THE TONE SYMBOLS—THOSE
SYMBOLS WHICH PICTURE OR EXPRESS THE
VARIOUS STATES OF FEELING

1. ADMIRATION:

Colloquial.

a—O, look at those lovely roses! Look at them!

b—I never listened to such beautiful music in all my life!
The purity of it! the sweetness of it!

c—What a magnificent sunset! Isn't it glorious!

Classical.

d—What a piece of work is man! How noble in reason!
how infinite in faculty; in form, and moving, how
express and admirable! in action, how like an
angel! in apprehension, how like a god! the beauty
of the world! the paragon of animals!

SHAKESPEARE, *Hamlet,* ii, 2.

2. ADMISSION:

Colloquial.

a—Well, yes, if you want to know, I was there.

b—I admit that I didn't state the case plainly.

c—I grant it, you are right.

Classical.

d—When I spoke that I was ill-temper'd, too.

SHAKESPEARE, *Julius Caesar,* iv, 3.

3. ADORATION: (See Admiration, Reverence, Affection.)

Colloquial.

a—Mother, dear mother, I adore the very ground you tread on.

Classical.

b—O speak again, bright angel, for thou art
As glorious to this night, being o'er my head,
As is a winged messenger of heaven.
                    SHAKESPEARE, *Romeo and Juliet,* ii, 2.

4. ADVICE:

Colloquial.

a—Of course, it's your money, and you can do what you like with it, but if I were you I would save it.

b—If I were you I would wear your pink, it is so much prettier than the red.

c—My advice is, gentlemen, to throw this whole thing up; if we succeed it will do us no good, and if we fail it will do us harm.

Classical.

d—I'll tell you what you shall do. Our general's wife is now the general; confess yourself freely to her; importune her help to put you in your place again.
                    SHAKESPEARE, *Othello,* ii, 3.

5. AFFECTION:

Colloquial.

a—Hello, old chum, I'm so glad to see you; how well you are looking! Shake again!

b—Good-by, mother. Hope you'll have a lovely trip. Don't mind me, I'll be all right.

c—Come here, little sister, and let me take you on my knees. You are the sweetest little, dearest little— um-um (kissing her).

Classical.

d—The dearest friend to me, the kindest man,
The best condition'd and unwearied spirit
In doing courtesies.

> SHAKESPEARE, *Merchant of Venice,* iii, 2.

e—This royal throne of kings, this sceptered isle,
This earth of majesty, this seat of Mars,
This other Eden, demi-paradise ; . . .
This blessed plot, this earth, this realm, this England !

> SHAKESPEARE, *Richard II,* ii, 1.

6. AGITATION : (See Excitement, Fear.)

7. AGGRIEVANCE : (See Reproach.)

Colloquial.

a—I feel hurt. It's unkind.

b—I stood by you through thick and thin, and now you turn around and abuse me. It's mean, to say the least.

c—Yes, sir, I introduced that gentleman to this house ; I procured him a good position, and now, sir, when he has risen to power he turns upon me. That's gratitude for you.

Classical.

d— Brutus hath riv'd my heart :
A friend should bear his friend's infirmities,
But Brutus makes mine greater than they are.

> SHAKESPEARE, *Julius Caesar,* iv, 3.

8. AGONY :

Colloquial.

a—O, open the door. You are crushing my finger ! O-O-O !

b—O, mother, the pain is awful ! O, my head, my head !

Classical.

c—O Desdemona ! dead ? Desdemona ! dead ? oh, oh !

> SHAKESPEARE, *Othello,* v, 2.

d—O all you host of heaven! O earth! what else?
And shall I couple hell? O fie! Hold, my heart;
And you, my sinews, grow not instant old,
But bear me stiffly up!

SHAKESPEARE, *Hamlet,* i, 5.

9. AMAZEMENT:

Colloquial.

a—Gone to be married. Married! Well, did you ever!

b—What! Our club beaten? It's impossible. Beaten?
I can't believe it.

c—What? The society will lose its charter? The members will be turned out? Disgraced? I am amazed!

Classical.

d—   What! fifty of my followers at a clap!
Within a fortnight?

SHAKESPEARE, *King Lear,* i, 4.

e—Gone to be married! Gone to swear a peace!
False blood to false blood joined! Gone to be
friends!
Shall Lewis have Blanch? and Blanch those provinces?

SHAKESPEARE, *King John,* iii, 1.

10. AMBITION: (See Determination, Assertion, Admiration.)

Colloquial.

a—Let us make this the greatest organization in America. We can, we will.

Classical.

b—We'll both together lift our heads to heaven;
And never more abase our sight so low,
As to vouchsafe one glance unto the ground.

SHAKESPEARE, *Henry VI,* II, i, 2.

11. ANGER:

Colloquial.

a—You cur! Strike that little boy again and I'll thrash
you on the spot!

b—Angry? Who wouldn't be angry? He called me a thief.

c—Keep calm? I'll not keep calm; do you think I shall see my honor attacked and not resent it? O, you—you—.

Classical.

d—Villains! you did not so, when your vile daggers
Hack'd one another in the sides of Caesar:
You show'd your teeth like apes, and fawn'd like hounds,
And bow'd like bondmen, kissing Caesar's feet;
Whilst . . . Casca like a cur, behind,
Struck Caesar on the neck. O you flatterers!

SHAKESPEARE, *Julius Caesar,* v, 1.

12. ANGUISH: (See Agony, Remorse.)

13. ANNOYANCE:

Colloquial.

a—I told you once. How many times do you want me to tell you?

b—Will you cease annoying me just for one minute? I've no patience with this sort of thing; it's childish.

Classical.

c—O, I could divide myself and go to buffets, for moving such a dish of skimmed milk with so honorable an action!

SHAKESPEARE, *Henry IV,* I, ii, 3.

14. ANTITHESIS: (See Comparison.)

Colloquial.

a—That's good, but this is bad.

b—George is sharp, Will is dull; George is thoughtful, Will is careless.

Classical.

c— Let's kill him boldly but not wrathfully;
Let's carve him as a dish fit for the gods,
Not hew him as a carcass fit for hounds.

SHAKESPEARE, *Julius Caesar,* ii, 1.

15. ANXIETY:

Colloquial.

a—Sh! here comes the teacher! If she catches us here
we are in for it. Listen! That's her footstep!
O, what will we do? Hark! She's going to the
next room. No—O, dear!

Classical.

b—Alack! I am afraid they have awak'd
And 'tis not done:—the attempt, and not the deed,
Confounds us. Hark! I laid their daggers ready,
He could not miss them.

SHAKESPEARE, *Macbeth,* ii, 2.

16. APPEAL: (See Entreaty, Coaxing.)

Colloquial.

a—The others wouldn't, but you will. O, do, please.

b—I appeal to you, sir, was it fair? Would you have
submitted to this treatment yourself?

Classical.

c—   I beseech you,
Wrest once the law to your authority:
To do a great right, do a little wrong.

SHAKESPEARE, *Merchant of Venice,* iv, 1.

17. APPREHENSION: (See Fear.)

Colloquial.

a—I am afraid it's lost; I guess we are in for it.

b—O what if we have made a mistake!

Classical.

c—   What if it be a poison?
SHAKESPEARE, *Romeo and Juliet,* iv, 3.

*d—*How if, when I am laid in the tomb,
I wake before the time that Romeo
Come to redeem me? There's a fearful point!
SHAKESPEARE, *Romeo and Juliet,* iv, 3.

18. APPRECIATION: (See Praise.)

Colloquial.

*a—*I can assure you I appreciate your kindness.
*b—*That was a very generous thing to do, and I shall not forget it. You are real kind.

Classical.

*c—*More is thy due than more than all can pay.
SHAKESPEARE, *Macbeth,* i, 4.

19. APPROVAL:

Colloquial.

*a—*That's splendid.
*b—*That's the very thing.
*c—*I approve of it in every respect.

Classical.

*d—*Well spoken; with good accent, and good discretion.
SHAKESPEARE, *Hamlet,* ii, 2.

20. APOLOGY: (See Frankness.)

Colloquial.

*a—*I am so sorry I did it.
*b—*I want to apologize for my conduct; it was unbecoming a gentleman.

Classical.

*c—*Give me your pardon, sir; I have done you wrong.
SHAKESPEARE, *Hamlet,* v, 2.

21. ARGUING:

Colloquial.

a—You say he did; I say he didn't. Haven't I eyes? Can't I see?

b—If he was in New York, he could not be in Chicago. And if he was not in Chicago, how can he be charged with this crime?

c—Grant your premises and your conclusion follows. But I question your premises.

d—Now your position is this: If Rogers wins it is genius, if Wilson wins, it is talent. Now is there any rhyme or reason in such a statement? No, and you know there isn't. Arguments? You haven't any.

e—Now, my dear sir, don't get excited. I am only trying to prove that what he said was not in accordance with his policy, that's all. There's no need of your losing your temper over it. Keep cool, keep cool.

Classical.

f—Say, Warwick was our anchor; what of that?
And Montague our topmast; what of him?
Our slaughter'd friends the tackles; what of these?
Why, is not Oxford here another anchor?
And Somerset another goodly mast?
SHAKESPEARE, *Henry VI*, III, v, 4.

22. ARROGANCE: (See Assertion, Admiration, Contempt.)

Colloquial.

a—There is not a person here my equal. I, I am above you all.

Classical.

b—   I am Sir Oracle,
And when I ope my lips, let no dog bark!
SHAKESPEARE, *Merchant of Venice*, iii, 3.

23. ASSENT:

Colloquial.

a—Why, yes, of course you may have it. It's a pleasure to be able to accommodate you.

b—Can you have this pen? Well—um—yes, I guess you may have it.

Classical.

c—Yes, Shylock, I will seal unto this bond.
SHAKESPEARE, *Merchant of Venice*, i, 3.

24. ASSERTION:

Colloquial.

a—That is not so. It is. It is not. It is. It is not.

b—Stop that. I'll not. You shall. I'll not. You shall. I'll not.

c—What that man says is false. He did do it. I saw him do it, and he knows he did it.

Classical.

d— I was born free as Caesar; so were you:
We both have fed as well; and we can both
Endure the winter's cold as well as he.
SHAKESPEARE, *Julius Caesar*, i, 2.

25. ASSURANCE:

Colloquial.

a—Let's have a look; I won't take it; upon my honor I won't.

b—You needn't be frightened. They'll treat you splendidly.

c—I assure you, you will be perfectly safe.

Classical.

d— I will not touch thine eyes
For all the treasure that thine uncle owes.
SHAKESPEARE, *King John*, iv, 1.

26. AUTHORITY: (See Command, Anger.)

Colloquial.

a—Go right home this instant. Do you hear me? Go
right home.

b—I command you to take your seat.

Classical.

c—Once more, on pain of death, all men depart.

SHAKESPEARE, *Romeo and Juliet,* i, 1.

27. AVERSION: (See Contempt.)

Colloquial.

a—I can't bear him. He's disgusting.

Classical.

b—   O, he's as tedious
As is a tired horse, a railing wife;
Worse than a smoky house: I had rather live
With cheese and garlick, in a windmill, far,
Than feed on cates, and have him talk to me,
In any summer-house in Christendom.

SHAKESPEARE, *Henry IV,* I, iii, 1.

28. AWE: (See Solemnity, Sadness, Sublimity.)

Colloquial.

a—Hush, boys! They are praying.

b—Don't speak, he's dying!

Classical.

c—Silence, how dead! and darkness, how profound!
   *   *   *   *   *   *   *
Creation sleeps!

YOUNG, *Night Thoughts.*

d—'Tis now the very witching time of night;
When churchyards yawn.

SHAKESPEARE, *Hamlet,* iii, 2.

29. BELITTLING: (See Dispraising.)

Colloquial.

a—Call that good? Why, it's the poorest picture I ever
looked at.

Classical.

b— I gave it to a youth,–
A kind of boy; a little scrubbed boy.

SHAKESPEARE, *Merchant of Venice,* v, 1.

30. BENEDICTION:

Colloquial.

a—May God's blessing accompany you.

b—Good luck to you.

Classical.

c— May he live
Longer than I have time to tell his years!
Ever beloved, and loving, may his rule be!
And, when old Time shall lead him to his end,
Goodness and he fill up one monument!

SHAKESPEARE, *Henry VIII,* ii, 1.

d— Hail to thee, lady! and the grace of Heaven,
Before, behind thee, and on every hand,
Enwheel thee round!

SHAKESPEARE, *Othello,* ii, 1.

31. BITTERNESS:

Colloquial.

a—I can never forgive him. He cut me to the soul.

Classical.

b—And is it thus? repays he my deep service
With such contempt? Made I him king for this?

SHAKESPEARE, *Richard III,* iv, 2.

32. BOASTING:

Colloquial.

a—Bah, we could beat them left handed.

b—Bah, you talk of fighting. Wait till you see us, then
you will know what fighting is.

c—One American is equal to three Frenchmen any time.

Classical.

d—   I'll play the orator as well as Nestor;
    Deceive more slily than Ulysses could;
    And, like a Sinon, take another Troy.

        SHAKESPEARE, *King Henry VI,* iii, 2.

33. BOLDNESS: (See Defiance.)

Colloquial.

a—Whether I get thrashed for it or not, I'll go right up
to the teacher and tell her what I think of her.

b—Yes, sir, I went right up to the President and con-
fronted him.

Classical.

c—   Let it fall . . . though the fork invade
    The region of my heart.

        SHAKESPEARE, *King Lear,* i, 1.

34. BRAVERY:

Colloquial.

a—It means death, sir, but I'll go.

b—What if there be ten to one, I'll fight.

Classical.

c—Once more unto the breach, dear friends, once more;
    Or close the wall up with our English dead!

        SHAKESPEARE, *Henry V,* iii, 1.

35. CALLING:

Colloquial.

a—Do you hear me up there? Are you in the tower?
    George! George! Come down, I say!

Classical.

b—   Awake! Awake!
    Ring the alarm-bell:—Murder and treason!
    Banquo, and Donalbain! Malcolm! Awake!

        SHAKESPEARE, *Macbeth,* ii, 3.

36. CALM: (See Repose.)

Colloquial.

a—Everything is so calm, so quiet, so still.

Classical.

b—

I feel within me
A peace above all earthly dignities,
A still and quiet conscience.

SHAKESPEARE, *Henry VIII,* iii, 2.

37. CAREFULNESS: (See Caution.)

Colloquial.

a—Be steady—so—steady.

b—There, I'll place that exactly on the line—so.

Classical.

c—

I'll observe his looks;
I'll tent him to the quick.

SHAKESPEARE, *Hamlet,* ii, 2.

38. CAUTION: (See Warning.)

Colloquial.

a—Look out there, or you'll fall: go slow; steady.

b—We'll have to be careful; very, very, careful.

c—Mark my word, that course will lead us into serious trouble.

Classical.

d—

Touch this sparingly, as 'twere far off;
Because, you know, my mother lives.

SHAKESPEARE, *Richard III,* iii, 5.

39. CERTAINTY: (See Assertion, Conviction.)

40. CHALLENGE: (See Defiance.)

Colloquial.

a—Come out if you dare and fight. I challenge you.

Classical.

b—Nay, answer me; stand, and unfold yourself.

SHAKESPEARE, *Hamlet,* i, **1.**

41. CLIMAX:

Colloquial.

a—He called me a liar, a thief, a murderer!

b—Oh, gentlemen, it was grand, sublime, masterful, wonderful.

c—I shall denounce him here, I shall denounce him at the convention, I shall denounce him in the Senate, I shall denounce him everywhere.

d—Yes, I did it yesterday, I did it today, and I'll do it tomorrow.

e—I shall do it tomorrow, I did it today, and I did it yesterday.

Classical.

f—The cloud-capp'd towers, the gorgeous palaces,
The solemn temples, the great globe itself,
Yea, all which it inherit, shall dissolve.

SHAKESPEARE, *The Tempest,* iv, 1.

g—See, what a grace was seated on this brow;
Hyperion's curls; the front of Jove himself;
An eye like Mars, to threaten and command;
A station like the herald Mercury,
New-lighted on a heaven-kissing hill;
A combination, and a form, indeed,
Where every god did seem to set his seal,
To give the world assurance of a man.

SHAKESPEARE, *Hamlet,* iii, 4.

42. COAXING: (See Entreaty, Appeal.)

Colloquial.

a—Oh, papa, please take me to the circus, do; I'll be so good if you do. Won't you? Do.

b—Please tell me what she said, do. I won't repeat it for the world. Tell me, O, do.

Classical.

c—I prythee call him back. . . . Good love, call him back.   SHAKESPEARE, *Othello,* iii, 3.

d—Sweet, sweet nurse, tell me, what says my love?

SHAKESPEARE, *Romeo and Juliet,* ii, 5.

43. COMMENDATION: (See Praise, Admiration.)

Colloquial.

a—There, that's the way to do it.

b—You have acted nobly.

c—You did that just splendidly.

Classical.

d—O valiant cousin! worthy gentleman!

SHAKESPEARE, *Macbeth,* i, 2.

44. COMPLAINT:

Colloquial.

a—He won't pay the slightest attention to me.

b—Not once have you kept your promise.

Classical.

c—My lord of Gloster, I have long borne
Your blunt upbraidings and your bitter scoffs:
By heaven, I will acquaint his majesty
Of those gross taunts that oft I have endured.

SHAKESPEARE, *Richard III,* i, 3.

45. COMPARISON:

Colloquial.

a—That is good, this is better, but this is best.

b—This one is brighter, but the other has the nobler countenance.

c—I should say this weighs about two pounds and this two and a half.

Classical.

d—   It [mercy] becomes
The throned monarch better than his crown;
His sceptre shows the force of temporal power,
The attribute to awe and majesty,
Wherein doth sit the dread and fear of kings;
But mercy is above this sceptred sway;
It is enthroned in the hearts of kings,
It is an attribute of God himself;
And earthly power doth then show likest God's
When mercy seasons justice.

SHAKESPEARE, *Merchant of Venice,* iv, 1.

e—Brutus, and Caesar: what should be in that Caesar?
Why should that name be sounded more than yours?
Write them together, yours is as fair a name;
Sound them, it doth become the mouth as well;
Weigh them, it is as heavy; conjure with them,
Brutus will start a spirit as soon as Caesar.

SHAKESPEARE, *Julius Caesar,* i, 2.

46. COMMAND: (See Authority.)

Colloquial.

a—Halt!

b—Stop that!

c—Back, back, you cowards! Would you lose your honor?
Back!

Classical.

d—Hold! for your lives!

SHAKESPEARE, *Othello,* ii, 3.

e—Stay! you that bear the corse, and set it down.

SHAKESPEARE, *Richard III,* i, 2.

47. CONCESSION: (See Frankness.)

Colloquial.

a—Yes, I'll grant that much.

b—I admit it was partly my fault, not all.

c—I will give you a piece of it, but not all of it.

Classical.

d—I grant I am a woman.

SHAKESPEARE, *Julius Caesar,* ii, 1

48. CONDEMNATION: (Solemn)

Colloquial.

a—You have brought upon yourself a terrible responsibility.

b—You have made everybody feel awful.

Classical.

c—Hear your sentence. . . .
We our kingdom's safety must so tender,
Whose ruin you have sought, that to her laws
We do deliver you. Get you, therefore, hence,
Poor, miserable wretches, to your death.
SHAKESPEARE, *Henry V*, ii, 2.

49. CONDEMNATION: (Angry)

Colloquial.

a—You ought to be thoroughly ashamed of yourself.
b—That's simply outrageous, wicked.
c—That's real mean of you.

Classical.

d—A murderer and a villain!
A slave, that is not twentieth part the tithe
Of your precedent lord; a vice of kings;
A cutpurse of the empire and the rule,
That from a shelf the precious diadem stole,
And put it in his pocket!
SHAKESPEARE, *Hamlet*, iii, 4.

50. CONCERN: (See Anxiety.)

Colloquial.

a—I hope nothing has happened to him.

Classical.

b—Didst thou not hear a noise?
SHAKESPEARE, *Macbeth*, ii, 2.

51. CONFIDENCE:

Colloquial.

a—I believe you; there's my hand.

Classical.

b—My life upon her faith!
SHAKESPEARE, *Othello*, i, 3.

c—Thou shalt have charge, and sovereign trust, herein.
SHAKESPEARE, *Henry IV*, I, iii, 2.

52. CONFUSION:

Colloquial.

a—Really I didn't mean to--I was going to—that is—I mean—no—yes—really—

Classical.

b—It is very sultry,—as 'twere,—I cannot tell how,— but—my lord—

SHAKESPEARE, *Hamlet,* v, 2.

53. CONSOLATION: (See Encouragement.)

Colloquial.

a—Oh, don't take it so to heart; it is not really so bad as it seems. Everything will come out all right.

b—Don't cry—I won't tell. Really I won't.

Classical.

c—The king shall have my service, but my prayers
For ever and forever shall be yours.

SHAKESPEARE, *Henry VIII,* iii, 2.

54. CONTEMPT:

Colloquial.

a—Do you think I could so lower myself as to shake hands with you. I had rather touch a toad.

b—Speak to you? Bah! What are you but a low, miserable cur.

Classical.

c—Remember whom you are to cope withal;—
A sort of vagabonds, rascals and runaways,
A scum of Bretagnes, and base lackey peasants.

SHAKESPEARE, *Richard III,* v, 3.

d—   You souls of geese,
That bear the shapes of men, how have you run
From slaves that apes would beat! . . .
All hurt behind; backs red, and faces pale
With flight and agued fear!

SHAKESPEARE, *Coriolanus,* i, 4.

55. CONVICTION:

Colloquial.

a—I am as positive of it as I stand here.

b—I'm right; I know it. I feel it.

c—As sure as the sun rises and sets that path will lead
you into trouble.

Classical.

d— Not all the water in the rough rude sea
Can wash the balm from an anointed king:
The breath of worldly men cannot depose
The deputy elected by the Lord.

SHAKESPEARE, *Richard II,* iii, 2.

e—There's a special providence in the fall of a sparrow.

SHAKESPEARE, *Hamlet,* v, 2.

f—There's a divinity that shapes our ends,
Rough-hew them how we will.

SHAKESPEARE, *Hamlet,* v, 2.

56. COURAGE:

Colloquial.

a—Whether they punish me or not, I am going to tell
the truth.

b—Let us be firm, even if it costs us our lives.

c—You may torture me, sir, but you cannot make me lie.

Classical.

d—I am armed and well prepared.—
Give me your hand, Bassanio; fare ye well! . . .
Repent not you that you shall lose your friend,
And he repents not that he pays your debt.

SHAKESPEARE, *Merchant of Venice,* iv, 1.

e— I cannot heave
My heart into my mouth; I love your majesty
According to my bond; nor more, nor less.

SHAKESPEARE, *King Lear,* i, 1.

57. COWARDLINESS: (See Fear.)

Colloquial.

a—I can't go across, I'm frightened. O, I'll get hurt, I
know I shall.

Classical.

b—   I'll go no more;
I am afraid to think what I have done;
Look on't again I dare not.

SHAKESPEARE, *Macbeth,* ii, 2.

c— Thou can'st not say I did it: never shake
Thy gory locks at me.

SHAKESPEARE, *Macbeth,* iii, 4.

58. CRUELTY: (See Malice.)

Colloquial.

a—Suffer? Well, suffer on. I'm glad of it.

b—I don't care if you are hurt—serves you right.

c—That's right, rain blows on him.

Classical.

d—I'll hear no more:—die, prophet, in thy speech;
For this, amongst the rest, was I ordain'd.

SHAKESPEARE, *Henry VI,* III, v, 6.

59. CURSING:

Colloquial.

a—A curse upon your wickedness!

Classical.

b—All the contagion of the south light on you!
You shames of Rome! You herd of—Boils and
plagues
Plaster you o'er; that you may be abhorred
Further than seen, and one infect another
Against the wind a mile!

SHAKESPEARE, *Coriolanus,* i, 4.

c—Bloody thou art, bloody will be thy end;
Shame serves thy life, and doth thy death attend.

SHAKESPEARE, *Richard III,* iv, 4.

60. DECISION: (See Determination, Assertion.)

Colloquial.

a—My mind is made up. I shall do it, and shall do it
at once.

b—I haven't and I don't mean to; there, that settles it.

Classical.

c—Tell them that I will not come today:
Cannot, is false; and that I dare not, falser;
I will not come today; tell them so, Decius.
SHAKESPEARE, *Julius Caesar,* ii, 2.

d—What I have written, I have written.
BIBLE, *John,* xix.

61. DEFIANCE:

Colloquial.

a—Try it if you dare—try it.

b—I defy you, sir; I defy the soldiers; I defy you all.

c—Prove it; you cannot. I challenge you to prove it.

d—I defy every one here to point out a single error in
my course.

Classical.

e—Defiance, traitors, hurl we in your teeth:
If you dare fight today, come to the field.
SHAKESPEARE, *Julius Caesar,* v, 1.

62. DEFERENCE: (See Respect.)

Colloquial.

a—After you, sir.

b—I bow to your experience.

Classical.

c—I shall in all my best obey you, madam.
SHAKESPEARE, *Hamlet,* i, 2.

d—Most potent, grave, and reverend signiors,
My very noble and approved good masters.
SHAKESPEARE, *Othello,* i, 3.

63. DELIGHT:

Colloquial.

a—Hurrah! Tomorrow's a holiday.

b—Why, did you ever! It's Mr. Thompson. I'm so glad! Sit down! Well, this is a pleasure. I am delighted. There is no other word to express it. I am delighted.

Classical.

c—Hoo! Marcius coming home!

SHAKESPEARE, *Coriolanus,* ii, 1.

d—I am giddy; expectation whirls me round,
The imaginary relish is so sweet,
That it enchants my sense.

SHAKESPEARE, *Troilus and Cressida,* iii, 2.

64. DENIAL:

Colloquial.

a—I deny it; I deny it absolutely.

Classical.

b—Cassius—I denied you not.
Brutus—You did.
Cassius—I did not.

SHAKESPEARE, *Julius Caesar,* iv, 3.

65. DERISION: (See Contempt, Sarcasm, Disdain.)

Colloquial.

a—You fight? Bah! You would run at the sound of a pop-gun.

Classical.

b—And who doth lead them but a paltry fellow, . . .
A milk sop, one that never in his life
Felt so much cold as overshoes in snow?

SHAKESPEARE, *Richard III,* v, 3.

66. DESPAIR:

Colloquial.

a—I've tried and tried and tried, but it is no use. I'm doomed.

Classical.

b—I have lived long enough: my way of life
Is fallen into the sear, the yellow leaf.
SHAKESPEARE, Macbeth, v, 3.

67. DEPRECATION:

Colloquial.

a—May I never see such a sight again.

Classical.

b—   O, woe is me!
To have seen what I have seen, see what I see!
SHAKESPEARE, Hamlet, iii, 1.

68. DEPRECIATION: (See Dispraising, Belittling.)

69. DETERMINATION: (See Assertion.)

Colloquial.

a—You say you will not; I say you shall, and, what is
more, I will compel you.

b—I'll do just as I please.

c—You may call me a liar, a fool, a hypocrite; you may
call me anything you wish, you cannot, shall not,
swerve me from my purpose.

Classical.

d—I'll have my bond; I will not hear thee speak:
I'll have my bond.
SHAKESPEARE, Merchant of Venice, iii, 3.

70. DIGNITY: (See Pride.)

Colloquial.

a—Do you know to whom you are speaking?
b—I have too much self-respect to do it.
c—You insult me, sir.

Classical.

d—   Do not fear our person;
There's such divinity doth hedge a king,
That treason can but peep to what it would.
SHAKESPEARE, Hamlet, iv, 5.

71. DISSATISFACTION:

Colloquial.

a—O, that won't do at all.

b—I'm completely dissatisfied. Nothing has gone right. Everything has failed, failed miserably.

c—O, that thing is no use. Take it back; we can never use that.

Classical.

d—O, it offends me to the soul, to hear a robustious peri-wig-pated fellow tear a passion to tatters, to very rags, to split the ears of the groundlings.

SHAKESPEARE, *Hamlet,* iii, 2.

72. DISCONTENT: (See Dissatisfaction.)

73. DISCOURAGING:

Colloquial.

a—O, don't go there. It's so hot and dusty. You'll be all tired out.

b—Take my advice and throw the whole thing over. It will fail sure.

Classical.

c—   I pray thee, good Mercutio, let's retire;
The day is hot, the Capulets abroad.

SHAKESPEARE, *Romeo and Juliet,* iii, 1.

74. DISPRAISING: (See Belittling, Dissatisfaction.)

Colloquial.

a—That's not good at all. That's miserable.

b—That picture is very poor indeed; the trees are yellow and the grass looks blue.

Classical.

c—That's villainous, and shows a most pitiful ambition.

SHAKESPEARE, *Hamlet,* iii, 2.

75. DISCRIMINATION: (See Comparison.)

76. DISGUST: (See Aversion.)

77. DISDAIN: (See Contempt.)

Colloquial.

a—I wouldn't be seen with you.

b—I refuse to have any talk with you whatever.

Classical.

c—I know thee not, old man; fall to thy prayers.

SHAKESPEARE, *Henry IV*, II, v, 5.

78. DISMISSAL: (See Command, Authority.)

Colloquial.

a—Now you may go.

b—Leave this room at once, sir.

c—Go away from here.

Classical.

d— Cassio, I love thee;

But never more be officer of mine.

SHAKESPEARE, *Othello,* ii, 3.

e—Rogues, hence, avaunt; vanish like hailstones, go!

SHAKESPEARE, *Merry Wives of Windsor,* i, 3.

79. DISAPPOINTMENT:

Colloquial.

a—O, that's too bad. I had set my whole heart on going. I'm so disappointed.

Classical.

b—There comes my fit again; I had else been perfect; . . .

But now, I am cabin'd, cribb'd, confined.

SHAKESPEARE, *Macbeth,* iii, 4.

80. DISMAY:

Colloquial.

a—We are lost; O, what will we do?

Classical.

b—France, friend with England! What becomes of me?
SHAKESPEARE, *King John,* iii, 1.

81. DISRESPECT: (See Contempt.)

Colloquial.

a—I don't care who you are. Get out of my way.
b—You are old and foolish.

Classical.

c—These tedious old fools.
SHAKESPEARE, *Hamlet,* ii, 2.

82. DOUBT: (See Perplexity.)

83. DREAD: (See Fear, Anxiety.)

Colloquial.

a—Look! It's a mad dog. O, what if it should come
this way?
b—The small-pox. Ugh! I shudder when I think of it.

Classical.

c—What, if it tempt you toward the flood, my lord,
Or to the dreadful summit of the cliff, . . .
And there assume some other horrible form?
SHAKESPEARE, *Hamlet,* i, 4.

84. EMULATION: (See Ambition, Admiration.)

Colloquial.

a—O, if I could only do like that.
b—There's an example worthy of our emulation.
c—Let us see then if we can't equal it. It is worth a
trial.

Classical.

d—When the blast of war blows in our ears,
Then imitate the action of the tiger.
SHAKESPEARE, *Henry V,* iii, 1.

85. ENCOURAGEMENT:

Colloquial.

a—That was fine—go it—go it—one more effort and the day is ours.

b—Don't give up. You have any number of chances yet.

c—Go right in and I'm sure you'll win.

Classical.

d—Be stirring as the time; be fire with fire;
Threaten the threatener, and outface the brow
Of bragging horror.
> SHAKESPEARE, *King John*, v, 1.

e—Good cheer, Antonio! What, man! courage yet!
> SHAKESPEARE, *Merchant of Venice*, iv. 1.

f—Why, how now, Adam! no greater heart in thee?
Live a little, comfort a little, cheer thyself a little;
if this uncouth forest yield anything savage, I will
either be food for it, or bring it for food to thee.
. . . Well said, thou look'st cheerily.
> SHAKESPEARE, *As You Like It*, ii, 6.

86. ENTREATY:

Colloquial.

a—Do, please, let me go this once. O, do.

b—I entreat you, I beg of you to give me a fair hearing.

Classical.

c—Speak with me, pity me, open the door.
> SHAKESPEARE, *Richard II*, v, 3.

87. ENVY:

Colloquial.

a—O, if I only had his horses.

Classical.

b—Heaven, that I had thy head!
> SHAKESPEARE, *Pericles*, i, 1.

88. EXCITEMENT: (See Uproar, Encouragement.)

Colloquial.

a—Go it! Go it—that's it; now, now!

b—Look out for those horses! Look out!

Classical.

c—Rescue, my lord of Norfolk, rescue, rescue!
The king enacts more wonders than a man,
Daring an opposite to every danger;
His horse is slain, and all on foot he fights,
Seeking for Richmond in the throat of death;
Rescue, fair lord, or else the day is lost.
SHAKESPEARE, Richard III, v, 4.

89. EXCLAMATION: (See Admiration, Indignation.)

Colloquial.

a—O, what a victory! Terrific! Tremendous!
b—Stop! I protest! Shame!

Classical.

c—Look! my lord! it comes!
SHAKESPEARE, Hamlet, i, 4.

90. EXCUSE:

Colloquial.

a—I am sorry I was late, but the clock was slow.
b—I am sorry I have delayed you, but really there were
so many visitors I couldn't help it.

Classical.

c—　　　　　　　What I have done,
That might your nature, honor, and exception
Roughly awake, I here proclaim was madness.
SHAKESPEARE, Hamlet, v, 2.

91. EXECRATION:

Colloquial.

a—Out you go, and don't you come near this house again,
you cur.
b—You, sir, have caused it all; out of my sight.

Classical.

c—Out of my sight! thou dost infect mine eyes.
SHAKESPEARE, Richard III, i, 2.

92. EXHORTATION: (See Entreaty.)

Colloquial.

a—Do right, do right. Whatever else you fail to do, do right. Do right. Never let your names be covered with shame.

b—Don't give up—don't—try again. Be brave! Be men!

Classical.

c—Cromwell, I charge thee, fling away ambition.

SHAKESPEARE, *Henry VIII*, iii, 2.

93. EXPECTATION:

Colloquial.

a—He is due here now. Look! Isn't that he? That's the same style of coat, the same hat. I hope—yes, it is he.

b—He said he would wave a red flag if we were victorious. What's that? I think I see something. Yes, and I think—I think—hurrah! We've won!

Classical.

c—What noise? . . . They cry—"a sail." My hopes do shape him for the governor. . . . They do discharge their shot of courtesy. Our friends at least. . . . Hark! . . . They give their greeting to the citadel.

SHAKESPEARE, *Othello*, ii, 1.

94. EXPLANATION:

Colloquial.

a—Well, you see it was this way. He came over here and he said to me, "What's the matter?" and I said to him, "I've lost your knife," and he said something I don't care to repeat, and then I struck him. That's exactly how it was.

Classical.

b—Your brother and my sister no sooner met, but they looked; no sooner looked, but they loved; no sooner loved, but they sighed; no sooner sighed, but they

asked one another the reason; no sooner knew the
reason but they sought the remedy: and in these
degrees they have made a pair of stairs to marriage.
SHAKESPEARE, *As You Like It*, v, 2.

95. EXTOLLING: (See Praise, Admiration.)

96. EXULTATION:

Colloquial.

a—Ha! ha! Now I've got you.

b—Hurrah! hurrah! hurrah! hurrah!

c—Exult! We have a right to exult. Our triumph is
nothing short of stupendous! We have carried
everything, everything! Not a scrap for the
enemy.

Classical.

d—Now, infidel, I have thee on the hip.
SHAKESPEARE, *Merchant of Venice*, iv, 1.

97. FATIGUE:

Colloquial.

a—I am so tired.

b—I am worn right out—completely exhausted.

Classical.

c—Dear master, I can go no further! O I die for food!
Here lie I down.
SHAKESPEARE, *As You Like It*, ii, 6.

98. FAREWELL:

Colloquial.

a—Good-by, remember me to all the folks.

Classical.

b—Adieu! brave Moor!
SHAKESPEARE, *Othello*, i, 3.

c—For ever and for ever, farewell, Cassius;
If we do meet again, why, we shall smile;
If not, why then this parting was well made.
SHAKESPEARE, *Julius Caesar*, v, 1.

99. FEAR: (See Anxiety.)

Colloquial.

a—Flames? Mercy on us! If they should spread to this room! Ah, look! They are coming in at the window!

Classical.

b—How is't with me, when every noise appals me?

SHAKESPEARE, *Macbeth*, ii, 2.

c—I have a faint cold fear thrills through my veins.

SHAKESPEARE, *Romeo and Juliet*, iv, 3.

100. FEARLESSNESS: (See Boldness, Bravery, Courage.)

101. FEEBLENESS:

Colloquial.

a—I am so weak. I can't stand.

Classical.

b—I am old now. . . . Mine eyes are not of the best.

SHAKESPEARE, *King Lear*, v, 3.

102. FLATTERY: (See Praise, Admiration.)

Colloquial.

a—Kate, you are perfection itself.
b—If we only had your help, we couldn't fail.

Classical.

c—(Goneril to King Lear):
I love you more than word can wield the matter,
Dearer than eyesight, space and liberty; . . .
A love that makes breath poor, and speech unable.

SHAKESPEARE, *King Lear*, i, 1.

103. FOREKNOWLEDGE:

Colloquial.

a—I knew it beforehand.
b—O, that's nothing new. I heard that long ago.

Classical.

c—I . . . knew the tailor that made the wings she flew
　withal.

SHAKESPEARE, Merchant of Venice, iii, 1.

104. FRANKNESS:

Colloquial.

a—I frankly confess I made a mistake, a very bad one.
　I admit it.

b—I'm the one to be blamed. It's my fault. Blame me.

Classical.

c—I owe you much; and, like a wilful youth,
　That which I owe is lost.

SHAKESPEARE, Merchant of Venice, i, 1.

105. GASPING:

Colloquial.

a—It—is—so—hard—to—breathe—I—gasp.

Classical.

b—　Help me into some house, Benvolio,
　Or I shall faint.

SHAKESPEARE, Romeo and Juliet, iii, 1.

106. GAYETY: (See Mirth.)

Colloquial.

a—Let us go right in for a jolly good time. Off we go.
　Hurrah!

b—Let us have a race to the corner. Altogether—one,
　two, three—away.

Classical.

c—　　　　　Come, musicians, play.
　A hall! a hall! give room, and foot it, girls.

SHAKESPEARE, Romeo and Juliet, i, 5.

107. GENEROSITY:

Colloquial.

a—No, really I want you to take it. You need it and I
　can get along without it.

Classical.

b—Try what my credit can in Venice do;
That shall be rack'd, even to the uttermost,
To furnish thee to Belmont, to fair Portia.

SHAKESPEARE, Merchant of Venice, i, 1.

108. GENIALITY: (See Mirth, Affection.)

Colloquial.

a—Bess, you little darling, come and sit on brudder's
knee. Come on. (Lifting her on knee.) Ah,
that's the girl. There you are. What's that?
Give you a ride on my foot? Of course brudder
will. Steady now. There! Up she goes and
down she goes; up she goes, down she goes. Now,
here goes a great big one. Whew! My! but wasn't
that fine? Ha, ha!

Classical.

b—My excellent good friends! How dost thou Guilden-
stern?
Ah Rosencrantz! Good lads, how do ye both?

SHAKESPEARE, Hamlet, ii. 2.

c—Feast with the best, and welcome to my house . . .
Now we sit to chat, as well as eat.

SHAKESPEARE, Taming of the Shrew, v, 2.

109. GLORIFICATION: (See Praise, Adoration.)

110. GRIEF: (See Sadness.)

Colloquial.

a—To think that a month ago he was with us, and
now he lies there dead. A wife, a mother, a child,
all mourning him. I—I can't go on.

b—She has lost her father, and he was all she had—
all she had.

Classical.

c—O mighty Caesar! Dost thou lie so low?
Are all thy conquests, glories, triumphs, spoils,
Shrunk to this little measure? Fare thee well.

SHAKESPEARE, Julius Caesar, iii, 1.

111. GRATITUDE: (See Thanks, Appreciation.)

Colloquial.

a—Thanks ever so much.

b—I am ever so much obliged. I am sure it was very kind of you indeed.

Classical.

c—We stand indebted . . .
In love and service to you evermore.
SHAKESPEARE, *Merchant of Venice*, iv, 1.

112. HATRED: (See Anger, Malice.)

113. HORROR:

Colloquial.

a—Never have I seen such a sight. He rushed in here all steeped in blood! His hair, his face, his hands, all covered with blood. Look! There it is— don't! don't!

b—Boys, it was pitch dark—just like it is tonight. We were near this very spot and the horrible thing came along. Oh, look! There it is!

Classical.

c—   Oh! horror! horror! horror!—
Tongue, nor heart, cannot conceive, nor name thee.
SHAKESPEARE, *Macbeth*, ii, 3.

d—What dreadful noise of water in my ears!
What sights of ugly death within mine eyes!
Methought I saw a thousand fearful wrecks;
A thousand men that fishes gnaw'd upon!
SHAKESPEARE, *Richard III*, i, 4.

114. IMPATIENCE: (See Annoyance.)

Colloquial.

a—Oh, stop bothering me, will you!

b—Impatient? It's time to be impatient. First one interrupts me, then another. There, now you go.

c—Hurry, girls, don't keep me waiting all day. Hurry or I'll be late.

Classical.

d—Out on ye, owls; nothing but songs of death?
SHAKESPEARE, *Richard III,* iv, 4.

e—O ye gods! ye gods! Must I endure all this?
SHAKESPEARE, *Julius Caesar,* iv, 3.

115. IMPUDENCE: (See Impertinence, Insolence.)

116. IMPERTINENCE:

Colloquial.

a—Young lady, your face is powdered.

Classical.

b—Will you hoist sail, sir? here lies your way.
SHAKESPEARE, *Twelfth Night,* i, 5.

117. INCREDULITY:

Colloquial.

a—Really, I can't believe it. It seems impossible.

b—No, you needn't try to make me believe that

Classical.

c—It is not so; thou hast misspoke, misheard; . . .
It cannot be; thou dost but say, 'tis so.
SHAKESPEARE, *King John,* iii, 1.

118. INDIGNATION: (See Anger, Contempt.)

Colloquial.

a—It's a shame.

b—I never heard of anything more high-handed. It's
outrageous, scandalous.

Classical.

c—   Shall we now
Contaminate our fingers with base bribes,
And sell the mighty space of our large honors
For so much trash as may be grasped thus?
I had rather be a dog and bay the moon,
Than such a Roman.
SHAKESPEARE, *Julius Caesar,* iv, 3.

119. INDECISION: (See Perplexity.)

120. INDIFFERENCE:

Colloquial.

a—I don't care what you do.

b—I am perfectly indifferent what course you take; you can do it or not, just as you like.

c—I'd just as soon stay as go, go as stay; it makes not a particle of difference, so choose for yourself.

Classical.

d—Man delights not me; no, nor woman neither.
Shakespeare, Hamlet, ii, 2.

121. INTERROGATION:

Colloquial.

a—What number did you say? Twenty-nine? Are you sure that's right? Is it not forty-nine? Is it the house next the corner? Has it green shutters?

Classical.

b—   Is whispering nothing?
Is leaning cheek to cheek? Is meeting noses?
. . . .

Skulking in corners? wishing clocks more swift?
Hours, minutes? noon, midnight?—is this nothing?
Shakespeare, Winter's Tale, i, 2.

c—Hath not a Jew eyes? hath not a Jew hands, organs, dimensions, senses, affections, passions? fed with the same food, hurt with the same weapons, subject to the same diseases, healed by the same means, warmed and cooled by the same winter and summer, as a Christian is? If you prick us, do we not bleed? If you tickle us, do we not laugh? If you poison us, do we not die?
Shakespeare, Merchant of Venice, iii, 1.

122. INSOLENCE: (See Contempt.)

Colloquial.

a—I wouldn't own such a name.

b—I wouldn't belong to such a miserable nationality.

Classical.

c—As you are old and reverend, you should be wise.

SHAKESPEAR, *King Lear* i, 4.

123. INVOCATION: (See Appeal, Entreaty.)

124. IRREVERENCE: (See Contempt.)

Colloquial.

a—I don't revere laws; I don't revere anything.

b—Bah, I don't think much of nature.

Classical.

c—You're a fishmonger.

SHAKESPEARE, *Hamlet,* ii, 2.

125. IRRESPONSIBILITY: (See Excuse.)

Colloquial.

a—It's not my fault.

b—Well, am I responsible? You surely didn't expect
me to do it, did you?

c—Don't blame me for it. I didn't do it.

Classical.

d—If Hamlet from himself be ta'en away,
And, when he's not himself, does wrong Laertes,
Then Hamlet does it not.

SHAKESPEARE, *Hamlet,* v, 2.

126. IRONY:

Colloquial.

a—You're brave, very, very!

b—You are so smart!—so smart!

Classical.

c—I fear I wrong the honorable men
Whose daggers have stabbed Caesar.
SHAKESPEARE, *Julius Caesar,* iii, 2.

127. JEALOUSY: (See Contempt, Anger, Malice, Threatening.)

128. JOY: (See Delight.)

Colloquial.

a—Throw up your caps! We've won! Hurrah!

b—I can't find words to express it. It was glorious! glorious!

c—Why, what do you think? Papa is going to take us to Europe. I could dance for joy.

Classical.

d—   More dances my wrapt heart
Than when I first my wedded mistress saw
Bestride my threshold.
SHAKESPEARE, *Coriolanus,* iv, 5.

129. LAMENTATION: (See Remorse, Reproach, Agony.)

130. LAUGHTER: (See Mirth.)

131. LOATHING: (See Contempt, Aversion.)

132. LOVE: (See Admiration, Adoration, Affection.)

Colloquial.

a—There, my little one, put your arms around me—so.

b—To see that grand old hero smiling there, with his silver locks—yes, man though I am, I could have kissed him.

Classical.

c—It is my lady, Oh, it is my love!
SHAKESPEARE, *Romeo and Juliet,* ii, 2.

d—My bounty is as boundless as the sea,
My love as deep; the more I give to thee
The more I have, for both are infinite.
SHAKESPEARE, *Romeo and Juliet,* ii, 2.

133. MALICE: (See Cruelty, Malediction.)

134. MALEDICTION: (See Execration, Malice.)

Colloquial.

a—Serves you right, you wretch. I hope you'll have
  bad luck and lots of it.

Classical.

b—   Poison be their drink!
  Gall, worse than gall, the daintiest that they taste!
  Their sweetest shade a grove of cypress trees!
  Their chiefest prospect murd'ring basilisks!
            SHAKESPEARE, *Henry VI*, II, iii, 2.

c—Oh, may such purple tears be always shed
  From those that wish the downfall of our house!
            SHAKESPEARE, *Henry VI*, III, v, 6.

d—There let him sink, and be the seas on him!
            SHAKESPEARE, *Richard III*, iv, 4.

135. MEDITATION:

Colloquial.

a—Let me see—four into thirty-nine goes (work the
  sum aloud)—four into thirty-five goes (work the
  sum aloud)—ninety-eight times seventy-four is—

b—Ought I to do it, or ought I not? If I do it, they
  will—they wouldn't ask me that. If I don't do
  it, they might—no—yes—they will avoid me.

Classical.

c—   To die,—to sleep,—
  No more; and, by a sleep, to say we end
  The heart ache, and the thousand natural shocks
  That flesh is heir to,—'tis a consummation
  Devoutly to be wished. To die,—to sleep,—
  To sleep; perchance to dream;—aye, there's the rub.
            SHAKESPEARE, *Hamlet*, iii, 1.

136. MELANCHOLY: (See Despair.)
Colloquial.

a—I've tried to do the right thing, but somehow everything goes against me. I feel right down miserable.

b—Hope? There's no hope. How dull and dead my whole life seems!

Classical.

c—I am a tainted wether of the flock,
Meetest for death; the weakest kind of fruit
Drops earliest to the ground, and so let me.

SHAKESPEARE, *Merchant of Venice,* iv, 1.

137. MIRTH: (See Gayety.)
Colloquial.

a—Laugh? I should think I did; to see that great fat man with his tall silk hat bump into that fat woman and then fall flat in the mud! It was so funny that I—ha, ha, ha!—

b—Fun! That doesn't half tell it. We laughed and sang and sang and laughed until I thought the roof would come down.

Classical.

c—A fool, a fool! I met a fool i' the forest,
A motley fool;—a miserable world;
As I do live by food, I met a fool.

SHAKESPEARE, *As You Like It,* ii, 7.

d—   Haste thee, nymph, and bring with thee
Jest, and youthful jollity,
Quips, and cranks, and wanton wiles,
Nods, and becks, and wreathéd smiles,
Such as hang on Hebe's cheek,
And love to lie in dimple sleek;
Sport that wrinkled Care derides,
And Laughter holding both his sides.
Come, and trip it as you go,
On the light fantastic toe.

MILTON, *L'Allegro.*

138. MISTRUST: (See Suspicion, Assertion.)

Colloquial.

a—I don't believe he's honest.

Classical.

b—Our fears in Banquo stick deep.

SHAKESPEARE, *Macbeth,* iii, **1.**

139. MODESTY:

Colloquial.

a—Oh, don't praise me; I did my duty, that's all.

b—Oh, I did pretty well, but then I ought to.

c—If I can do half as well as she I shall be satisfied.

Classical.

d—I am no orator as Brutus is;

. . . .

For I have neither wit, nor words, nor worth,
Action, nor utterance, nor the power of speech
To stir men's blood; I only speak right on.

SHAKESPEARE, *Julius Caesar,* iii, **2.**

140. MOANING: (See Agony.)

Colloquial.

a—Oh, the pain, the pain, the pain!

Classical.

b—All the perfumes of Arabia will not sweeten this
little hand. Oh! Oh! Oh!

SHAKESPEARE, *Macbeth,* v, 1.

141. MOCK-DEFERENCE: (See Sarcasm.)

Colloquial.

a—Really, you are so very, very, very superior that I
bow to your majesty.

Classical.

b—Shall I bend low, and in a bondman's key
Say this—
Fair sir, you spit on me on Wednesday last;

You spurn'd me such a day; another time
You called me dog; and for these courtesies
I'll lend you this much moneys?

SHAKESPEARE, *Merchant of Venice,* i, 3.

142. MOCKERY: (See Ridicule, Sarcasm.)

Colloquial.

a—Cry away, you great big baby—boo-hoo, boo-hoo, hoo-hoo!

Classical.

b—Aye, and that tongue of his that bade the Romans
Mark him, and write his speeches in their books,
Alas! it cried, *give me some drink, Titinius,*
As a sick girl.

SHAKESPEARE, *Julius Caesar,* i, 2.

143. OBSTINACY: (See Determination, Prejudice.)

Colloquial.

a—I will not budge; not a jot, not an inch.
b—I don't want to go, and I won't go; so there.

Classical.

c—In the way of bargain, mark ye me,
I'll cavil on the ninth part of a hair.

SHAKESPEARE, *Henry IV,* I, iii, 1.

144. OMINATION:

Colloquial.

a—Look, how black it is! There will be a storm.
b—I feel it in my bones. Something terrible is going to happen.
c—I don't want to frighten you, but there is danger ahead.

Classical.

d—O Caesar! these things are beyond all use,
And I do fear them.

SHAKESPEARE, *Julius Caesar,* ii, 2.

145. PAIN: (See Agony.)

Colloquial.

a—Oh, it hurts—Oh! Oh!

Classical.

b—I bleed still!   I am hurt to the death—
    SHAKESPEARE, *Othello,* ii, 3.

146. PENITENCE: (See Regret.)

147. PERMISSION: (See Assent.)

Colloquial.

a—You may take it.   You have my fullest permission.

Classical.

b—Take thy fair hour, Laertes; time be thine,
    And thy best graces spend it at thy will.
    SHAKESPEARE, *Hamlet,* i, 2.

148. PERPLEXITY:

Colloquial.

a—This is the house.   No, it can't be.   Yes, there are
    the same old steps.   But I am sure it wasn't a
    red brick.   No—yes, this must be it.   No—well,
    if I'm not mixed!

Classical.

b—Where have I been?   Where am I? . . . I know
    not what to say.
    SHAKESPEARE, *King Lear,* iv, 7.

149. PERSUASION: (See Entreaty, Advice.)

Colloquial.

a—Come on, do, and have some fun.   You'll have a
    glorious time.   Nothing like it in your life be-
    fore.   Come on.

Classical.

b—Take thrice thy money; bid me tear the bond.
    SHAKESPEARE, *Merchant of Venice,* iv, 1.

150. PITY: (See Solicitude, Grief, Sadness.)

Colloquial.

a—Oh, look at that poor bird. Its leg is broken. That's too bad.

b—Poor fellow! He had awfully bad luck. I feel sorry for him.

Classical.

c—   Oh, I have suffered
With those that I saw suffer! a brave vessel,
Who had, no doubt, some noble creatures in her,
Dash'd all to pieces. Oh! the cry did knock
Against my very heart! Poor souls! they perish'd.
                        SHAKESPEARE, *The Tempest,* i, 2.

151. POLITENESS:

Colloquial.

a—Allow me to assist you.

Classical.

b—May it please your highness sit?
                        SHAKESPEARE, *Macbeth,* iii, 4.

152. PRAISE: (See Admiration, Acceptance.)

Colloquial.

a—Your essay was fine.

b—That's what I call courage.

Classical.

c—Brave Macbeth, (well he deserves that name).
                        SHAKESPEARE, *Macbeth,* i, 2.

d—   O wise and upright judge!
How much more elder art thou than thy looks!
                        SHAKESPEARE, *Merchant of Venice,* iv, 1.

153. PREJUDICE: (See Assertion.)

Colloquial.

a—It is because it is, and that's all there is to it.

b—That may be all true, gentlemen, but just the same I prefer my own way. I was brought up in it and I am going to stay in it.

Classical.

c—I can give no reason, nor I will not.

SHAKESPEARE, *Merchant of Venice*, iv, 1.

154. PRIDE: (See Arrogance, Boasting.)

Colloquial.

a—I am proud to say that they all, all must bow to me.

Classical.

b—Aye, every inch a king!

SHAKESPEARE, *King Lear*, iv, 6.

155. PRAYER: (See Appeal, Entreaty, Reverence, Awe, Love.)

156. PROMISING: (See Assertion.)

Colloquial.

a—I promise you I'll never tell as long as I live.

b—If you do as I ask, I'll give you this pencil.

c—I promise you to do exactly as you ask me.

Classical.

d—For he, today, that sheds his blood with me
Shall be my brother.

SHAKESPEARE, *Henry V*, iv, 3.

e—I never more will break an oath with thee

SHAKESPEARE, *Merchant of Venice*, v, 1.

157. PROTEST:

Colloquial.

a—Stop, I object. It's unfair.

Classical.

b—   Revoke thy gift;
Or whilst I can vent clamor from my throat
I'll tell thee, thou dost evil.

SHAKESPEARE, *King Lear*, i, 1.

158. RAGE:

Colloquial.

a—You low, driveling cur! I'll stop your slanders, you
—O you—

Classical.

b—You slave, you cur! . . . Do you bandy looks with
    me, you rascal!

SHAKESPEARE, King Lear, i, 4.

c—Away to heaven, respective lenity,
    And fire-eyed fury be my conduct now!
    Now, Tybalt, take the villain back again.

SHAKESPEARE, Romeo and Juliet, iii, 1.

d—Go, prick thy face, and over-red thy fear,
    Thou lily-livered boy. What soldiers, patch?
    Death of thy soul! those linen cheeks of thine
    Are counselors to fear. What soldiers, whey-face?

SHAKESPEARE, Macbeth, v, 3.

159. REBUFF: (See Refusal.)

Colloquial.

a—No! There, that's flat.

Classical.

b—Thou shalt have nothing but the forfeiture.

SHAKESPEARE, Merchant of Venice, iv, 1.

160. RECKLESSNESS: (See Indifference.)

Colloquial.

a—I don't care a snap of the finger whether I break my
    neck or not.

Classical.

b—Slave, I have set my life upon a cast,
    And I will stand the hazard of the die.

SHAKESPEARE, Richard III, v, 5.

161. REFUSAL, POLITE:

Colloquial.

a—I don't like to refuse you, but really I must.

b—I am sorry, but I cannot accept your kind offer.

c—No, thank you.

Classical.

d—This ring, good sir,—alas, it is a trifle;
    I will not shame myself to give you this.

SHAKESPEARE, Merchant of Venice, iv, 1.

162. REFUSAL: (See Assertion, Dismissal.)

Colloquial.

a—No, I won't have it. I refuse it.

Classical.

b—No, no; forsooth.

SHAKESPEARE, *Taming of the Shrew,* iv, 3.

163. REGRET: (See Remorse, Agony.)

Colloquial.

a—Oh, boys, if we had only done what was right!

b—I regret it; I regret it from my soul. We should have treated him respectfully. For one, I am sorry, deeply sorry.

c—Oh, pshaw! why didn't I see that before? I might have won if I had. That's too bad!

Classical.

d—   O Cromwell, Cromwell!
Had I but served my God with half the zeal
I served my king . . . He would not, in mine age,
Have left me naked to my enemies.

SHAKESPEARE, *King Henry VIII,* iii, 2.

164. REJECTION: (See Refusal, Denial, Dismissal.)

Colloquial.

a—Send it back; I will have nothing to do with it.

Classical.

b—Away with it.

SHAKESPEARE, *Taming of the Shrew,* iv, 3.

165. RELIANCE: (See Trust, Confidence.)

Colloquial.

a—I have the utmost faith in him. He is as true as steel.

b—I'm going to take your word for it.

Classical.

c—   A man he is of honesty and trust;
            To his conveyance I assign my wife.

SHAKESPEARE, *Othello*, i, 3.

166. REMORSE: (See Agony, Regret.)

Colloquial.

a—Oh, if I had only known; if I had only known!

b—Oh, what would I not give to recall those words!

Classical.

c—O coward Conscience, how thou dost afflict me!

SHAKESPEARE, *Richard III*, v, 3.

167. RENUNCIATION: (See Refusal, Dismissal.)

Colloquial.

a—I have absolutely renounced it.

b—I have done with it.

Classical.

c—   Here I disclaim all my paternal care,
            Propinquity, and property of blood,
            And as a stranger to my heart and me
            Hold thee, from this, forever.

SHAKESPEARE, *King Lear*, i, 1.

168. REPOSE:

Colloquial.

a—I could lie here and dream and dream and dream
   (falls asleep).

Classical.

b—My soul is heavy, and I fain would sleep.

SHAKESPEARE, *Richard III*, i, 4.

169. REPROACH: (See Indignation, Reproof, Aggrievance.)

Colloquial.

a—Oh, shame, shame!

b—After she has sent you this lovely present, to talk of
   her like that! You ought to be ashamed of yourselves!

c—Sir, you prated long and loud of bravery, and this is how you show it—by desertion.

d—Oho, aha, I see! Aha! You've been kissing some-one, and I know who! Oh, shame! shame! Kiss-ing the boys! kissing the boys! Oh, shame! shame! shame!

Classical.

e—   O proper stuff!
This is the very painting of your fear:
This is the air-drawn dagger, which, you said,
Led you to Duncan.

SHAKESPEARE, *Macbeth,* iii, 4.

f—O shame! where is thy blush?

SHAKESPEARE, *Hamlet,* iii, 4.

170. RESENTMENT: (See Reproach.)

Colloquial.

a—That was a very mean thing for you to do.

Classical.

b—Your words and performances are no kin together.
. . . I think it is scurvy.

SHAKESPEARE, *Othello,* iv, 2.

171. RESIGNATION:

Colloquial.

a—I am resigned to my fate.

b—I'm used to it now, so I accept the situation and say nothing.

Classical.

c—If it be now, 'tis not to come; if it be not to come, it will be now; if it be not now, yet it will come; the readiness is all.

SHAKESPEARE, *Hamlet,* v, 2.

172. RESPECT:

Colloquial.

a—I shall obey you, sir.

Classical.

b—We both obey.

SHAKESPEARE, *Hamlet,* ii, 2.

c—Mine honored lord!

SHAKESPEARE, *Hamlet,* ii, 2.

173. RESPONSIBILITY:

Colloquial.

a—I accept the entire responsibility.

Classical.

b—We must bear all.

SHAKESPEARE, *Henry V*, iv, 1.

174. REPROOF: (See Indignation, Advice.)

Colloquial.

a—Never stand in front of a lady in that manner; it's discourteous.

b—That was very ungentlemanly indeed. You ought to be more careful.

Classical.

c—Do you take the court for Paris-garden? ye rude slaves, leave your gaping.

SHAKESPEARE, *Henry VIII*, v, 4.

175. REQUEST: (See Interrogation, Authority, Command.)

Colloquial.

a—May I take this book?

b—I want you to go there and ask him for my letters.

c—Will you oblige me with your pencil?

Classical.

d—   Grant me two things, I pray you:
Not to deny me, and to pardon me.

SHAKESPEARE, *Merchant of Venice*, iv, 1.

e—Give me your gloves . . . and . . . I'll take this ring from you.

SHAKESPEARE, *Merchant of Venice*, iv, 1.

176. RETALIATION:

Colloquial.

a—There, that's what you get for striking me.

b—You strike, gentlemen, I strike back; you taunt, I return it; you curse, I return that. Whatever you give you'll get; rest assured of that. And it will serve you right.

Classical.

c—And there's for twitting me with perjury.

SHAKESPEARE, *Henry VI,* III, v, 5.

177. RETORT:

Colloquial.

a—Well, I never lie; that's one thing I don't follow your example in.

Classical.

b—OCT.: Not that we love words better, as you do.
BRU.: Good words are better than bad strokes, Octavius.

SHAKESPEARE, *Julius Caesar,* v, 1.

178. REVENGE: (See Malice, Triumph, Retaliation.)

179. REVERENCE: (See Awe, Solemnity, Sadness.)

180. RIDICULE: (See Sarcasm, Irony, Mockery.)

Colloquial.

a—The gentleman says he saw the thunder; I have no doubt he will soon assert he heard the lightning, and looking forward to the past he will solemnly swear he saw the footprints of a hand.

b—He says he saw a ghost? Bah! He saw a sheet held up by some jackanapes of a boy, and he calls that a ghost. The whole thing is ridiculous, absurd.

Classical.

c—What's this? A sleeve? 'Tis like a demi-cannon. What up and down, carv'd like an appletart?
Why, what o' world's name, tailor, call'st thou this?

SHAKESPEARE, *Taming of the Shrew,* iv, 3.

181. SADNESS:

Colloquial.

a—It was the saddest death I ever witnessed. The children touching the face of the dead and calling, "Papa," "Papa"; the mother choking with sobs; the sheriff standing there with his writ—but I can't go on, I—I—

Classical.

b—The sun for sorrow will not show its head;
Go hence, to have more talk of these sad things.
                SHAKESPEARE, *Romeo and Juliet,* v, 3.

182. SARCASM: (See Ridicule, Irony, Mockery.)

Colloquial.

a—The gentleman is so very considerate, very; so
amiable, so gentle. His remarks are so profound,
so all-embracing, that I think we shall soon find
him editing a baby's primer.

b—Brilliant? Of course you are; so, so brilliant. Really,
it's a wonder you're not President.

Classical.

c—What, will the aspiring blood of Lancaster
Sink in the ground? I thought it would have mounted.
See how my sword weeps for the poor king's death!
                SHAKESPEARE, *Henry VI,* III, v, 6.

183. SATISFACTION: (See Admiration.)

Colloquial.

a—Ah, that's just what I wanted, the very thing. Why,
if you had thought for a year you couldn't have
brought me anything I should like better. It's
perfectly charming.

b—That, sir, is absolutely satisfactory. It realizes our
hopes to the letter. It is perfection itself.

Classical.

c—This gentle and unforced accord of Hamlet
Sits smiling to my heart.
                SHAKESPEARE, *Hamlet,* i, 2.

184. SCORN: (See Contempt.)

Colloquial.

a—I scorn your offer, and you too, you hypocrite.
b—I want nothing to do with you, you wretch.

Classical.

c—You common cry of curs! whose breath I hate
As reek o' the rotten fens,—whose loves I prize
As the dead carcasses of unburied men,
That do corrupt my air,—I banish you!

> SHAKESPEARE, *Coriolanus,* iii, 3.

185. SECRECY:

Colloquial.

a—Don't breathe this to a soul.

Classical.

b—But you'll be secret? SHAKESPEARE, *Hamlet,* i, 5.

186. SELF-DENUNCIATION: (See Admission, Indignation, Remorse.)

Colloquial.

a—I am absolutely ashamed of myself.
b—I admit it, I am a coward, a wretch—it was downright mean of me.

Classical.

c— I am pigeon-livered, and lack gall
To make oppression bitter.

> SHAKESPEARE, *Hamlet,* ii, 2.

187. SHIVERING AND SHUDDERING:

Colloquial.

a—O—ugh! it's cold.

Classical.

b—Tom's a-cold . . . Tom's a-cold.

> SHAKESPEARE, *King Lear,* iii, 4.

188. SLOTH:

Colloquial.

a—Oh, it's too much trouble to move. I'm sleepy—so sleepy. I could lounge here all day.

189. SOLEMNITY: (See Sadness.)

Colloquial.

a—I said to the doctor, "Is there any hope?" "None," he answered. We kept quite still. The poor fellow was breathing his last.

b—Don't joke; it's too solemn a thing; the boy may die.

c—I have just heard that Mamie is dead.

Classical.

d—   Sweets to the sweet; farewell:
I hop'd thou should'st have been my Hamlet's wife;
I thought thy bride-bed to have deck'd, sweet maid,
And not t'have strew'd thy grave.

SHAKESPEARE, Hamlet, v, 1.

190. SOLICITUDE: (See Pity, Sympathy.)

Colloquial.

a—Aren't you well, Willie? Feeling sick? There, don't cry.

b—Is he feeling any better today? Did he sleep at all last night? Is there anything I can do for him? I do hope you'll tell me.

Classical.

c—How does my royal lord? How fares your majesty?

SHAKESPEARE, King Lear, iv, 7.

191. STARTLING: (See Excitement.)

Colloquial.

a—Why, how you startled me!

Classical.

b—Hark! Peace!

SHAKESPEARE, Macbeth, ii, 2.

192. STRUGGLING:

Colloquial.

a—Let go of me, do you hear? Let go! There, take that!

Classical.

b—HAMLET (*struggling with* LAERTES):
I prithee take thy fingers from my throat!
Away thy hand!

SHAKESPEARE, Hamlet, v, 1.

193. STUBBORNNESS: (See Prejudice, Determination, Obstinacy.)

Colloquial.

a—I'll not change my view, no matter what your arguments are.

Classical.

b—There is no power in the tongue of man
To alter me; I stay here on my bond.
> SHAKESPEARE, *Merchant of Venice,* iv, 1.

194. SUBLIMITY: (See Awe.)

Colloquial.

a—And then, sir, as far as the eye could see, up, up, up, mountains behind mountains. It was sublime; I could not speak.

Classical.

b—Roll on, thou deep and dark blue ocean, roll;
Boundless, endless, and sublime.
> BYRON, *Childe Harold.*

c— For likest gods they seem'd,
Stood they or moved, in stature, motion, arms,
Fit to decide the empire of great heaven.
> MILTON, *Paradise Lost,* Book vi.

195. SURPRISE: (See Amazement.)

196. SUSPICION:

Colloquial.

a—I believe that fellow's a thief.

Classical.

b—I do not like these several councils.
> SHAKESPEARE, *Richard III,* iii, 2.

197. SUSPENSE: (See Anxiety.)

198. SYMPATHY: (See Pity, Solicitude.)

Colloquial.

a—I am truly sorry for you. It was most unkind of them.

Classical.

b—I am sorry that thou art not well.

SHAKESPEARE, *Romeo and Juliet,* ii, 5.

199. TENDERNESS: (See Affection.)

200. TERROR: (See Horror.)

Colloquial.

a—What? Would you burn my child? Stop! Stop!

b—The boat is sinking. Help! Help!

Classical.

c—O look! methinks I see my cousin's ghost
Seeking out Romeo, that did spit his body
Upon a rapier's point:—stay, Tybalt, stay.

SHAKESPEARE, *Romeo and Juliet,* iv, 3.

d—Avaunt! and quit my sight! . . . Hence, horrible
shadow!
Unreal mockery! hence!

SHAKESPEARE, *Macbeth,* iii, 4.

201. THANKS:

Colloquial.

a—I thank you very much indeed.

b—This gold watch for me? Oh, thanks!

Classical.

c—For all, our thanks.

SHAKESPEARE, *Hamlet,* i, 2.

202. THREAT:

Colloquial.

a—If you do that I'll tell the teacher.

b—If you make the slightest mistake, mark my words,
you shall pay for it; you shall pay for it.

c—If he swerve a hairbreadth from the truth I'll expose
him before you all.

Classical.

d—Unmanner'd dog! stand thou when I command:
Advance thy halberd higher than my breast,

Or by St. Paul, I'll strike thee to my foot,
And spurn upon thee, beggar, for thy boldness.
SHAKESPEARE, *Richard III,* i, 2.

e—Unhand me, gentlemen;—
By heaven, I'll make a ghost of him that lets me.
SHAKESPEARE, *Hamlet,* i, 4.

203. TRANQUILLITY:
Colloquial.

a—How tranquil everything is! Not a ripple on the
water, no breeze, so still; I am going to lie down
and dream.

Classical.

b—How sweet the moonlight sleeps upon this bank.
Here will we sit, and let the sounds of music
Creep in our ears; soft stillness and the night
Become the touches of sweet harmony.
SHAKESPEARE, *Merchant of Venice,* v, 1.

204. TRIUMPH:
Colloquial.

a—There, I told you my course would be approved.

Classical.

b— It shall go hard,
But I will delve one yard below their mines,
And blow them at the moon.
SHAKESPEARE, *Hamlet,* iii, 4.

205. TRUST: (See Confidence.)

206. TYRANNY: (See Cruelty, Command.)
Colloquial.

a—Make him do it; force him.

b—Do as you are bid and ask no questions.

c—You ask for rights here. I will answer you—you
shall have none; I'll see to that.

Classical.

d—I tell thee what, get thee to church o' Thursday,
Or never after look me in the face.
Speak not, reply not, do not answer me.
SHAKESPEARE, *Romeo and Juliet,* iii, 5.

207. UPROAR: (See Excitement.)
Colloquial.

a—It was pandemonium. No other word describes it. The roaring, the shouting, the hooting, all in one tremendous uproar.

Classical.

b—   Now storming fury rose,
And clamor such as heard in heaven till now
Was never; arms on armor clashing bray'd
Horrible discord, and the madding wheels
Of brazen chariots raged: dire was the noise.
                    MILTON, *Paradise Lost,* Book **VI.**

c—The owl shriek'd at thy birth, an evil sign;
The night-crow cried, forboding luckless time;
Dogs howl'd, and hideous tempests shook down trees;
The raven rook'd her on the chimney's top,
And chattering pies in dismal discords sung.
                    SHAKESPEARE, *Henry VI,* III, v, 6.

208. URGING: (See Appeal, Entreaty.)
Colloquial.

a—Go on, go on, go on.

Classical.

b—On, on, you noblest English.
                    SHAKESPEARE, *Henry V,* iii, 1.

209. VINDICATION:
Colloquial.

a—You have acted exactly as you should.

Classical.

b—You are right, justice, and you weigh this well;
Therefore still bear the balance and the sword.
                    SHAKESPEARE, *Henry IV,* II, v, 2.

210. WARNING: (See Threat.)
Colloquial.

a—You better go home or you'll catch it.
b—If you persist, I warn you, you are lost.

c—Beware, gentlemen, beware. I warn you, in less than
a week they will be here.

Classical.

d—   But, hear you, leave behind
Your son, George Stanley: look your heart be firm,
Or else his head's assurance is but frail.

SHAKESPEARE, *Richard III,* iv, 4.

e—Beware the Ides of March.

SHAKESPEARE, *Julius Caesar,* i, 2.

211. WELCOME: (See Delight.)

Colloquial.

a—Why, how do you do? I am delighted to see you.

Classical.

b—A hundred thousand welcomes: I could weep,
And I could laugh; I am light, and heavy; welcome.

SHAKESPEARE, *Coriolanus,* ii, 1.

212. WHISPERING:

Colloquial.

a—Sh! Don't stir; they'll hear you.

Classical.

b—Hark! Who lies i' the second chamber?

SHAKESPEARE, *Macbeth,* ii, 1.

213. WOE: (See Grief.)

Colloquial.

a—Oh, gentlemen, it was piteous; the moans, the agoniz-
ing looks!

Classical.

b—O piteous spectacle! O bloody times!

SHAKESPEARE, *Henry VI,* III, ii, 5.

214. WONDER: (See Amazement, Admiration.)

Colloquial.

a—Well, if that isn't wonderful!

b—It's marvelous! It's a miracle!

Classical.

c—O day and night, but this is wondrous strange!

SHAKESPEARE, *Hamlet,* i, 5.

DEVELOPING SPECIFIC POWERS OF PORTRAYAL.

Frequently it will be found that a student while effective in portraying one class of emotions is weak in another. To assist such student examples especially valuable for different classes of feelings are now given. As many tones are combinations of simple emotions in various proportions, the same example will be found sometimes under different heads.

1. *To Develop Brightness, Animation, Vivacity.* Practice Tone Drills Nos. 63, 106, 108, 128, 137; also Nos. 1, 5, 85, 88, 93, 94, 96, 147, 183, 207, 214.

2. *To Develop Facility in the Expression of Admiration, Love, Affection and Kindred Feelings.* Practice Tone Drills Nos. 1, 3, 5, 111, 132, 194; also Nos. 10, 18, 19 41b, 43, 53, 63, 84, 85, 102, 108a, 152, 190, 201.

3. *To Develop Expression of Sympathy, Regret, Grief, Agony and the Like.* Practice Tone Drills Nos. 8, 53, 110, 140, 145, 150, 181, 190; also Nos. 20, 66, 79, 80, 86, 90, 97, 101, 136, 163, 166, 186, 198, 213.

4. *To Develop Expression of Assertion, Conviction, Intention, Determination and the Like.* Practice Tone Drills Nos. 24, 55, 60, 64, 69, 164, 165; also Nos. 46, 48, 51, 61, 78, 91, 143, 152, 153, 156, 157, 159, 162, 167, 173, 193, 202, 206, 209, 210.

5. *To Develop Expression of the Various Forms of Dissatisfaction and Dislike, Indignation, Aggrievance and Contempt.* Practice Tone Drills Nos. 11, 27, 49, 54, 58, 118, 158, 176, 180, 184; also Nos. 7, 13, 26, 29, 31, 44, 46c, 59, 65, 71, 74, 77, 81, 91, 114, 122, 124, 134, 141, 142, 160, 170, 177, 182.

6. *To Develop Expression of Emotions Demanding Perturbation, Excitement.* Practice Tone Drills Nos. 88, 96a, 99, 191, 208; also Nos. 15, 52, 57, 80, 83, 85, 89, 91, 105, 113, 144, 187, 200, 207, 212.

7. *To Develop Expression of Entreaty From Request to Appeal.* Practice Tone Drills Nos. 16, 42, 53, 86, 92, 149, 175.

8. *To Develop Power in the Expression of Climax.* Practice Tone Drills Nos. 24, 41, 45a, 64, 69a, 145, 208; also Nos. 22, 40, 60, 88, 89, 162a, 176b, 214b.

9. *To Develop Expression of Awe, Solemnity, Dignity, Sublimity.* Practice Tone Drills 28, 30a, c, 48, 110, 181, 189, 194; also Nos. 55d, e, f, 56, 62, 70, 144, 163a, d, 171c.

FIVE TO TEN MINUTE GENERAL DRILL ON TONES.

10. Practice Tone Drills Nos. 1a, 5a, 8a, 11a, d, 16a, 19a, 21a, 22a, 24a, b, 26a, 28a, b, 35, 41a, b, 43a, 46a, b, c, 49a, 53a, 55b, 63a, b, 86a, 88a, b, 89a, b, 96a, b, 99a, 106a, 110, 126, 132a, b, 135, 137a, b, c, 140a, 150a, 158, 168a, 181, 182b, 190a, b, 191, 200a, 207, 208, 214a.

TEN TO TWENTY MINUTE GENERAL DRILL ON TONES.

11. All of Five Minute Drill, as above, also Tone Drills Nos. 3, 5c, 7a, 13a, 15, 20a, 23c, 27, 32, 34a, 37a, 40, 41c, 42a, 47a, 48a, 51, 52, 54a, 57a, 59, 60a, 61a, 65a, 69a, 70a, 80, 83b, 84, 91a, 92b, 93b, 97a, 101, 105, 114a, 116, 118, 121, 124a, 136a, 139b, 144, 148, 153, 157, 177, 180a, 187, 206a, 202a, 203a.

Note: In some instances Colloquial Drills only have been specified. Where desired a Classical example under same Tone may be used.

TONE DRILLS FOR VOCAL DEVELOPMENT.

12. *To Free the Vocal Muscles.* Practice Tone Drills Nos. 8, 63, 86, 110, 128, 132, 137, 145, 166, 181, 194, 200, 207.

13. *To Secure Flexibility.* Practice Tone Drills Nos. 1, 5, 9, 16, 20, 25, 42, 47, 94, 106, 111, 126, 132, 141, 169d, 180, 182, 190, 201.

14. *To Secure Forward Placing of Tone.*   Practice Tone Drills Nos 24, 26, 46, 63, 64, 89, 157, 200, 208.

15. *To Secure Resonance and Volume*   Practice Tone Drills Nos. 8, 10, 19, 32, 33, 34, 35, 40, 41, 61, 96, 110, 137, 152, 154, 181, 189, 194, 207.

16. *To Develop Musical Quality.*   Practice Tone Drills Nos. 36, 110, 136, 150, 166, 168, 181, 189, 207, 213.

INTERPRETATION

1. *Interpretation Implies Conception and Execution.*—By conception is meant the clear and complete apprehension of all that the author intended in his composition. By execution is meant the complete portrayal of the conception to the listener. Conception implies knowing, execution implies showing. It is plain that before a person can portray a picture or tell a story effectively to others he must himself know completely such story or picture. Execution is, therefore, lame and impotent without conception.

2. *A United Aim—Unity—Implies that Nothing Stands for Itself.*—Every line, every word, every syllable of a worthy composition is a necessary part of the whole, has some use, is for some purpose. They all coöperate in producing the writer's conception; they have a United Aim. If, then, the student does not realize this coöperative aim he cannot be said to read well. Without understanding the coöperative purpose of all, he cannot tell the relative value of words, phrases, sentences and parts, and his interpretation (?) will be a hap-hazard affair in which the writer's thoughts and feelings run the risk of not being expressed at all. Here is a short poem from Tennyson:

BREAK, BREAK, BREAK.

Break, break, break,
   On thy cold gray stones, O Sea!
And I would that my tongue could utter
   The thoughts that arise in me.

O well for the fisherman's boy,
  That he shouts with his sister at play!
O well for the sailor lad,
  That he sings in his boat on the bay!

And the stately ships go on
  To their haven under the hill;
But O for the touch of a vanish'd hand,
  And the sound of a voice that is still.

Break, break, break,
  At the foot of thy crags, O Sea!
But the tender grace of a day that is dead
  Will never come back to me.

Suppose the student ignores the existence of a united aim
in this poem and reads each line as related to nothing but
itself. He comes to the line "O well for the fisherman's lad
that he shouts with his sister at play." "Ah," says this hap-
hazard student. "Shouting at play, why that's a jolly thing,
so I'll show my audience how a boy can shout. I'll just read
that in a rollicking, roaring, shouting style that will make
plain the fun the boy and his sister are having." And he
does it!

Had this student perceived that poetry and all good writing are not patchwork, but harmonic growth, he would have
read and reread this poem until he had found coöperative
purpose, a united aim. Sooner or later he would have discovered that every syllable helps to set forth melancholy's
wail and that, therefore, the slightest intrusion of jollity
would horribly mutilate one of the poet's purest creations.
Conception then demands a clear understanding of the United
Aim. Without it a student is a ship without a rudder; he
will drift.

3. *The United Aim Comprises Both a Dominant Thought and a Dominant Feeling.*—In every piece of literature there is the idea itself—the thing told, and there is the emotional attitude or feeling of the author (or character) towards this idea or thing. Thus, in the preceding poem we have seen that there is the tale of loneliness itself (the thought) and the feeling of melancholy in respect to this loneliness. In Lincoln's Dedication of Gettysburg Cemetery we have the story of the national importance of the occasion—Dominant Thought, and the feeling of solemnity in respect to this importance—Dominant Feeling, the two comprising the United Aim.

ILLUSTRATION OF TONING A SELECTION.

4. To make plain the process of toning let us take an example—this poem on William Tell:

"Place there the boy," the tyrant said;
"Fix me the apple on his head.
    Ha! rebel, now!
There's a fair mark for your shaft;
To yonder shining apple waft
    An arrow." And the tyrant laughed.
        With quivering brow
Bold Tell looked there; his cheek turned pale;
His proud lips throbbed as if would fail
        Their quivering breath.
"Ha! doth he blanch?" fierce Gesler cried,
"I've conquered, slave, thy soul of pride."
No voice to that stern taunt replied,
        All mute as death.
"And what the meed?" at length Tell asked.
"Bold fool, when slaves like thee are tasked,
        It is my will.

But that thine eye may keener be,
And nerved to such nice archery,
If thou cleav'st yon, thou goest free.
   What! pause you still?
Give him a bow and arrow there;
One shaft—but one." Gleams of despair
Rush for a moment o'er the Switzer's face:
Then passed away each stormy trace,
And high resolve came in their place.
   Unmoved, yet flushed,
"I take thy terms," he muttered low,
Grasped eagerly the proffered bow—
   The quiver searched,
Sought out an arrow keen and long,
Fit for a sinewy arm and strong,
And placed it on the sounding thong,
   The tough yew arched.
He drew the bow, whilst all around
That thronging crowd there was no sound,
   No step, no word, no breath.
All gazed with an unerring eye,
To see the fearful arrow fly;
The light wind died into a sigh,
   And scarcely stirred.
Afar the boy stood, firm and mute;
He saw the strong bow curved to shoot,
   But never moved.
He knew the daring coolness of that hand,
He knew it was a father scanned
   The boy he loved.
The Switzer gazed—the arrow hung,
"My only boy!" sobbed on his tongue;
   He could not shoot.
"Ha!" cried the tyrant, "doth he quail?

Mark how his haughty brow grows pale!"
But a deep voice rung on the gale—
      "Shoot in God's name!"
Again the drooping shaft he took,
And turned to Heaven one burning look,
      Of all doubts reft.
"Be firm, my boy!" was all he said.
The apple's left the stripling's head;
      Ha! Ha! 'tis cleft!
And so it was, and Tell was free.
Quick the brave boy was at his knee
      With rosy cheek.
His loving arms his boy embrace;
But again that tyrant cried in haste,
"An arrow in thy belt is placed;
      What means it? Speak!"
The Switzer raised his clenched hand high,
Whilst lightning flashed across his eye
      Incessantly.
"To smite thee, tyrant, to the heart,
Had Heaven willed it that my dart
      Had touched my boy."
"Rebellion! Treason! Chain the slave!"
A hundred swords around him wave,
Whilst hate to Gesler's features gave
      Infuriate joy.
But that one arrow found its goal,
Hid with revenge in Gesler's soul;
      And Lucerne's lake
Heard his dastard soul outmoan
When Freedom's call abroad was blown,
And Switzerland, a giant grown,
      Her fetters brake.
From hill to hill the mandate flew,

> From lake to lake the tempest grew,
>   With wakening swell,
> Till proud oppression crouched for shame,
> And Austria's haughtiness grew tame,
> And Freedom's watchword was the name
>   Of William Tell.

Before proceeding with the analysis of part of this poem it must be clearly understood:

(a) We are considering the feelings, not the thoughts.

(b) The phraseology set down as describing the states of feeling is not the only phraseology that could be used.

(c) The analysis is not the only analysis. It is given as a practical illustration of the scope and power of the tone principle in the study of literature for the purpose of interpretation.

(d) Conception does not necessarily demand that the particular feeling or its tone shall be written down. A student will often know the feeling aright, but be unequal to describing it in words.

(e) Writing down the feeling, however, insures greater accuracy and will give splendid mental training. The student will then know that he knows.

Coming now to the analysis, it is first necessary to determine the United Aim. After carefully reading the poem we conclude the author intends that every word shall in some way contribute to telling the story of William Tell and the apple—Dominant Thought, and from the viewpoint of sympathy with Tell—Dominant Feeling. This, then, is our United Aim which we shall use as our guide and arbiter.

> "Place there the boy."

This is spoken by the tyrant, and evidently to one of his soldiers. The feeling here, the state dominating Gesler, is one of command; and we so note.

"the tyrant said,"

This is the author himself speaking. What is the feeling here? First we must refer to our United Aim. This decrees that the poet intends to exhibit sympathy for Tell. Then the feeling will be one of indignation. By this is shown our opinion of the tyrant in placing the boy's life in peril. We manifest sympathy for Tell and hatred of Gesler.

"Fix me the apple on his head."

The feeling here, the state dominating Gesler, is one of command:

"Ha! rebel, now!"

This is Gesler to Tell. The words "ha" and "now" tell us of what? Exultation. Gesler says here in reality, "At last, you expert shooter, I've a chance to take the pride out of you."

"rebel"

Plainly this is spoken with contempt.

"There's a fair mark for your shaft;"

Here Gesler does not mean what he says. He knows the mark is not fair but most unfair. Irony is the state, colored with taunting.

"To yonder shining apple waft an arrow."

This is evidently delivered in a tone of command.

And the tyrant laughed.

Here we must think a moment. Does the author intend that we shall utter these words with the feeling accompanying ordinary explanation, or does he desire something more? Does he ask us to suggest on "laughed" the sarcastic, tantalizing way in which Gesler laughed, or, again, does he wish us to show indignation at the fact of the laughing, or, yet again, does he desire to convey to the listener amazement that Gesler could actually exhibit glee at his devilish scheme, or, still again, does he intend indignation to accompany delivery of "the tyrant" and amazement on "laughed"?

Here is a variety of possibilities; how shall we decide? We have agreed that the poet intends as part of his United Aim, sympathy for Tell, hatred of Gesler. Would not the feeling here be indignation, and also amazement bordering on horror, that a man commands a father to shoot a son and laughs at it? The words might be paraphrased colloquially thus, "And would you believe it, the wretch actually had the fiendishness to laugh." Applying this to the author's words, we have "And the tyrant" given with indignation, "laughed" with amazement. It may be argued that this analysis is too subtle, that one state only would underlie these words; but if a story-teller is intense, deeply in earnest, this variety of emotion will be warranted and natural. It is asked would not "laughed" take a tone suggestive of Gesler's particular taunting way, and the answer is that Gesler's fiendish proceeding would surely focus the attention more upon the awfulness than upon the manner.

> With quivering brow
> Bold Tell looked there; his cheek turned pale;
> His proud lips throbbed as if would fail
> Their quivering breath.

Is this the ordinary calm description? No, for the situation is too unusual, too intense for that. The feeling here is deep concern.

> "Ha, doth he blanch?"

Here we have fierce exultation.

> fierce Gesler cried.

Here, explanation tinged with indignation at Gesler.

> "I've conquered,"

Fiendish exultation.

> "slave,"

Contempt here.

> "Thy soul of pride."

Here, exultation and contempt.

> No voice to that stern taunt replied—
> All mute as death.

Is this calm narration? or sympathy? or awe? The occasion, surely, is too vital to tell it colloquially. Pity might creep in, but the stronger drives out the weaker, the mind is above all swayed with the atmosphere of hush, stillness and concern that envelops the occasion. Plainly the feeling is one of awe.

> "And what the meed?"

Tell is struggling to control himself. Agony has given place to indignation, but he is trying hard to master himself. His interrogation would show suppressed indignation.

> At length Tell asked.

This is simple explanation, colored with pity.

> "Bold fool, when slaves like thee are tasked,

Contempt.

> It is my will.

Authority.

Here the analysis must stop. Let the student complete it for himself. Sufficient has been given to show not only the method of tone analysis but to demonstrate its value in securing accuracy and completeness in the conception of the feeling in literature.

Note.—Before toning the remainder of the poem, the student is expected to have thoroughly familiarized himself with the Tone Drills. In analysis, when in doubt as to the name of a feeling, consult the Tone Drills. Where, however, a student finds a phrase that will more effectively call up the tone than those given in the table, let him use it. Also he may sometimes find more than one word necessary to describe some of the mingled emotions. In such cases phrase freely.

5. *Exercises in Toning.*—Proceeding from the easy to the hard, let the student take representative selections and set down as accurately as he can the states or tones demanded.

6. *Interpretative Conception.*—For actual delivery the student must realize that the simple setting down of the tones demanded by a selection is not sufficient. A student has not a true and complete interpretative conception of the feeling in a piece of literature until he has likened it in some way to his own experience, to something he has seen, or heard, or done, or felt, or said. Thus, in William Tell, an effective conception of the feeling accompanying the words "Place there the boy" is not realized by merely saying the state is one of command. He must know command. In effect he must say to himself, "The state is about like my own when I have told some person I have control over to 'do as I bid you,' or 'put that down,' or 'go there at once,'" and the words "the tyrant said" (if indignation be the state decided upon) are not conceived interpretatively until the student, consciously or unconsciously, shall have said, "That's like my own feeling when I have seen some outrageous act—a woman struck, or the like—and have burst out, 'that's a shame,' 'that's an outrage,' 'you cur.'" This process of likening may not necessarily be a conscious one, but, conscious or unconscious, an effective conception demands it. If it be contended that this is debasing or cheapening literature the answer is that such contention is based on the absurd notion that everyday experiences are necessarily vulgar. It is surely **not** degrading literature to arrive at an interpretation **of**

Hamlet's love for his father by going into our own experience and realizing our love for our own father.

7. *Aids to Interpretative Conception.*—Interpretative conception is aided to a marked degree by the practice upon the Tone Drills. In most cases these examples cause in the student just such a process as we have demanded, leading him at once into his experience and enabling him vividly and responsively to know the desired emotion and its tone.

THOUGHT IN EXPRESSION

1.   All good reading and speaking implies not only a right rendering of the feeling, but also a recognition of the true groups—Grouping or Phrasing,—and an appreciation of Prominence.

2.   *Group the Words That Make an Idea.*—In speaking naturally words fall into groups. Thus: "If it is wet there will be no meeting." Here "If it is wet" is one group, "there will be no meeting" is another. To say "If it is wet there" would confuse the listener, and any other arrangement but the one given would also confuse. Grouping helps to make clear the meaning.

3.   *Give Prominence to the Words That So Treated Make the Important Idea Stand Out.*—In speaking naturally that which is important receives such utterance as to make it prominent. In "It is not only hot but red hot" we make the first "hot" and "red" prominent because so treated they bring out the main idea.

As a rule, prominence is given to the word or words that contain the *new* idea, the words containing the old idea being delivered as if in parenthesis. Thus in our example the first "hot" is a new idea and is given prominence. The second "hot," being an old idea, is delivered parenthetically.

In the following sentence the main ideas desired to be conveyed to the listener are, that "Belshazzar . . . made a great feast," "and drank wine," and these words, therefore, constitute the groups demanding prominence, the subsidiary groups being "the king," "to a thousand of his lords" and "before the thousand." The words connected by hyphens

84

make up the group-word, and are to be delivered as if one polysyllabic word, with the emphasis on the accented syllable of the emphatic word:

Belshazzar—(the-king) — made-a-great-feast—(to-a-thousand-of-his-lords)—and-drank-wine—(before-the-thousand).

EXERCISE.

In the selection that follows,

a. Indicate the groups.

b. Indicate the words or groups that demand prominence in delivery.

c. Read aloud with careful regard to grouping and prominence.

BELSHAZZAR'S FEAST.

Daniel v.

Belshazzar the king made a great feast to a thousand of his lords and drank wine before the thousand. Belshazzar, while he tasted the wine, commanded to bring the golden and silver vessels which Nebuchadnezzar, his father, had taken out of the temple which was in Jerusalem; that the king and his lords, his wives and his concubines, might drink therein.

Then they brought the golden vessels that were taken out of the temple of the house of God which was at Jerusalem; and the king and his lords, his wives and his concubines, drank in them.

They drank wine and praised the gods of gold and of silver, of brass, of iron, of wood and of stone. In the same hour came forth the fingers of a man's hand, and wrote over against the candlestick upon the plaister of the wall of the king's palace, and the king saw part of the hand that wrote.

Then the king's countenance was changed in him, and his

thoughts troubled him; and the joints of his loins were loosed, and his knees smote one against another.

The king cried aloud to bring in the enchanters, the Chaldeans and the soothsayers. The king spake and said to the wise men of Babylon: "Whosoever shall read this writing and show me the interpretation thereof, shall be clothed with purple, and have a chain of gold about his neck, and shall rule as one of three in the kingdom." Then came in all the king's wise men, but they could not read the writing nor make known to the king the interpretation.

Then was King Belshazzar greatly troubled, and his countenance was changed in him, and his lords were perplexed.

Now the queen, by reason of the words of the king and his lords, came into the banquet house. The queen spake and said: "O king, live forever; let not thy thoughts trouble thee, nor let thy countenance be changed. There is a man in thy kingdom in whom is the spirit of the holy gods, and in the days of thy father light and understanding and wisdom, like the wisdom of the gods, was found in him; and the king Nebuchadnezzar, thy father; the king, I say, thy father, made him master of the magicians, enchanters, Chaldeans and soothsayers; forasmuch as an excellent spirit, and knowledge, and understanding, interpreting of dreams, and showing of dark sentences, and dissolving of doubts, were found in the same Daniel, whom the king named Belteshazzar. Now let Daniel be called and he will show the interpretation."

Then was Daniel brought in before the king. The king spake and said unto Daniel: "Art thou that Daniel which art of the children of the captivity of Judah, whom the king, my father, brought out of Judah? I have heard of thee, that the spirit of the gods is in thee, and that light and understanding and excellent wisdom is found in thee. And now the wise men, the enchanters, have been brought in before me, that they should read this writing and make known unto me the interpretation thereof; but they could not shew the interpretation of the thing. But I have heard of thee that thou canst give interpretations and dissolve doubts; now if thou canst read the writing, and make known to me the interpretation thereof, thou shalt be clothed with purple, and have a chain of gold about thy neck, and shalt rule as one of three in the kingdom."

Then Daniel answered and said before the king: "Let thy gifts be to thyself, and give thy rewards to another; nevertheless, I will read the writing unto the king and make known to him the interpretation. O thou king, the Most High God gave Nebuchadnezzar, thy father, the kingdom, and greatness, and glory, and majesty; and because of the greatness that he gave him, all the peoples, nations, and languages trembled and feared before him: whom he would, he slew, and whom he would, he kept alive; and whom he would, he raised up, and whom he would, he put down. But when his heart was lifted up and his spirit was hardened, that he dealt proudly, he was deposed from his kingly throne, and they took his glory from him; and he was driven from the sons of men; and his heart was made like the beasts, and his dwelling was with the wild asses; he was fed with grass like oxen, and his body was wet with the dew of heaven; until he knew that the Most High God ruleth in the kingdom of men, and that He setteth up over it whomsoever He will. And thou, his son, O Belshazzar, hast not humbled thine heart, although thou knowest all this, but hast lifted up thyself against the Lord of heaven; and they have brought the vessels of His house before thee, and thou and thy lords, thy wives and thy concubines, have drunk wine in them; and thou hast praised the gods of silver and gold, of brass, iron, wood and stone, which see not, nor hear, nor know; and the God in whose hand thy breath is, and whose are all thy ways, hast thou not glorified. Then was the part of the hand sent from before Him, and this writing was inscribed. And this is the writing that was inscribed: MENE, MENE, TEKEL, UPHARSIN. This is the interpretation of the thing: MENE, God hath numbered thy kingdom and finished it; TEKEL, thou art weighed in the balances and are found wanting; PERES, thy kingdom is divided and given to the Medes and Persians."

Then commanded Belshazzar, and they clothed Daniel with purple, and put a chain of gold about his neck, and made proclamation concerning him that he should rule as one of three in the kingdom. In that night Belshazzar, the Chaldean king, was slain, and Darius, the Mede, received the kingdom, being about threescore and two years old.

DRILLS IN PROMINENCE

Read aloud each of the following, taking care to give prominence to that word or to those words which so treated will best bring out the sense.

1. Look in thy heart and write.—*Sir Philip Sidney.*

2. A great writer does not reveal himself here and there, but everywhere.—*James Russell Lowell.*

3. A puppy plays with every pup he meets, but an old dog has few associates.—*Josh Billings.*

4. No man can be provident of his time who is not prudent in the choice of his company.—*Jeremy Taylor.*

5. He who gives advice to a self-conceited man stands himself in need of counsel.—*La Rochefoucauld.*

6. He that would write what is worthy to be read more than once should blot frequently.—*Horace.*

7. All orators are dumb when beauty pleadeth.—*William Shakespeare.*

8. Drive thy business; let not that drive thee.—*Benjamin Franklin.*

9. Tell me what you are busy about and I will tell you what you are.—*Wolfgang von Goethe.*

10. No book is worth anything which is not worth much. —*John Ruskin.*

11. The books which help you most are those which make you think the most.—*Theodore Parker.*

12. Read a page and think an age.

13. 'Tis the good reader that makes the good book.— *Ralph Waldo Emerson.*

14.   You will find poetry nowhere unless you bring some with you.—*Joseph Joubert.*

15.   For the want of a nail the shoe was lost; for the want of a shoe the horse was lost; for the want of a horse the man was lost.—*Benjamin Franklin.*

16.   We find in life exactly what we put in it.—*Ralph Waldo Emerson.*

17.   An old warrior is never in haste to strike the first blow.—*Pietro Trapassi Metastasio.*

18.   He that will not look before must look behind.—*Gaelic Proverb.*

19.   When clouds are seen wise men put on their cloaks.— *William Shakespeare.*

20.   As turning the logs will make a fire burn, so changes of study a dull brain.—*Henry Wadsworth Longfellow.*

21.   Character is what we are in the dark.

22.   Rich gifts wax poor when givers prove unkind.—*William Shakespeare.*

23.   If men are so wicked with religion, what would they be without it?—*Benjamin Franklin.*

24.   Knowledge comes, but wisdom lingers.—*Alfred Tennyson.*

25.   Wisdom is the principal thing; therefore get wisdom. —*The Bible.*

26.   The fool doth think he is wise, but the wise man knows himself to be a fool.—*William Shakespeare.*

27.   An intense hour will do more than dreamy years.— *Henry Ward Beecher.*

28.   A cow is a very good animal in the field, but we turn her out of the garden.—*Samuel Johnson.*

29.   The foolish and the dead alone never change their opinion.—*James Russell Lowell.*

30.   Leave what you've done for what you have to do;

don't be consistent, but be simply true.—*Oliver Wendell Holmes.*

31.   Fortune gives her hand to the bold man.—*Virgil.*

32.   Be bold, first gate. Be bold, and evermore be bold, second gate. Be not too bold, third gate.—*Inscriptions on the Gates of Busyrane.*

33.   The man who has never been in danger can not answer for his courage.—*La Rochefoucauld.*

34.   I will listen to anyone's convictions, but pray keep your doubts to yourself.—*Wolfgang von Goethe.*

35.   The reward of one duty is the power to fulfill another. —*George Eliot.*

36.   Only so much do I know as I have lived.—*Ralph Waldo Emerson.*

37.   Be not ashamed to own thy follies, but ashamed not to end them.—*Horace.*

38.   It is not flesh and blood, but the heart, that makes brothers.—*Johann Schiller.*

39.   Animals feed, men eat; but only men of intelligence know how to eat.—*Brillat-Savarin.*

40.   Always rise from the table with an appetite, and you will never sit down without one.—*William Penn.*

41.   There is nothing difficult in the world; the only fear is that men will lack perseverance.—*Confucius.*

42.   He who has determined has half his work done.

43.   He who lets the goat be laid on his shoulders is soon forced to carry the cow.—*Italian Proverb.*

44.   Nature gives woman so much power that the law wisely gives them little.—*Johnson.*

45.   He who is slow in promising is surest to keep his word.—*Rousseau.*

46.   Nothing except a battle lost can be half so melancholy as a battle won.—*Wellington.*

47.   He that would have his virtue published, is not the servant of virtue, but glory.—*Johnson.*

48.   Think twice before you speak once and you will speak twice the better for it.

49.   The rays of happiness, like those of light, are colorless when unbroken.—*Longfellow.*

50.   A man of little learning is like the frog who, having never seen the ocean, thinks its well a great sea.—*Burmese Proverb.*

51.   Thy friend has a friend and thy friend's friend has a friend, so be discreet.—*Talmud.*

52.   Let our object be our country, our whole country, and nothing but our country.—*Daniel Webster.*

53.   Circumstances?   I make circumstances.—*Napoleon.*

54.   The moment the skill of the artist is perceived, the spell of the art is broken.—*Macaulay.*

55.   Make all you can, save all you can, give all you can. —*Wesley.*

56.   We can only escape the arbitrariness of the judge by placing ourselves under the despotism of the law.—*Napoleon.*

57.   Honor and shame from no condition rise; act well your part, there all the honor lies.—*Pope.*

58.   He who saith there is no such thing as an honest man, you may be sure is himself a knave.—*Bishop Berkeley.*

59.   He jests at scars that never felt a wound.—*Shakespeare.*

60.   No really great man ever thought himself so.—*Hazlitt.*

61.   True politeness consists in treating others just as you love to be treated yourself.—*Chesterfield.*

62.   You had better return a fan gracefully than give a thousand pounds awkwardly.—*Chesterfield.*

63.   The great man is he who does not lose his child's heart.—*Mencius.*

64. Who speaketh kind words hath many friends, but the harsh man hath but few.—*Burmese Proverb*.

65. So live with thy friend that if he become thine enemy he can do thee no harm.—*Tully*.

66. No friend is a friend until he shall prove a friend.—*Beaumont and Fletcher*.

67. He who hunts for flowers, will find flowers; he who loves weeds may find weeds.—*Beecher*.

68. Little minds are hurt by little things; great minds rise above them.—*La Rochefoucauld*.

69. Words pass away but actions remain.—*Napoleon*.

70. Woman can do everything, because she rules those who command everything.—*French Proverb*.

71. Go to your rich friend's house when invited, to your poor friend's house without invitation.—*Portuguese*.

72. Be courteous to all, but intimate with few.—*Washington*.

73. Even the fool is wise after the event.—*Homer*.

74. The nickel plating gives no power to the engine.

75. Be not forgetful to entertain strangers; for thereby some have entertained angels unawares.—*Bible*.

76. A beautiful eye makes silence eloquent, a kind eye makes contradiction an assent, an enraged eye makes beauty deformed.—*Addison*.

77. To most men experience is like the stern lights of a ship, which illumine only the track it has passed.—*Coleridge*.

78. He who sedulously attends, pointedly asks, calmly speaks, coolly answers, and ceases when he has no more to say, is in possession of some of the best requisites of man.—*Lavater*.

79. Faithful are the wounds of a friend, but the kisses of an enemy are deceitful.—*Bible*.

80.   It is much easier to ruin a man of principle than a man of none, for he may be ruined through his scruples.—*Colton*.

81.   Physic, for the most part, is nothing else but the substitute of exercise and temperance.—*Addison*.

82.   People who are always taking care of their health are like misers, who are hoarding up a treasure which they have never spirit enough to enjoy.—*Sterne*.

83.   A man must first govern himself, ere he be fit to govern a family; and his family, ere he be fit to bear the government in the commonwealth.—*Sir Walter Raleigh*.

84.   Possession is eleven points in the law.—*Cibber*.

85.   If Heaven had looked upon riches to be a valuable thing, it would not have given them to such a scoundrel.—*Swift*.

86.   He who covets what belongs to another deservedly loses his own.—*Phædrus*.

87.   It matters not how long you live, but how well.—*Publius Syrus*.

88.   The manly part is to do with might and main what you can do.—*Emerson*.

89.   We do not count a man's years until he has nothing else to count.—*Emerson*.

90.   Necessity is the argument of tyrants; it is the creed of slaves.—*Pitt*.

ENGLISH PRONUNCIATION

	A	B	C	D
1. a in all	1. balk	1. dawn	1. fall	1. gaudy
2. a in ask	2. bask	2. dance	2. fast	2. glance
3. a in air	3. bare	3. dare	3. fair	3. glare
4. a in at	4. bat	4. dab	4. fat	4. gap
5. a in alms	5. balm	5. dark	5. father	5. guard
6. a in pale	6. babe	6. date	6. fade	6. gate
7. e in cede	7. beet	7. deed	7. feed	7. geese
8. e in earn	8. bird	8. dirge	8. fern	8. girl
9. u in urn	9. burn	9. durst	9. fur	9. gurgle
10. e in net	10. bet	10. debt	10. fed	10. get
11. i in tide	11. bide	11. dine	11. fine	11. guide
12. i in did	12. bit	12. din	12. fit	12. gill
13. o in mode	13. bode	13. dote	13. foal	13. goat
14. o in odd	14. boss	14. dot	14. fop	14. got
15. u in cute	15. abuse	15. duke	15. few	15. gewgaw
16. u in cut	16. but	16. duck	16. fun	16. gun
17. oo in cool	17. boot	17. doom	17. fool	17. goose
18. oo in hook	18. book	18. took	18. full	18. good
19. ow in owl	19. bow	19. doubt	19. fowl	19. gout
20. oi in oil	20. boil	20. doily	20. foil	20. goiter

VOWEL PRACTICE.

In the preceding Vowel Table utter alternately the sounds in:

1 and 5	2 and 5	4 and 10	7 and 12	10 and 12	16 and 9
1 and 2	2 and 4	4 and 12	8 and 9	15 and 17	17 and 16
1 and 14	2 and 14	4 and 5	10 and 6	14 and 9	17 and 18
1 and 19	3 and 6	5 and 14	10 and 3	14 and 16	18 and 16

TABLE OF CONSONANTS.

1. p as in peep	13. s as in sauce
2. b as in bib	14. z as in zone
3. t as in tot	15. sh as in show
4. d as in did	16. zh as in azure
5. ch as in church	17. l as in lull
6. j as in judge	18. m as in mum
7. k as in kick	19. n as in none
8. g as in gig	20. ng as in ring
9. f as in fife	21. r as in roar
10. v as in vivid	22. w as in we
11. th as in thin	23. wh as in why
12. th as in then	24. y as in yet

25. h as in hat

CONSONANT PRACTICE.

Utter distinctly, giving a quick, decisive accent to first syllable:

1. (Lips). Peepuh, beebuh; feefuh, veevuh; wewuh, wheewhuh; kweekwuh; meemuh.

2. (Tongue). Teetuh, deeduh; thethuh, theethuh; seesuh, zeezuh; reeruh; sheeshuh, zheezhuh; neenuh; cheechuh, jeejuh, leeluh.

3. (Jaw). Yeeyuh; keekuh, geeguh.

4. (Abdominal muscles). Heehuh.

5. Practice 1, 2, 3 and 4 of above, using ah and ō in place of "ee," as—pahpuh, bahbuh, etc.; pōpuh, bōbuh, etc.

DRILLS ON SELECTED CONSONANTS.

T, Th, D.
t as in toot.
th as in thick, myth.
th as in though, smooth.
d as in did.

Errors in Pronunciation:

t sometimes incorrectly sounded like d in dun and fad.

d sometimes incorrectly sounded like t in tin and fit.

th in thick and myth sometimes incorrectly sounded like th in smooth and though.

th in though and smooth sometimes incorrectly sounded like th in thick and myth.

Distinction Drill:

(a) sooth, soothe; bath, bathe; both, booth; breath, breathe.
thank, than; think, then; thatch, that.
tin, din; ten, den; tot, dot; tart, dart.

Utter the following vigorously:

(b)	(c)
thin, tin, din	dead, debt, death
than, tan, Dan	heed, heat, heath
thank, tank, dank	shed, sheet, sheath
those, toes, doze	need, neat, beneath
thread, tread, dread	had, hat, hath
thigh, tie, die	ladder, latter, lather
the, tee, dee	bode, boat, both
their, tare, dare	ore, oat, oath
thicket, ticket	pad, pat, path
theme, team, deem	broad, brought, broth
then, ten, den	rod, rot, wroth
thick, tick, Dick	hard, heart, hearth

(d)	(e)
not thatch but thatcheth	to the two that thatcheth
not tether but tethereth	to the two that tethereth
not theorize but theorizeth	to the two that theorizeth
not thicken but thickeneth	to the two that thickeneth
not thieve but thieveth	to the two that thieveth
not thin but thinneth	to the two that thinneth

not thirst but thirsteth   to the two that thirsteth
not thrash but thrasheth   to the two that thrasheth
not thread but threadeth   to the two that threadeth
not threaten but threateneth to the two that threateneth
not throw but throweth   to the two that throweth
not thrill but thrilleth   to the two that thrilleth
not thrive but thriveth   to the two that thriveth
not throb but throbeth   to the two that throbeth
not throttle but throttleth   to the two that throttleth
not thrum but thrumeth   to the two that thrumeth
not thrust but thrusteth   to the two that thrusteth
not thwart but thwarteth   to the two that thwarteth
not thunder but thundereth   to the two that thundereth
not thwack but thwacketh   to the two that thwacketh

Accent Drill:

(a). Tutored, tortured, tattered, tittered, tettered, tottered, torrid, torrent, abated, abetted, attainted, attuned, attired, tautology, tabouret, taciturn, tact, tactics, tantamount, tertiary, tether, strait, tincture.

(b). Didactic, death, defeating, dedicate, dedication, deodorize, data.

Sentences:

(a). To do the truth daily try to think the truth.
(b). To dare, to do, to die.
(c). Two duties do.
(d). He ate edible tamarinds.
(e). They threaten to not abate one jot or tittle.
(f). To think the thought is theoretically to tell the thought, though this thinking the thought telleth not the tale thoroughly.
(g). Theophilus Thistle, the successful thistle sifter, thrust three thousand thistles through the thick of his thumb;

see that thou thrust not three thousand thistles through the thick of thy thumb.

R.

r in rear, roar, row, oar, urn.

Errors in Pronunciation:

Sometimes incorrectly sounded like a in father and like aw in awl.

Distinction Drill:

Utter in pairs decisively, the mind intently upon the distinction:

car, caw; mar, maw; farther, father;
leer, Leah; carve, calve; bore, boa.

Accent Drill:

Pronounce the following, attacking vigorously the accented syllable:

armour, farther, further, shriller, robber, rarely, ewer, berry, rural, arrowroot, arable, burner, approach, bursar, mercer, merger, roiler, rather, murderer, regulator, interpreter, quarter-master, rearing, riderless, rhubarb, phrenzy, rampart, uproarious, oratorical, mirror, uprising, Christian, discerner, rhinoceros, burgomaster, forefinger, harbinger, wharfinger, encroacher, furnisher, hydrographer, chirographer, chevalier, chandelier, fusilier, gondolier, carabinier, rapier, harrier, harquebusier, hearkener, foreigner, extortioner, sojourner, usurper, forswearer, demurrer, harbourer, purchaser, animadverter.

Sentences:

The cart caught the father farther from his hearth than Hawth expected.

Hark! a hawk!

O, horrible! horrible! most horrible!

S.
s in sit, hiss.

Error in Pronunciation:

Sometimes incorrectly sounded like z in zone and ooze.

Distinction Drill:

Utter in pairs decisively, the mind intently upon the distinction:

hiss, his; brace, braze; sounds, zounds; haste, hazed; face, phase; fleece, flees; mace, maize; race, raise; cease, seize; ceaseth, seizeth; muscle, muzzle; use (noun), use (verb).

Accent Drill:

Pronunce the following, attacking vigorously the accented syllable:

passing, massing, asbestos, asceticism, assassins, assets, assessor, associate, assuage, assuasive, basilisk, basis, brassiness, bristles, siesta, disuse (noun), essential, justice, isosceles, slices, losses, mischievousness, pessimism, presence, sassafras, seasons, sensations, sensuous, sparseness.

Sentences:

He says his sowing zone has several associated sections sizing similarly.

Sometimes his hisses seem seriously sent.

SH.
sh in ash, she.

Error in Pronunciation:

Sometimes sounded like zh in seizure.

Distinction Drill:

Utter in pairs. decisively, the mind intently upon the distinction:

tressure, treasure; glacier, glazier: barouche, by rouge;

ashery, azure; meshy, measure; leash, leisure; innovation, invasion; addition, adhesion; concession, concision; my rash, mirage.

Accent Drill:

Pronounce the following, attacking vigorously, the accented syllable:

enmeshed, sheltering, shiftlessness, shriveling, shrunken, splashing, crashing, conscientious, constitutional, splashing, crushing, swishing, bashfulness, refreshments, ocean, nauseous, personification, considerations, commemoration, admonition, misapprehension, additional, expansion, inattention, shiverer, provisional, shrievalty, explanation, harshness, relaxation, hashish, rashness, confessional.

Sentences:

She visually vitiated the abashed glazier's glacier.
The nation's vision of vanishing pleasure.

Z.
z in gaze, zero.

Errors in Pronunciation:

Sometimes incorrectly sounded like s in sit.

Distinction Drill:

See Distinction Drill under sound "s."

Accent Drill:

Pronounce the following, attacking vigorously, the accented syllable:

mesmerism, easiness, visage, prosaic, disposing, Moses, cruising, malfeasance, enthusiasm, protoplasmic, laziness, cousin, business-like, drizzling, miserable, amazement, measles, fizzle, miserly, emblazoned, displeasing, nosegay, apprizing, appeased, visitant, proposing, interpose, irresolute, museum, unwisdom, disease, dizziness, divisible, mizzen-mast.

Sentence Drill:
see under s.

ZH.
zh in rouge, seizure, vision.

Error in Pronunciation:
Sometimes incorrectly sounded like sh in she, ash.

Distinction Drill:
See Distinction Drill for sound "sh."

Accent Drill:
Pronounce the following, attacking vigorously the accented syllable:

vision, seizure, cortege, displeasure, immeasurable, cohesion, transfusion, delusion, unusually, incision, fusionists, provisionally, visualizing, sub-division, revision, casually, cohesion, abrasion, osier, casuistry, abscission, persiflage, erasure, leisurely, infusion, treasured, persuasion, explosion, confusion, collision, bourgeoisie.

Sentences:
See under "sh."

W.
w as in wood, wet.

Errors in Pronunciation:
Sometimes incorrectly sounded like v in veal.

Distinction Drill:
Utter in pairs decisively, the mind intently upon the distinction:

Very, wary; veal, weal; vale, wail; veered, weird; averred, a word; vague, wake; vassal, wassail; vane, wane; vaunt, want; vaulter, Walter; vest, west; vent, went.

Accent Drill:

Pronounce the following, attacking vigorously the accented syllable:

wolverine, wabble, wafer, wagoner, worldliness, wainscoting, waving, interwoven, intertwining, wanderer, awakening, awarding, war-arrow, war-whoop, withershins, work-woman, war-ship, warrior, unwavering, warrantable, bewitching, watchword, watchfulness, water-way, waving, witchingly, wilderness, waywardness, wealthy, wearisomeness, weather-wise, weevil, well-wisher, westwardly, wishy-washy.

Sentences:

With worthiness we welcome Willie Varden.

We were very well versed.

WH.
wh as in whip.

Errors in Pronunciation:

Sometimes incorrectly sounded like w in wool, v in very.

Distinction Drill:

Utter in pairs decisively, the mind intently upon the distinction:

wether, whether; wye, why; wat, what; weed, wheat; wealth, whelp; weal, wheel; wear, where; wine, whine; wide, white; weal, wheel, veal; wary, wherry, very; wine, whine, vine.

Accent Drill:

Pronounce the following, attacking vigorously the accented syllable:

whacking, whatnot, whatever, wheaten, wheel-barrow, whichsoever, wheresoever, wherewithal, whimperer, whimsically, whipper-snapper, whirlwind, whisper, whistler, whirte-weed, whittle-shawl, wharfinger, over-whelming, wheyish, whirligig, awhile.

Sentences:

When the wee whistler was very well whipped.

Why were virtue's warnings whimsically vetoed?

ACCENT DRILL ON VOWELS.

Note. Webster's Dictionary, the Standard and the Century differ in respect to the correct pronunciation of many words. In these exercises, with few exceptions, the pronunciation is that preferred by the Standard.

1. Pronounce the words in the following exercise with decision, attacking vigorously the accented syllable, that is, the syllable that demands the primary accent.

2. Vary the method by uttering each syllable separately, then the whole word.

a in all.

Forestall, disenthrall, altering, psalter, lawyer, applaud, defraud, because, withdraw, foresaw, cauliflower, warrior, laudanum, laureate, gaudy, caulking, bawling, caucus, almanac, allspice, balking, appalling.

a in alms, father.

Cantata, almond, laughter, Alabama, martyrdom, disarmament, bourgeois (citizen), oleomargarine, disembark, promenade, becalmed, armful, embalming, lava.

a in ask.

Impassable, casket, master, basket, slanting, enhance, taskmaster, unasked, basswood, castor, everlasting, lancer, dancer, fastening, aghast, blasting, glass-blowing, impassably, passover, vastness, passport, password, pastoral, pasturage, plastering.

a in at.

Catamaran, chastisement, valentine, paramount, caravan, caricature, passenger, allopathic, coadjutant, combative, disenfranchisement, circumambulate, abjectness, abracadabra, adamantine, aldermanic, somnambulism, anachronism, animalcule, approbative, atavism, biographical.

a in fare.

Parentage, prepare, impairment, despairing, tearing, shareholder, ensnare, unaware, doctrinaire, unbearable, prayerfully, unfairly, heirloom, bearishness, carefully, comparing.

e in eke.

Chimera, coliseum, convenience, credence, cuirassier, cuisine, retreating, experience, inferior, apotheosis, cerement, chameleon, abstemious, adamantean, anæsthesia, capuchin, chevalier, egregious, encyclopedia, homogeneity, mausoleum, monocotyledon.

e in earn.

Alternately, earnestness, versatile, ermine, earning, unconcern, discerning, fertile, infernal, myrtle, mercifully, mercury, merchandise.

oo in hoof, fool.

Pollutedness, overshoot, bamboozle, moonlight, rudiment, proof-reader, disapprove, alluvial, plumage, oolong, ruthless, hoosier, denouement, abstruse, assurance, hallelujah, prurient, youthfulness, foolishness, toothsome, superfluity, spoonful, soothsayer, roofing, rootlet, overrule, caboose, unloosening.

oo in book.

Overtook, footprint, mistook, woodchuck, woolgathering, bullock, bulwark, bushwacker, bulletin, bullion, wolfish, rookery, womanliness, roommate, afoot, brooklet, bookbindery, bulldozing, cookery, unwomanly, crookedness, fulsomeness, hoodwink, unhooking, forsook.

o in odd, cot.

Chronological, cochineal, commonwealth, incomparable, origin, orator, coronet, agnosticism, anemometer, confiscate, monogram, isosceles, mnemonics, anthropophagi, cacophony, chirography, chiropodist, contumacy, contumely, corollary, cosmopolite, epizootic.

u in bud, fun.

Covetousness, coverlet, crushing, cuttle-fish, buttresses, accompaniment, agriculturist, annunciate, cupboard, bungalow, adumbrate, buckwheat, bulkhead, cutpurse, consummate, buncombe, enunciate, abutment, annulment, fulminate, perfunctorily, assumption, butternut, buzzard, circumference, covenanter.

u as in burr, urn.

Furtively, furniture, gurgling, hurtfulness, incursion, insurgent, bifurcate, objurgatory, pursuivant, courteousness, burden, murkiness, murmuring, nurturing, purposeful, surgeon, discourteous, appurtenance, burdensome, burgess, burgomaster, cursorily, curvature, surplice, concur, furrier, furtherance.

a in babe.

Contemporaneously, crystallization, defalcation, decoration, desperado, equivocation, exhortation, expatriate, monomaniac, vagaries, aeronaut, altercation, amelioration, apparatus, naturalization, plagiarism, aquarium, archangel, assailant, attache, aviary, bayonet, candelabra, carbonaceous, chicanery, civilization, commissariat.

i in bide.

Indecipherable, benighted, nightingale, ninetieth, piracy, derisive, dynamite, declining, diadem, admiringly, inquire, nitrogen, notoriety, revivalist, conniving, unreliable, acclimatize, ammoniacal, annihilate, declivous, demoniacal, perspiring, indecisive, environment, icicle, undeniable, unlicensed, unlikelihood.

o in bode.

Locomotive, opponent, equatorial, quotient, loathsome, inappropriate, devotedness, orotund, opprobriousness, socialism, encomium, bureaucracy, chauvinism, spoliater, poulterer, cognomen, condolence, corporeal, corrosive, decorous, diplomacy, diplomatist, misquoted, proposal, infusoria, localize.

oi in boi.

Cloister, poignant, clairvoyance, reconnoiter, avoirdupois, boisterous, avoidance, buoyancy.

ow in owl.

Counterfeit, foundling, counselor, mountainous, abounding, befouled.

u in duke.

Nuisance, dubious, indubitable, maturity, illuminate, obtuse, enthusiasm, acumen, attuning, beauteous, circuitous, peculiar, archdukedom, assiduity, circumlocution, circuitousness, astute, amusement, spurious, ambiguity, minutiæ.

e in met.

Adolescence, amendatory, anemograph, antebellum, betterment, prevalent, blessedness, breathless, brethren, celestial, celluloid, censurable, centenary, cherish, chemistry, cleverness, clericalism, coalesce, commendable, competitive, complexity, incomprehensible, inconsequential, condescendingly, enviousness, epidemic, equestrianism, forensic.

i in it.

Admittance, militarism, astringency, astigmatism, asynchronism, belligerent, benediction, billings-gate, brilliancy, chivalrous, Christendom, commiserate, conditionally, deliciousness, diligence, revisiting, explicitly, fiftieth, sacreligious, forbidding, glistening, gypsum, impossibility, pillory, inconspicuous, insufficiency, rivulet, physicist, novitiate, asphyxiate, aborigines, antithesis, archbishop, asphyxia, benignant, carnivorous, gibberish, lyrical, peninsula, brigand, cachinnatory, centrifugal, centripetal, chivalrous, commiserate, contiguously, convivial, equivocal, delirious, demolition, disputant, electricity, equanimity, erysipelas.

WORDS OFTEN MISPRONOUNCED.

Abattoir, abdomen, abjectly, abjuratory, absolutory, acclimate, acclivous, acetic, acumen, adept, Adonis, aerated, aerial, aeriform, aerolite, aeronaut, agape, albumen, allude, ally, alternate (noun), alternate (verb), alternately, amenable, ammoniacal, annex, annunciation, antipodes, aorist, apotheosis, applicative, aquiline, arid, artificer, ascetic, aspirant, association, atelier, atomic, atrophy, attache, augury, auscultatory, auxiliary, Ave Maria, avoirdupois.

Bade, bayou, belles-lettres, bellows, bestial, bicephalous, bijou, bipartite, bitumen, borealis, brevet, brigand, brooch, caffeine, chameleon, caoutchouc, capuchin, casualty, casuistry, celibacy, ceramic, chastisement, cherubic, chiffonier, chimera, chivalrous, chyle, chyme, clandestine, clangor, classicism, coadjutor, connoisseur, consummate, contemplative, contrary, contrarily, controvert, contumacy, contumely, corrugate, corsair, courteous, covetous, crematory, critique, cuirassier, cuisine.

Data, debonair, debris, debut, debutante, decade, defalcate, deficit, delusive, demesne, demoniacal, denouement, derisive, dilapidate, dissentient, dissoluble, docile, domicile, dubious.

Eclat, edelweiss, effigy, egotism, eligible, elision, elixir, elusive, embroglio, empyrean, encyclical, enervate, ennui, ensemble, entrée, enumerate, enunciation, epitome, equable, equipoise, ermine, esoteric, exchequer, exclusive, exculpate, exeunt, exonerate, exorable, exoteric, expiatory, explicable, exquisite.

Facial, falchion, falcon, feline, fête, fetich, febrile, fiduciary, finale, finance, financier, flaccid, flagitious, formidable, frontal, frontier, fulsome, fustian.

Gallows, gape, gasometer, génie, genii, genuine, germane, ghoul, gibe, gondola, gondolier, granary, gubernatorial, guerdon.

Heinous, hierarchy, holocaust, homeopathic, homeopathist, homicidal, homogeneity, horizon, hospitable, hostage, hydropathy, hyperbole, hypocrisy.

Illusive, immobile, impetus, impious, implacable, importune, imprecatory, inalienable, incognito, incommensurable, incomparable, incomputable, incorrigible, inculcate, indict, indigenous, indisputable, indocile, indubitable, inebriety, inexorable, inexplicable, ingot, inquire, integer, integral, interlocutory, interloper, interminable, internecinal, internecine, interpolate, interregnum, inundate, inveigle, irascible, irrefragable, irremediable, irreparable, irrevocable.

Jasmine, jeremiad, jocose, jocund, juvenile.

Kaleidoscope.

Legendary, legislature, lethargic, leviathan, lithe, lithography, litterateur, lucubratory.

Mangy, mausoleum, mauve, metallurgy, metamorphose, meteorite, meteorology, mezzo-soprano, mimetic, minority, mobilize, monad, monogyny, mulct.

Naive, nasal, natatory, necromancy, noxious, numismatic, nuptial, nymph.

Obesity, obligatory, oblique, obscenity, occult, ocean, onerous, opera-bouffe, ophthalmy, opponent, outre, oyer.

Pacificatory, paleontology, palladium, palsied, panegyric, panegyrist, parachute, patron, patronage, pedagogics, pellucid, pharyngeal, picayune, piquancy, placable, placate, plagiarism, plethora, porphyry, posthumus, prebendary, precedence, precedency, precise, prelude, precocity, predecessor, predilection, presume, primogeniture, priority, pristine, privacy, probity, process, procurator, procuress, prolix, promulgate, prophecy, proscenium, protege, protestation, protocol, provocation, provocative, psalm, pseudonym, psychical, publicist, puerile, puissance, pyramidal, pyrotechnics, pyroxene.

Quay, query.

Rabies, rapier, ratiocination, recitative, recluse, recondite, refragable, refutable, regime, renaissance, renunciation, reparable, repartee, repetitive, reprobatory, requital, reservoir, residuum, resume, retributive, reveillé, ribald, robust, romance, rotund, ruin.

Sacerdotal, salic, salutatory, sarcophagus, saturnine, schism, schismatic, scintillate, senile, seraphic, seraphim, serpentine, servile, sesame, silhouette, sinecure, solecism, sonata, soporific, squalor, stalwart, suicidal, superfluous, supine, supple, surfeit, syncope.

Tepid, thyme, tout-ensemble, troth, trousseau, truculent, truffle, tubercular, turbine.

Ukase, ultimatum, undulatory, unguent, ursuline.

Vehemence, verbatim, vibrative, vibratory, vocable.

Zodiacal, zoolite.

VOCAL DEVELOPMENT

The Untrained Voice is Unequal to Demands.—The un-
cultivated voice rarely does the bidding of its owner; what
the speaker desires to do and what his untrained voice actually does are, usually, very far apart. The speaker may be
truly in earnest, but ineffective because his voice fails to carry
the sound, or is unpleasantly high or rasping, or breathy or
wheezy. Or, again, his stream of sound may be so thin that
it fails to convey sincerity.

The Voice Can Be Improved.—Nature's kindness in regard
to the voice is the same as in respect to all other organs. She
has generously given to it a capacity for growth and refine-
ment; also she has very generously withheld from us the
limits of that capacity.

*Organs Directly or Indirectly Necessary to the Production
of Voice.*—*Diaphragm* (muscle at base of chest and forming
roof of abdominal cavity) ; *abdominal muscles* (extending
across abdomen and waist in front) ; *costal and intercostal
muscles* (joined to the ribs and aiding in the rise and fall of
short ribs) ; *pectoral muscles* (extending over chest) ; *thorax*
(cavity containing the lungs) ; *lungs* (with their air cells and
tubes all joining and ending in two tubes, one from each
lung, called the bronchi) ; the *bronchi* (which also join, forming the windpipe) ; *windpipe or trachea* (a large tube) ;
larynx, or vocal box, in which sound is made (Adam's apple) ;
true vocal cords (two white ligaments stretching across voice
box; expired air passes on but one side of each, and in pure

111

tones the cords are but a hair breadth apart, while in breathing tones distance increases with the predominance of breath) ; *mouth* proper, *nasal cavities, hard palate, soft palate, tongue, teeth, lips, jaw.*

VOCAL DRILLS

Relax throat; let the sounds seem to make themselves.

To Secure Coöperation of Abdominal Muscles.

1.   (a).   Laugh out heartily—*o, ah, oo,* once, twice, three times, five times.   Direct tone to front of mouth.   Place hand just below waist and note how, when laugh is hearty, the abdominal muscles coöperate.   If throat is scraped, it is a sign of incorrect use.   Remedy: use for a time a match about one to one and one-half inches long, placed perpendicularly between the teeth.

(b).   Laugh out heartily, yet freely and easily: *All, ask, air, at, alms, ale, eel, earn, urn, ebb, isle, it, oak, odd, use, up, ooze, hook, owl, oil.*

(c).   Slide the voice upwards on sounds in 1b; also on sounds, syllable by syllable, in the following:

"I cannot, my lords, I will not, join in congratulation on misfortune and disgrace. This, my lords, is a perilous and tremendous moment. It is not a time for adulation. The smoothness of flattery cannot save us in this awful and rugged crisis. It is now necessary to instruct the throne in the language of truth. We must, if possible, dispel the delusion and darkness which envelop it, and display, in its full danger and genuine colors, the ruin which is brought to our doors. Can ministers still presume to expect support in their infatuation? Can Parliament be so dead to its dignity and duty as to give its support to measures thus obtruded and forced upon it? Measures, my lords, which have brought this late flour-

ishing empire to scorn and contempt. But yesterday and
Britain might have stood against the world; now, none so
poor as to do her reverence."

To Free the Vocal Muscles.

2. (a). Let head fall and revolve it lifelessly.

(b). Yawn—*skah, skaw, glahgle, glawgle, klahk, klawk,
gahg, gawg, lahl, lawl.*

(c). Sob 2b.

(d). Practice Tone Drills Nos. 8, 63, 86, 110, 128, 132,
137, 145, 166, 181, 194, 200, 207.

To Secure Flexibility.

3. (a). Slide the voice upwards, without pause, on the
sounds *blee, blo, blah; lahl, lawl, lile; e, o, ah, oo;* also on
sounds in 1b and 1c. Maintain throughout a feeling of
brightness and geniality.

(b). Practice Tone Drills Nos. 1, 9, 5, 16, 20, 25, 42, 47,
94, 106, 111, 126, 132, 141, 169d, 180, 182, 190, 201.

To secure Forward Placing of Tone.

4. (a). Utter decisively and brightly, with mind upon
projecting sounds to some specific point: *bābā, bēbē, bībī;
dādā, dēdē, dīdī; fāfā, fēfē, fīfī; jājā,* etc.; *kākā,* etc.; *lālā,*
etc.; *sāsā,* etc.; *tātā,* etc.; *nānā,* etc.; *vāvā,* etc.; *māmā,* etc.;
wāwā, etc.; *kwākwā,* etc; *rārā,* etc.

(b). Utter *ip, it, ik,* decisively.

(c). Utter explosively—*puh, tuh, kuh.*

(d). Utter decisively, *skah, skaw, glahgle, glawgle, klahk,
klawk, gahg, gawg.*

(e). Utter sounds in 1b with the aim of hitting top corner
of room with each sound. Utter one syllable at a time.

(f). Practice Drills in Sections 8 and 9.

(g). Practice 1a, 1b and 1c.

(h). Practice Tone Drills 24, 26, 46, 63, 64, 89, 157, 200,
208.

To Free the Jaw.

5. (a). With jaw relaxed utter *blee-blee, blo-blo, blah-blah* (1) aloud; (2) silently.

(b). Utter *e-yah, e-yaw, e-yoi* (1) aloud, (2) silently.

(c). Utter 2b.

To Free the Tongue.

6. (a). Utter *lahl, lawl, lile.*

(b). Yawn—*aw, ah.*

(c). Utter *tētē, tōtō, tahtah; thēthē, thōthō, thahthah; nēnē, nōnō, nahnah, kēkē,* etc.; *lēlē,* etc.; *rērē,* etc.

(d). Utter: "Theophilus Thistle the successful thistle sifter thrust three thousand thistles through the thick of his thumb; see that thou thrust not three thousand thistles through the thick of thy thumb."

(e). Practice the Articulation Drill for letter "T."

To Free the Lips.

7. (a). Utter decisively *e, o, ah, oo.*

(b). Utter decisively *bēbē, bōbō, bahbah; fēfē, fōfō, fahfah; mēmē, mōmō, mahmah; kwēkwē, kwōkwō, kwah-kwah; vēvē,* etc.; *wēwē,* etc.; *wheewhee,* etc.

To Free the Nasal Passage.

8. (a). With the aim of causing vibration in the upper part of the nasal chamber utter the sounds *nun, neen, nane, noon.*

(b). Slide the sound *"un"* up and down the scale.

(c). Hum a tune, throat free, lips gently meeting.

To Secure Resonance and Volume.

9. (a). Practice breathing exercises.

(b). Prolong sounds *e, o, ah, oo.*

(c). Prolong sounds, syllable by syllable, in 1b and 1c.

(d). Go up and down scale note by note with each sound in 7a, 1b.

(e). Utter *moo-ane, moo-een, moo-ine, moo-un, moo-ohn,* up and down scale.

(f). Hum a tune, throat open, lips gently meeting.

(g). Sob sounds in 4d, 6a.

(h). Practice Tone Drills Nos. 8, 10, 19, 32, 33, 34, 35, 40, 41, 61, 96, 110, 137, 152, 154, 181, 189, 194, 207.

To Develop Musical Quality.

10. (a). Practice softly and with the mind upon producing sweetness of tone the Drills, Section 9, b, c, d, e, f.

(b). Moan sounds in 5a, 6a, 7a, 8a.

(c). Practice Tone Drills Nos. 36, 110, 136, 150, 166, 168, 181, 189, 207, 213.

BREATHING EXERCISES.

11. (a). Lying flat upon back, body relaxed, gently exhaust the air in lungs through a quill toothpick, a clay pipestem or some other article with an aperture not larger than a pin's head. Pause a second, refill lungs slowly through the nostrils. Vary the rate—fast, slow, medium.

(b). *Costal Breathing.*—Distend sides while inhaling through nostrils, relax gradually with slow exhalation.

(c). *Chest Breathing.*—Relax chest muscle; inhale and expand chest to fullest capacity. Exhale gradually.

(c). *Waist Breathing.*—Inhale, at same time expanding entire circle of waist.

(d). *Dorsal Breathing.*—Inhale as if endeavoring to thrust out the muscles of the back by the force of the air.

(e). *Abdominal Breathing.*—Breathe deeply, forcing the abdominal muscles outward. Let them sink when expelling the breath.

(f). *Full Breathing.*—Inhale slowly, expanding all parts.

(g). *Modes of Exhaling.*—Breathe out letter h (a) gently, (b) with steady force, (c) abruptly like a pistol shot.

BODILY DEVELOPMENT AND RESPONSIVENESS

1. *Effective Expression Demands Bodily Development.* —Rarely does the body, untrained, express itself adequately. There is usually awkwardness in attitude or gesture and general ungainliness. These destroy harmony in expression. They invite attention to themselves and not to the thought and feeling. Plainly some method of bodily development and control must be followed that will remedy this.

2. *Mental Processes an Aid to Bodily Development.*— Deeply feeling beauty, sublimity, grandeur and allied emotions will, in some degree, assist bodily expression. Also, all emotional expression in itself tends to render the body coordinately active.

3. *The Practice of the Tone Drills* with the specific purpose of bodily expression is invaluable in developing variety and ease.

4. *Specific Bodily Drills a Further Aid.*—Besides the mental processes certain specific bodily movements are especially valuable in attaining physical responsiveness.

EXERCISES.

5. (a). Arms full length above head, thumbs, crossed, try to touch the toes without bending the knees—slow movement throughout.

(b). Bend body from waist and revolve from right to left, left to right.

(c). Arms above head, let hands drop lifelessly; similarly forearm, then whole arm. Let body sink lifelessly almost to ground.

(d). Make lifeless and revolve whole arm, hand.

(e). Make figure 8 with whole arm, with hand.

(f). Make script alphabet—small letters—with whole arm; with hand.

(g). Bend head forward and revolve it, lifelessly, from right to left, from left to right.

(h). Extend arm to front, palm upwards; open and shut fingers nine times.

(i). Arms at side, hands shut, extend arms and open hands —at side, arms at angle of 30 degrees from body, then at 90 degrees (parallel with shoulder blades), then at 120 degrees. Also at same angles obliquely and in front.

METHOD OF STUDY AND PRACTICE OF EXPRESSION

1. *Determine the United Aim:*
    - (a). The Dominant Thought. What does the selection aim to show, prove, tell, etc.?
    - (b). The Dominant Feeling. What is the emotional attitude of the author (or character) towards the Dominant Thought?
2. *Determine the Groups.* What words are closely related?
3. *Determine the Ideas (and Their Words) That Demand* (a) *Prominence,* (b) *Pause.*
4. *Determine the Tones in Which the Various Ideas Should Be Delivered.* What are the various feelings in the selection and what tones will best show these?
5. *Make the Ideas Yours.* Understand with absolute clearness every idea in the selection.
6. *Make the Feelings Yours.* Exercise the imagination upon every idea. Go into your own experience and see if the emotion has not been yours in some simple form.

(Groups may be indicated by parentheses, prominent words by underlining, tones by marginal notes.)

METHOD OF PRACTICING DELIVERY.

1. Have a listener. If impracticable, imagine one.
2. Tell *ideas,* not words.
3. Intensely desire to have the idea grasped by listener.
4. Aim to convey to the listener the feelings in the selection. Manifest vividly the true feeling toward the ideas expressed.

PART II
SELECTIONS
CHOSEN FOR THEIR VALUE AS
STUDIES IN DOMINANT TONES
AND AFFORDING
A REPRESENTATIVE COURSE IN EXPRESSION

This section of selections is intended to furnish, on a more sustained scale, further drill upon the phases of feeling. To this end each selection is classified under its dominant tone.

This does not mean that there is but one tone in the selection but that the tone given predominates. Thus, in "The Field of Waterloo," the phrase "Wellington had the favorable side" partakes of Conviction, but the dominant tone of the entire selection is Explanation, under which head it is classified.

Strictly speaking there is no such thing as a distinctly marked evolution in the expression of phases of feeling. A child, by the time he can read, will be able to express joy, affection, anger, admiration, impatience, assertion, gayety equally well, *if the phrasing in which the feeling is couched is identical with his own experience*. A few forms of feeling such as horror and remorse may be considered as later stages because of their comparative rarity in experience, but on the whole the power to express varieties of feeling cannot be considered as being a steady growth, each month or year opening up new fields of emotion. The difficulty of expression lies not so much in the kind of feeling as in *the lack of vividness with which it appeals to experience*. Order of sequence, therefore, will depend upon the relative frequency with which a given kind of feeling has come vividly into our lives. But, the experience of no two lives being identical, the determining factor is individuality, and no order can be said to be applicable universally.

Broadly speaking the Dominant Tones may be arranged for a course of study in three different ways:

First—In the order set forth in the book, which aims to combine the law of proceeding from the familiar to the unfamiliar (so far as that law applies to kinds of emotion), with the law of variety.

Second—By a close adherence to the principle of Contrast, following Joy with Solemnity, Geniality with Indignation and so on.

Third—By grouping kindred emotions, and arranging them from the mild to the intense, as Calmness, Solemnity, Sublimity; Geniality, Gayety, Joy, Exultation; Gloom, Awe, Horror; Indifference, Belittling, Ridicule, Contempt; Admiration, Aspiration, Affection, Love, Adoration.

It will be noted that under the majority of tones there are two or three selections, one from the field of oratory, one from lyric or narrative poetry, and sometimes one from dramatic literature, usually Shakespeare. This permits a teacher or student to choose selections adapted either to a public speaker's course or to a course in reading. Power in either field, however, is best attained by the study of selections from both fields.

It will be seen that of the selections under a particular tone, frequently one selection is more difficult than another. This fact will suggest, at once, a rational sequence of study.

While the selections under this head are intended, primarily, as studies in dominant tones, they afford opportunity for the study and application of all the principles and rules of oral expression.

TONE OF EXPLANATION.

(See Tone Drill No. 94.)

[The tone of Explanation in its purest form indicates simply a
desire to make plain, to tell what the thing is or how it happened.
It is akin to Frankness. Usually there is a tinge of Geniality.]

The Battlefield of Waterloo.

VICTOR HUGO.

Those who would get a clear idea of the battle of Waterloo
have only to lay down upon the ground in their mind a
capital A.   The left stroke of the A is the road from Nivelles,
the right stroke is the road from Genappe, the cross of the A
is the sunken road from Ohan to Braine-l'Alleud.   The top
of the A is Mount Saint Jean, Wellington is there; the left-
hand lower point is Hougomont, Reille is there with Jerome
Bonaparte; the right-hand lower point is La Belle Alliance,
Napoleon is there.   A little below the point where the cross
of the A meets and cuts the right stroke, is La Haie Sainte.
At the middle of this cross is the precise point where the final
battle-word was spoken.   There the lion is placed, the involuntary symbol of the supreme heroism of the Imperial Guard.
The triangle contained at the top of the A, between the two
strokes and the cross, is the plateau of Mount Saint Jean.
The struggle for this plateau was the whole of the battle.
The wings of the two armies extended to the right and left
of the two roads from Genappe and from Nivelles; D'Erlon
being opposite Picton, Reille opposite Hill.   Behind the point
of the A, behind the plateau of Mount Saint Jean, is the
forest of Soignes.   As to the plain itself, we must imagine a
vast undulating country; each wave commanding the next,
and these undulations rising toward Mount Saint Jean are
there bounded by the forest.

Both generals had carefully studied the plain of Mount
Saint Jean, now called the plain of Waterloo.   Already in the

preceding year, Wellington, with the sagacity of prescience, had examined it as a possible site for a great battle. On this ground and for this contest Wellington had the favorable side, Napoleon the unfavorable. The English army was above, the French army below.

The Bashful Man.

HENRY MC KENZIE.

I labor under a species of distress, which, I fear, will at length drive me utterly from refined society. This distress is an extreme bashfulness and awkwardness. However, having determined to conquer these disadvantages, three days ago I accepted an invitation to dine with Sir Thomas Friendly. He has two small sons and five tall daughters, all grown-up, and living at Friendly Hall.

As I approached the house, a dinner bell alarmed my fears, lest I had spoiled the dinner by want of punctuality. At my first entrance I summoned all my fortitude, and made my rehearsed bow to Lady Friendly; but, unfortunately, bringing back my left foot into the third position, I trod upon the gouty toe of poor Sir Thomas, who had followed close at my heels. The confusion this accident occasioned in me is hardly to be conceived.

The cheerfulness of her ladyship, and the familiar chat of the young ladies, insensibly led me to throw off my reserve and sheepishness, till, at length, I ventured to join in the conversation, and even to start fresh subjects. The library being richly furnished with books in elegant bindings, I conceived Sir Thomas to be a man of literature; and ventured to give my opinion concerning the several editions of the Greek classics—in which the Baronet's ideas exactly coincided with my own! To this subject I was led by observing an edition of Xenophon, in sixteen volumes; which (as I had never before heard of such a thing) greatly excited my curiosity, and I approached to examine what it could be. Sir Thomas saw what I was about, and (as I supposed) willing to save me trouble, rose to take down the book, which made me more eager to prevent him; and, hastily laying my hand on the first volume, I pulled it forcibly—when, lo! instead of books, a board, which, by leather and gilding, had been made to look like sixteen volumes, came tumbling down, and, unluckily, pitched upon a Wedgewood inkstand on the table under it. In vain did Sir Thomas assure me there was no harm done. I saw the ink streaming from an inlaid table on the Turkey carpet; and, scarce knowing what I did, attempted to stop its progress with my cambric handkerchief. In the height of this confusion, we were informed that dinner was served up.

In walking through the hall and suite of apartments to the dining-room, I had time to collect my scattered senses; till I was desired to take my seat at table, betwixt Lady Friendly and her eldest daughter. I will not relate the several blunders which I made during the first course, or the distresses occasioned by my being desired to carve a fowl, or help to various dishes that stood near me, spilling a sauce-boat, and knocking down a salt-cellar; rather let me hasten to the second course, where fresh disasters quite overwhelmed me.

I had a piece of rich sweet pudding on my fork, when Miss Louisa Friendly begged to trouble me for part of a pigeon that stood near me. In my haste, scarce knowing what I did, I whipped the pudding into my mouth—hot as a burning coal! It was impossible to conceal my agony; my eyes were starting from their sockets! At last, in spite of shame and resolution, I was obliged to——drop the cause of torment on my plate. Sir Thomas and the ladies all compassionated my misfortune, and each advised a different application. One recommended oil, another water, but all agreed that wine was perhaps the best for drawing out the heat; and a glass of sherry was brought me from the side-board—I snatched it up with eagerness; but oh! how shall I tell the sequel? Whether the butler by accident mistook, or purposely designed to drive me mad, I know not; but he gave me the strongest brandy, with which I filled my mouth, already flayed and blistered. Totally unused to every kind of ardent spirits, with my tongue, throat, and palate as raw as beef, what could I do? I could not swallow, and, clapping my hands upon my mouth, the burning liquor squirted from me, like a fountain, over all the dishes, and I was crushed by bursts of laughter from all quarters.

In vain did Sir Thomas reprimand the servants, and Lady Friendly chide her daughters; the measure of my shame and their diversion was not yet complete. To relieve me from the intolerable state of perspiration which this accident had caused, without considering what I did, I wiped my face with that ill-fated handkerchief, still wet from the consequences of the fall of Xenophon, and covered my features with streaks of ink in every direction! The Baronet himself could not support this shock, but joined his lady in the general laugh; while I sprang from the table in despair, rushed out of the house, and ran home, in an agony of confusion and disgrace, which the most poignant sense of guilt could not have excited.

Othello's Defence.

WILLIAM SHAKESPEARE.

Most potent, grave, and reverend signiors,
My very noble and approved good masters,
That I have ta'en away this old man's daughter,
It is most true; true, I have married her:
The very head and front of my offending
Hath this extent, no more. Rude am I in my speech,

And little blest with the soft phrase of peace;
For since these arms of mine had seven year's pith,
Till now some nine moons wasted, they have used
Their dearest action in the tented field;
And little of this great world can I speak,
More than pertains to feats of broil and battle;
And therefore little shall I grace my cause
In speaking for myself.   Yet, by your gracious patience,
I will a round unvarnish'd tale deliver
Of my whole course of love; what drugs, what charms,
What conjuration and what mighty magic—
For such proceeding I am charged withal—
I won his daughter.
Her father loved me, oft invited me,
Still questioned me the story of my life
From year to year, the battles, sieges, fortunes,
That I have passed.
I ran it through, even from my boyish days
To the very moment that he bade me tell it;
Wherein I spake of most disastrous chances,
Of moving accidents by flood and field,
Of hair-breadth 'scapes i' the imminent deadly breach,
Of being taken by the insolent foe,
And sold to slavery, of my redemption thence,
And portance in my travel's history:
Wherein of antres vast and deserts idle,
Rough quarries, rocks, and hills whose heads touch heaven,
It was my hint to speak,—such was the process;
And of the Cannibals that each other eat,
The Anthropophagi, and men whose heads
Do grow beneath their shoulders.   This to hear
Would Desdemona seriously incline:
But still the house-affairs would draw her thence;
Which ever as she could with haste dispatch,

She 'ld come again, and with a greedy ear
Devour up my discourse: which I observing,
Took once a pliant hour, and found good means
To draw from her a prayer of earnest heart
That I would all my pilgrimage dilate,
Whereof by parcels she had something heard,
But not intentively: I did consent,
And often did beguile her of her tears
When I did speak of some distressful stroke
That my youth suffer'd.   My story being done,
She gave me for my pains a world of sighs:
She swore, in faith, 'twas strange, 'twas passing strange;
'Twas pitiful, 'twas wondrous pitiful:
She wish'd she had not heard it, yet she wish'd
That heaven had made her such a man: she thank'd me,
And bade me, if I had a friend that loved her,
I should but teach him how to tell my story,
And that would woo her.   Upon this hint I spake:
She loved me for the dangers I had pass'd,
And I loved her that she did pity them.
This only is the witchcraft I have used.
Here comes the lady; let her witness it.   —Othello, i., 3.

TONE OF GENIALITY.
(See Tone Drill No 108.)

[The tone of Geniality manifests a feeling of good will. It says
to the listener, more eloquently than words, ''I wish you well, it
is a pleasure to talk to you, I delight in your company.'']

Agreeable People.
T. DE WITT TALMAGE.

Agreeable people! I see by your looks, my friends, that
you belong to this class. These good-humored husbands
before me are all what they ought to be, good-natured as a

May morning; and when the wife asks for a little spending-money, the good man of the purse says, "All right; here's my pocket-book. My dear, take as much as you want, and come soon again." These wives at eveningtide always greet their companions home with a smile and say, "My dear, your slippers are ready and the muffins warm. Put your feet up on this ottoman. Bless the dear man!" These brothers always prefer the companionship of their own sisters to that of any one else's sister, and take them out almost every evening to lectures and concerts. And I suppose that in no public building to-night in this city, or in any other city, is there a more mild, affable, congenial and agreeable collection of people than ourselves.

The world has a great many delightful people who are easily pleased. They have a faculty of finding out that which is attractive. They are like a bee that no sooner gets out of the hive than it pitches for a clovertop. They never yet walked into a picture-gallery but they were refreshed and thankful. They saw some exquisite gem that kindled their admiration. There was some pleasant face in a picture that for hours kept looking over their shoulder. They will never forget how in one of them a vine in filial affection, with its tender arm hugged up an old grandfather of a tree that was about to feel the stiff breeze. They never came from a concert but there was at least one voice that they admired, and wondered how in one throat God could have placed such exhaustless fountains of harmony.

They like the spring, for it is so full of bird and bloom, and, like a priestess, stands swinging her censer of perfume before God's altar; and the summer is just the thing for them, for they love to hear the sound of mowing-machines, and battalions of thunderbolts grounding arms among the mountains; and autumn is their exultation, for its orchards are golden with fruit, and the forests march with banners dipped in sunsets and blood-red with the conflicts of frost and storm.

And they praise God for winter, that brings the shout of children, playing blind-man's buff, with handkerchief they can see through, around a blazing fire, and the snow shower that makes Parthenons and St. Mark's Cathedrals out of a pigeon-coop, and puts brighter coronets than the Georges ever wore on the brow of the bramble, and turns the wood-shed into a "royal tower" filled with crown jewels; and that sends the sleigh-riding party, in buffalo robes, behind smoking steeds. Three cheers for the goodnatured!

Henry V.'s Wooing.

WILLIAM SHAKESPEARE.

I' faith, Kate, my wooing is fit for thy understanding: I am glad thou canst speak no better English.; for, if thou couldst, thou wouldst find me such a plain king that thou wouldst think I had sold my farm to buy my crown. I know no ways to mince it in love, but directly to say "I love you:" then if you urge me farther than to say "Do you in faith?" I wear out my suit. Give me your answer; i' faith, do: and so clap hands and a bargain: how say you, lady?

If I could win a lady at leap-frog, or by vaulting into my saddle with my armour on my back, under the correction of bragging be it spoken, I should quickly leap into a wife. Or if I might buffet for my love, or bound my horse for her favours, I could lay on like a butcher and sit like a jack-an-apes, never off. But, before heaven, Kate, I cannot look greenly nor gasp out my eloquence, nor have I no cunning in protestation; only downright oaths, which I never use till urged, nor never break for urging. If thou canst love a fellow of this temper, Kate, whose face is not worth sun-burning, that never looks in his glass for love of anything he sees there, let thine eye be thy cook. I speak to thee plain soldier: if thou canst love me for this, take me; if not, to say to thee that I shall die, is true; but for thy love, by the Lord, no; yet I love thee too.

And while thou livest, dear Kate, take a fellow of plain and uncoined constancy; for he perforce must do thee right, because he hath not the gift to woo in other places: for these fellows of infinite tongue, that can rhyme themselves into ladies' favours, they do always reason themselves out again. What! a speaker is but a prater; a rhyme is but a ballad; a straight back will stoop; a black beard will turn white; a curled pate will grow bald; a fair face will wither; a full eye will wax hollow: but a good heart, Kate, is the sun and the moon; or, rather, the sun, and not the moon; for it shines bright and never changes, but keeps his course truly. If thou would have such a one, take me; and take me, take a soldier; take a soldier, take a king. And what sayest thou then to my love? speak, my fair, and fairly, I pray thee.

Put off your maiden blushes; avouch the thoughts of your heart with the looks of an empress; take me by the hand, and say "Harry of England, I am thine:" which word thou shalt no sooner bless mine ear withal, but I will tell thee aloud "England is thine, Ireland is thine, France is thine, and Henry Plantagenet is thine;" who, though I speak it before his face, if he be not fellow with the best king, thou shalt find the best king of good fellows. Come, your answer in broken music; for thy voice is music, and thy English broken; therefore, queen of all, Katharine, break thy mind to me in broken English, wilt thou have me? I kiss your hand, and I call you my queen.—Henry V, v., 2.

TONE OF ASSERTION.
(See Tone Drill No. 24.)

[The tone of Assertion denotes the feeling of aggressive positiveness. The ego dominates. The speaker means what he says and wishes the listener to know it.]

* A Gentleman.
GEORGE W. CURTIS.

A gentleman is not an idler, a trifler, a dandy; he is not a scholar only, a soldier, a mechanic, a merchant; he is the flower of men, in whom the accomplishment of the scholar, the bravery of the soldier, the skill of the mechanic, the sagacity of the merchant, all have their part and appreciation. A sense of duty is his mainspring, and like a watch crusted with precious stones, his function is not to look pretty, but to tell the time of day.

Philip Sidney was not a gentleman because his grandfather was Duke of Northumberland, and his father lord-deputy of Ireland, but because he was himself generous, simple, truthful, noble, refined. He was born with a gold spoon in his mouth, but the gold is only the test. In the mouths of the base, it becomes brass and iron. George IV, called with bitter irony, the first gentleman in Europe, was born with the gold spoon, but his acrid humors turned it to the basest metal, betraying his mean soul. George Stephenson was born with the pewter spoon in his mouth, but the true temper of his soul turned it into pure gold. The test of a gentleman is his use, not his uselessness; whether that use be direct or indirect, whether it be actual service or only inspiring and aiding action.

"To what purpose should our thoughts be directed to various kinds of knowledge," wrote Philip Sidney, in 1578, "unless room be afforded for putting it into practice so that public advantage may be the result?" And Algernon Sidney

* From "Literary and Social Essays." Copyright, 1895, by Harper & Bro.

said, nearly a century later, "I have ever had it in my mind that when God cast me into such a condition as that I cannot save my life but by doing an indecent thing, He shows me the time has come wherein I should resign it."

And when that time came he did resign it; for every gentleman instinctively serves justice and liberty. He feels himself personally disgraced by an insult to humanity, for he, too, is only a man; and however stately his house may be and murmurous with music, however glowing with pictures and graceful with statues and reverend with books—however his horses may outtrot other horses, and his yachts outsail all yachts—the gentleman is king and master of these and not their servant; he wears them for ornament, like the ring on his finger or the flower in his buttonhole, and if they go, the gentleman remains. He knows that all their worth comes from human genius and human training; and loving man more than the works of man, he instinctively shuns whatever in the shape of man is degraded, outraged or forsaken. He does not make the poverty of others the reason for robbing them; he does not make the oppression of others the reason for oppressing them, for his gentility is his religion; and therefore with simple truth and tender audacity the old English dramatist Dekkar calls Him who gave the name to our religion, and who destroyed the plea that might makes right—"the first true gentleman that ever breathed."

Peaceful Agitation.

CHARLES MACKAY.

We want no flag, no flaunting rag, for Liberty to fight;
We want no blaze of murderous guns, to struggle for the
    right.
Our spears and swords are printed words, the mind our battle-
    plain;
We've won such victories before,—and so we shall again.

The greatest triumphs sprung from force will stain the
    brightest cause:
'Tis not in blood that Liberty inscribes her civil laws.
She writes them on the people's heart in language clear and
    plain:—
True thoughts have moved the world before,—and so they
    shall again.

We yield to none in earnest love of Freedom's cause sublime;
We join the cry "Fraternity!" we keep the march of Time,
And yet we grasp not pike nor spear, our victories to obtain;
We've won without their aid before,—and so we shall again.

We want no aid of barricade to show a front to Wrong;
We have a citadel in Truth, more durable and strong.
Calm words, great thoughts, unflinching faith, have never
    striv'n in vain;
They've won our battles many a time,—and so they shall
    again.

Peace, Progress, Knowledge, Brotherhood—the ignorant may
    sneer,
The bad deny: but we rely to see their triumph near.
No widows' groans shall load our cause, nor blood of brethren
    stain;
We've won without such aid before,—and so we shall again.

Brutus's Speech in the Forum.

WILLIAM SHAKESPEARE.

Romans, countrymen, and lovers! hear me for my cause,
and be silent, that you may hear: believe me for mine honour,
and have respect for mine honour, that you may believe;
censure me in your wisdom, and awake your senses, that you
may the better judge.   If there be any in this assembly, any

dear friend of Cæsar's, to him I say that Brutus' love to
Cæsar was no less than his.   If then that friend demand why
Brutus rose against Cæsar, this is my answer: not that I
loved Cæsar less, but that I loved Rome more.   Had you
rather Cæsar were living, and die all slaves, than that Cæsar
were dead, to live all freemen?   As Cæsar loved me, I weep
for him; as he was fortunate, I rejoice at it; as he was
valiant, I honour him; but as he was ambitious, I slew him.
There is tears for his love; joy for his fortune; honour for
his valour; and death for his ambition.   Who is here so base
that would be a bondman?   If any, speak; for him have I
offended.   Who is here so rude that would not be a Roman?
If any, speak; for him have I offended.   Who is here so vile
that will not love his country?   If any, speak; for him have
I offended.   I pause for a reply.   Then none have I offended.
I have done no more to Cæsar than you shall do to Brutus.
The question of his death is enrolled in the Capitol; his glory
not extenuated, wherein he was worthy, nor his offences
enforced, for which he suffered death.

Here comes his body, mourned by Mark Antony; who,
though he had no hand in his death, shall receive the benefit
of his dying, a place in the commonwealth; as which of you
shall not?   With this I depart,—that, as I slew my best
lover for the good of Rome, I have the same dagger for
myself, when it shall please my country to need my death.
—Julius Cæsar, iii., 2.

TONE OF GAYETY.
(See Tone Drill No. 106.)

[The tone of Gayety manifests sprightliness, abandon, fun. It is closely allied to Geniality and Joy.]

Amusement.

T. DE WITT TALMAGE.

I say nothing against amusement. Persons of your temperament and mine could hardly live without it. I have noticed that a child who has no vivacity of spirit, in after life produces no fruitfulness of moral character. A tree that has no blossoms in the spring will have no apples in the fall.

A good game at ball is great sport. The sky is clear. The ground is just right for fast running. The club put off their coats and put on their caps. The ball is round and hard and stuffed with illimitable bounce. Get ready the bats and take your positions. Now, give us the ball. Too low? Don't strike. Too high? Don't strike. There it comes like lightning. Strike! Away it soars, higher, higher. Run! Another base. Faster. Faster. Good! All around at one stroke. All hail to the man or the big boy who invented ball playing.

After tea, open the checker board. Now look out, or your boy Bob will beat you. With what masterly skill he moves up his men. Look out now or he will jump you. Sure enough, two of your men gone and a king for Bob. With what cruel pleasure he sweeps the board. What! Only two more men left? Be careful now. Only one more move possible. Cornered sure as fate! And Bob bends over, and looks you in the face with a most provoking banter, and says, "Pop, why don't you move?"

Call up the dogs, Tray, Blanchard, and Sweetheart. A

good day for hunting. Get down, Tray, with your dirty
feet! Put on powder flask and shoulder the gun. Over the
hill and through the wood. Boys, don't make such a racket;
you'll scare the game. There's a rabbit! Squat. Take good
aim. Bang! Missed him. Yonder he goes. Sic 'em, sic 'em!
See the fur fly. Got him at last. Here, Tray! Here, Tray!

John, get up the bays. All ready. See how the buckles
glisten and the horses prance, and the spokes flash in the
sun. Now, open the gate. Away we go. Let the gravel fly,
and the tires rattle over the pavement, and the horses' hoofs
clatter and ring. Good roads, and let them fly. Crack the
whip! G'long! Nimble horses with smooth roads, in a
pleasant day, and no toll-gate—clatter, clatter, clatter.

I never see a man go out with a fishing rod to sport but
I silently say: "May you have a good time, and the right
kind of bait, and a basketful of catfish and flounders." I
never see a party taking a pleasant ride but I wish them a
joyous round, and say: "May the horse not cast a shoe,
nor the trace break, and may the horse's thirst not compel
them to stop at too many taverns." In a world where God
lets His lambs frisk, and His trees toss, and His brooks leap,
and His stars twinkle, and His flowers make love to each
other, I know He intended men at times to laugh and sing
and sport.

Jaques on the Fool

WILLIAM SHAKESPEARE.

A fool, a fool!———I met a fool i' the forest,
A motley fool; (a miserable world!)
As I do live by food, I met a fool,
Who laid him down and bask'd him in the sun,
And rail'd on lady Fortune in good terms,
In good set terms,—and yet a motley fool.
"Good-morrow, fool," quoth I; "No, sir," quoth he,

"Call me not fool, till heaven hath sent me fortune."
And then he drew a dial from his poke,
And looking on it with lack-lustre eye,
Says very wisely, "It is ten o'clock:
Thus may we see," quoth he, "how the world wags:
'Tis but an hour ago since it was nine,
And after one hour more 't will be eleven,
And so from hour to hour we ripe and ripe,
And then from hour to hour we rot and rot;
And thereby hangs a tale."   When I did hear
The motley fool thus moral on the time,
My lungs began to crow like chanticleer,
That fools should be so deep contemplative;
And I did laugh, sans intermission,
An hour by his dial.—O, noble fool!
A worthy fool!   Motley's the only wear.

—As You Like It, ii., 7.

TONE OF INTERROGATION.
(See Tone Drill No. 121.)

[The tone of Interrogation indicates that the speaker desires something answered.   The interrogation *sign* does not always imply the *tone* of Interrogation.   Frequently this sign demands the tone of Assertion.   The distinction will be seen in the selections that follow. Interrogation is usually found with some other tone, notably with Amazement and Indignation.]

English Treatment of Ireland.

SYDNEY SMITH.

We preach to our congregations, sir, that a tree is known by its fruits.   By the fruits it produces I will judge your system. What has it done for Ireland?   Has your system of exclusion made Ireland rich?   Has it made Ireland loyal?   Has it made Ireland free?   Has it made Ireland happy?   How is the wealth of Ireland proved? Is it by the naked, idle, suffering savages, who are slumbering on the mud floor of their cabins? In what does the loyalty of Ireland consist? Is it in the eagerness with which they would range themselves under the hostile banner of any invader, for your destruction and for your distress?

Is it liberty when men breathe and move among the bayonets of English soldiers? Is their happiness and their history anything but such a tissue of murders, burnings, hanging, famine, and disease, as never existed before in the annals of the world? This is a system which, I am sure, with very different intentions, and different views of its effects, you are met this day to uphold. These are the dreadful consequences which those laws your petition prays may be continued have produced upon Ireland.

Telemachus to the Allied Chiefs.

FENELON.

Fellow-soldiers and confederated chiefs. I grant you, if ever man deserved to have the weapon of stratagem and deceit turned against him, it is he who has used it himself so often—the faithless Adrastus! But shall it be said that we, who have united to punish the perfidy of this man,—that we are ourselves perfidious? Shall fraud be counteracted by fraud? Is a promise never to be kept but when a plausible pretence to break it is wanting? Shall an oath be sacred only when nothing is to be gained by its violation? If you are insensible to the love of virtue, and the fear of the gods, have you no regard to your interest and reputation? If, to terminate a war, you violate your oath, how many wars will this impious conduct excite? Who will hereafter trust you? What security can you ever give for your good faith? A solemn treaty?—You have trampled one under foot! An oath? You have committed perjury when perjury was profitable, and have defied the gods.

What have you to fear? Is not your courage equal to victory, without the aid of fraud? Your own power joined to that of the many under your command,—is it not sufficient? Let us fight,—let us die, if we must—but let us not conquer unworthily. Adrastus, the impious Adrastus, is in our power, provided—provided we disdain to imitate the cowardice and treachery which have sealed his ruin.

Shylock's Justification.

WILLIAM SHAKESPEARE.

He hath disgraced me, and hindered me half a million; laughed at my losses, mocked at my gains, scorned my nation, thwarted my bargains, cooled my friends, heated mine enemies; and what's his reason? I am a Jew. Hath not a Jew eyes? hath not a Jew hands, organs, dimensions, senses, affections, passions? fed with the same food, hurt with the same weapons, subject to the same diseases, healed by the same means, warmed and cooled by the same winter and summer, as a Christian is? If you prick us, do we not bleed? if you tickle us, do we not laugh? if you poison us, do we not die? and if you wrong us, shall we not revenge? If we are like you in the rest, we will resemble you in that. If a Jew wrong a Christian, what is his humility? Revenge. If a Christian wrong a Jew, what should his sufferance be by Christian example? Why, revenge.—M. V., iii., 1.

TONE OF SOLEMNITY.
(See Tone Drill No. 189.)

[The tone of Solemnity denotes the appreciation of the gravity of a situation or thing. The ego is humble or is submerged in sympathetic contemplation.]

Death of Copernicus.

EDWARD EVERETT.

At length he draws near his end. He is seventy-three years of age, and he yields his work on "The Revolutions of the Heavenly Orbs" to his friends for publication. The day at last has come on which it is to be ushered into the world. It is the 24th of May, 1543.

On that day—the effect, no doubt, of the intense excitement of his mind, operating upon an exhausted frame—an effusion of blood brings him to the gates of the grave. His last hour has come; he lies stretched upon the couch from which he will never rise.

The beams of the setting sun glance through the Gothic windows of his chamber; near his bedside is the armillary sphere which he has contrived to represent his theory of the heavens; his picture painted by himself, the amusement of his earlier years, hangs before him; beneath it are his astralobe and other imperfect astronomical instruments; and around him are gathered his sorrowing disciples.

The door of the apartment opens; the eye of the departing sage is turned to see who enters: it is a friend who brings him the first printed copy of his immortal treatise. He knows that in that book he contradicts all that has ever been distinctly taught by former philosophers; he knows that he has rebelled against the sway of Ptolemy, which the scientific world has acknowledged for a thousand years; he knows that the popular mind will be shocked by his innovations; he knows that the attempt will be made to press even religion into the service against him; but he knows that his book is true.

He is dying, but he leaves a glorious truth as his dying bequest to the world. He bids the friend who has brought it place himself between the window and his bedside, that the sun's rays may fall upon the precious volume, and he may behold it once more before his eye grows dim. He looks upon it, takes it in his hands, presses it to his breast, and expires.

But no, he is not wholly gone. A smile lights upon his dying countenance; a beam of returning intelligence kindles in his eye; his lips move; and the friend who leans over him can hear him faintly murmur the beautiful sentiments which the Christian lyrist of a later age has so finely expressed in verse:—

"Ye golden lamps of heaven, farewell, with all your feeble
     light;
  Farewell, thou ever-changing moon, pale empress of the
     night;
  And thou, effulgent orb of day, in brighter flames arrayed;
  My soul, which springs beyond thy sphere, no more demands
     thy aid.
  Ye stars are but the shining dust of my divine abode,
  The pavement of these heavenly courts where I shall reign
     with God."
So died the great Columbus of the heavens.

From Thanatopsis.

WILLIAM CULLEN BRYANT.

Yet a few days, and thee
The all-beholding sun shall see no more
In all his course; nor yet in the cold ground,
Where thy pale form was laid, with many tears,

Nor in the embrace of ocean, shall exist
Thy image.   Earth, that nourished thee, shall claim
Thy growth, to be resolved to earth again;
And, lost each human trace, surrendering up
Thine individual being, shalt thou go
To mix forever with the elements;
To be a brother to the insensible rock,
And to the sluggish clod, which the rude swain
Turns with his share, and treads upon.   The oak
Shall send his roots abroad, and pierce thy mould.
      Yet not to thine eternal resting-place
Shalt thou retire alone,—nor couldst thou wish
Couch more magnificent.   Thou shalt lie down
With patriarchs of the infant world,—with kings,
The powerful of the earth,—the wise, the good,
Fair forms, and hoary seers of ages past,
All in one mighty sepulchre.   The hills,
Rock-ribbed, and ancient as the sun; the vales
Stretching in pensive quietness between;
The venerable woods; rivers that move
In majesty, and the complaining brooks,
That make the meadows green; and, poured round all,
Old ocean's gray and melancholy waste,—
Are but the solemn decorations all
Of the great tomb of man!   The golden sun,
The planets, all the infinite host of heaven,
Are shining on the sad abodes of death,
Through the still lapse of ages.   All that tread
The globe are but a handful to the tribes
That slumber in its bosom.   Take the wings
Of morning, traverse Barca's desert sands,
Or lose thyself in the continuous woods
Where rolls the Oregon, and hears no sound
Save his own dashings,—yet the dead are there!

And millions in those solitudes, since first
The flight of years began, have laid them down
In their last sleep,—the dead reign there alone.
So shalt thou rest; and what if thou withdraw
In silence from the living, and no friend
Take note of thy departure? All that breathe
Will share thy destiny. The gay will laugh
When thou art gone, the solemn brood of care
Plod on, and each one, as before, will chase
His favorite phantom; yet all these shall leave
Their mirth and their employments, and shall come
And make their bed with thee.

TONE OF INDIGNATION.
(See Tone Drill No. 118.)

[The tone of Indignation is the antithesis of the tone of Geniality.
It proclaims a feeling *against* some person or thing. Its legitimate
province is the exposure of sham and the denunciation of wrong.]

Crossing the Rubicon.

SHERIDAN KNOWLES.

A gentleman speaking of Cæsar's benevolent disposition,
and of the reluctance with which he entered into the civil war,
observes: "How long did he pause upon the brink of the
Rubicon?" How came he to the brink of that river? How
dared he cross it? Shall a private man respect the boundaries of private property, and shall a man pay no respect
to the boundaries of his country's rights? How dared he
cross that river? Oh! but he paused upon the brink. He
should have perished on the brink before he had crossed it!
Why did he pause? Why does a man's heart palpitate when
he is on the point of committing an unlawful deed? Why
does the very murderer, his victim sleeping before him, and

his glaring eye taking the measure of the blow, strike wide of the mortal part? Because of conscience! 'Twas that made Cæsar pause upon the brink of the Rubicon! Compassion! What compassion? The compassion of an assassin, that feels a momentary shudder as his weapon begins to cut! Cæsar paused upon the brink of the Rubicon! What was the Rubicon? The boundary of Cæsar's province. From what did it separate his province? From his country. Was that country a desert? No; it was fertile and cultivated, rich and populous! Its sons were men of genius, spirit and generosity! Its daughters were lovely, susceptible and chaste! Friendship was its inhabitant! Love was its inhabitant! Domestic affection was its inhabitant! Liberty was its inhabitant! All bounded by the stream of the Rubicon! What was Cæsar who stood upon the brink of that stream? A traitor, bringing war and pestilence into the heart of that country! No wonder that he paused,—no wonder if, his imagination wrought upon by his conscience, he had beheld blood instead of water, and heard groans instead of murmurs! No wonder if some gorgon horror had turned him into stone upon the spot! But, no! he cried, "The die is cast!" He plunged! he crossed! and Rome was free no more!

The Partition of Poland.

CHARLES JAMES FOX.

Now, sir, what was the conduct of your own allies to Poland? Is there a single atrocity of the French in Italy, in Switzerland, in Egypt, if you please, more unprincipled and inhuman than that of Russia, Austria and Prussia, in Poland? What has there been in the conduct of the French to foreign powers; what in the violation of solemn treaties; what in the plunder, devastation, and dismemberment of unoffending countries; what in the horrors and murders perpetrated upon the subdued victims of their rage in any district which they have overrun,—worse than the conduct of those great powers in the miserable, devoted and trampled-on Kingdom of Poland, and who have been, or are, our allies in this war for religion, social order, and the rights of Nations? O, but you "regretted the partition of Poland!" Yes, regretted!—you regretted the violence, and that is all you did. You united yourself with the actors; you, in fact, by your acquiescence, confirmed the atrocity. But they are all your allies; and though they overran and divided Poland, there was nothing, perhaps, in the manner of doing it, which stamped it with peculiar infamy and disgrace. The hero of Poland, perhaps, was merciful and mild! Was he?

Let unfortunate Warsaw, and the miserable inhabitants of the suburb of Praga in particular, tell! What do we understand to have been the conduct of this magnanimous hero, with whom, it seems, Bonaparte is not to be compared? He entered the suburb of Praga, the most populous suburb of Warsaw, and there let his soldiery loose on the miserable, unarmed and unresisting people. Men, women and children,—nay, infants at the breast,—were doomed to one indiscriminate massacre! Thousands of them were inhumanly, wantonly butchered! And for what? Because they had dared to join in a wish to meliorate their own condition as a People, and to improve their Constitution, which had been confessed, by their own sovereign, to be in want of amendment And such is the hero upon whom the cause of "religion and social order" is to repose! And such is the man whom we praise for his discipline and his virtue, and whom we hold out as our boast and our dependence; while the conduct of Bonaparte unfits him to be treated with even as an enemy!

Rienzi to the Romans.

MARY RUSSELL MITFORD.

Friends!
I come not here to talk. Ye know too well
The story of our thraldom. We are slaves!
The bright sun rises to his course, and lights
A race of slaves! He sets, and his last beam
Falls on a slave: not such as, swept along
By the full tide of power, the conqueror leads
To crimson glory and undying fame,—
But base, ignoble slaves!—slaves to a horde
Of petty tyrants, feudal despots; lords,
Rich in some dozen paltry villages;
Strong in some hundred spearmen; only great
In that strange spell—a name! Each hour, dark fraud,
Or open rapine, or protected murder,
Cry out against them. But this very day,
An honest man, my neighbor,—there he stands,—
Was struck—struck like a dog, by one who wore
The badge of Ursini! because, forsooth,
He tossed not high his ready cap in air,
Nor lifted up his voice in servile shouts,
At sight of that great ruffian! Be we men
And suffer such dishonor? Men, and wash not
The stain away in blood? Such shames are common.
I have known deeper wrongs. I, that speak to ye,
I had a brother once, a gracious boy,
Full of all gentleness, of calmest hope,
Of sweet and quiet joy; there was the look
Of Heaven upon his face, which limners give
To the beloved disciple. How I loved
That gracious boy! Younger by fifteen years
Brother at once and son! He left my side,

A summer bloom on his fair cheeks—a smile
Parting his innocent lips. In one short hour,
The pretty, harmless boy was slain! I saw
The corse, the mangled corse, and then I cried
For vengeance! Rouse, ye Romans! Rouse, ye slaves!
Have ye brave sons?—Look in the next fierce brawl
To see them die! Have ye fair daughters?—Look
To see them live, torn from your arms, distained,
Dishonoured; and, if ye dare call for justice,
Be answered by the lash. Yet this is Rome,
That sat on her Seven Hills, and from her throne
Of beauty ruled the world! Yet we are Romans!
Why, in that elder day, to be a Roman
Was greater than a king! And once, again,—
Hear me, ye walls, that echoed to the tread
Of either Brutus!—once again, I swear,
The eternal city shall be free! her sons
Shall walk with princes!

TONE OF ADMIRATION.
(See Tone Drill No. 1.)

[The tone of Admiration proclaims the speaker's great delight or pleasure in the person or thing contemplated. It has a tinge of Amazement.]

The Ice Storm.

MARK TWAIN.

After all, there are at least one or two things about New England weather (or, if you please, effects produced by it) which we residents would not like to part with. If we had not our bewitching autumn foliage, we should still have to credit the weather with one feature which compensates for all its bullying vagaries—the ice-storm—when a leafless tree is clothed with the ice from the bottom to the top—ice that is as bright and clear as crystal; every bough and twig is strung with ice-beads, frozen dew-drops, and the whole tree sparkles, cold and white, like the Shah of Persia's diamond plume.

Then the wind waves the branches, and the sun comes out and turns all these myriads of beads and drops to prisms, that glow, and hum and flash with all manner of colored fires, which change and change again, with inconceivable rapidity, from blue to red, from red to green, and green to gold; the tree becomes a sparkling fountain, a very explosion of dazzling jewels, and it stands there the acme, the climax, the supremest possibility in art or nature of bewildering, intoxicating, intolerable magnificence! One cannot make the words too strong.

Month after month I lay up hate and grudge against the New England weather; but when the ice-storm comes at last, I say: "There, I forgive you now; the books are square between us; you don't owe me a cent; go and sin some more; your little faults and foibles count for nothing; you are the most enchanting weather in the world."

God and Beauty.

RICHARD S. STORRS, JR.

How perfectly replete is God's mind with all the laws and types of beauty.

We go into a collection of flowers and fruits, like those which we often see exhibited in the city or populous village, and there observe the innumerable varieties of color and of form assembled before us. Crimson, purple, scarlet, violet, every possible shade and tint of the green, the purest white, the richest, most velvety dark-blue or black, pearl color, gold color, lilac, vermillion, shades that melt into and are lost in each other, shades that are far too delicate to be defined by the relatively coarse apparatus of words—all are here, in inexhaustible richness, in seemingly inextricable confusion and medley, yet in really absolute proportion and harmony. Very often several are combined in one flower; and always when combined, in most beautiful, even musical, agreement and concord. The cup of the blossom is of white, edged with crimson; the petals are of scarlet, drooping gracefully out of their silver sheath; and even these are tufted and crested at the end, as if by a patient, assiduous tastefulness that could not let them go, with a golden finish.

We try to make the flower immortal and almost pine because it is not. We would stop, if we could, the steady and silent wheels of time, before they crushed the fragile glory. God will not let the flower live because he has another yet nobler thought, of more complete beauty, which he would show us. He hangs around such sights of beauty the stately grace and majesty of the earth—its woods and plains, its streams and seas, the sunshine flashing over all, the sunsets gorgeous in their pomp of pillared amethyst, opal, gold. He pours the beauty of the moonlight, even upon a resting world, weird and fantastic, yet lovely as a dream. He spreads the infinite canopy of the night, and touches it everywhere with dots of splendor. He makes each season a moving panorama of sights and sounds, of brilliant gleams or fragrant odors, full, constantly, of beauty to him who studies it.

He does not do this for the observation of man alone, remember; he does it for the utterance of his own interior and spontaneous thought. The whole creation teems thus with beauty, because his own mind teems with it evermore. He fills the forest depths, which no man sees, with foliage, yearly reproduced and yearly lost, age after age; with blossoming vines; with brilliant and tuneful birds; with grasses and mosses, all delicate and all transient. He paves the sea itself with shells, and edges the coasts with coral reefs, and makes the fish, which no man sees except through some strange violence of storms, a very mirror of every tint most sumptuous and splendid. In the midst of the forests, in the depths of the solid structure of the tree, he hides the curling and delicate grains which art laboriously searches out and displays. Amid rough rocks he drops the diamond; under the rude and earthly shell, he spreads the sheen of precious pearl; around gray cliffs the modest harebells wreathe their necklace at his command. The tiniest insect is covered over with beauty, his wings inlaid and plaited with gold, his breast and crest tipped with silver and pearl, the infinitesimal lines of his eye burnished beyond all human art!

And then God goes to other worlds, with his united creative energy, and there he erects a still different structure. He lays the very foundations differently, of masses and proportions, that he may build the whole edifice anew, and may spread with the same divine prodigality another series of inimitable decorations.

The Vale of Cashmere.

THOMAS MOORE.

Who has not heard of the Vale of Cashmere,
　With its roses the brightest that earth ever gave,
Its temples, and grottos, and fountains as clear
　As the love-lighted eyes that hang over their wave?
Oh to see it at sunset,—when warm o'er the Lake
　Its splendour at parting a summer eve throws,
Like a bride, full of blushes, when lingering to take
　A last look of her mirror at night ere she goes!—
When the shrines through the foliage are gleaming half-
　　shown,
And each hallows the hour by some rites of its own.
Here the music of prayer from a minaret swells,
　Here the Magian his urn, full of perfume, is swinging,

And here, at the altar, a zone of sweet bells
   Round the waist of some fair Indian dancer is ringing.
Or to see it by moonlight,—when mellowly shines
The light o'er its palaces, gardens, and shrines;
When the water-falls gleam, like a quick fall of stars,
And the nightingale's hymn from the Isle of Chenars
Is broken by laughs and light echoes of feet
From the cool, shining walks where the young people meet,—
Or at morn, when the magic of daylight awakes
A new wonder each minute, as slowly it breaks,
Hills, cupolas, fountains, called forth every one
Out of darkness, as if but just born of the Sun.
When the Spirit of Fragrance is up with the day,
From his Haram of night-flowers stealing away;
And the wind, full of wantonness, woos like a lover
The young aspen-trees, till they tremble all over.
When the East is as warm as the light of first hopes,
   And Day, with his banner of radiance unfurled,
Shines in through the mountainous portal that opes,
   Sublime, from that Valley of bliss to the world!

Cleopatra's Barge.

WILLIAM SHAKESPEARE.

The barge she sat in, like a burnish'd throne,
Burn'd on the water: the poop was beaten gold;
Purple the sails, and so perfumed that
The winds were love-sick with them; the oars were silver,
Which to the tune of flutes kept stroke and made
The water which they beat to follow faster,
As amorous of their strokes. For her own person,
It beggar'd all description: she did lie
In her pavilion, cloth-of-gold of tissue,
O'er-picturing that Venus where we see
The fancy out-work nature: on each side her

Stood pretty dimpled boys, like smiling Cupids,
With divers-colour'd fans, whose wind did seem
To glow the delicate cheeks which they did cool,
And what they undid did.

Her gentlewomen, like the Nereides,
So many mermaids, tended her i' the eyes,
And made their bends adornings: at the helm
A seeming mermaid steers: the silken tackle
Swell with the touches of those flower-soft hands,
That yarely frame the office. From the barge
A strange invisible perfume hits the sense
Of the adjacent wharfs. The city cast
Her people out upon her; and Antony,
Enthroned i' the market-place, did sit alone,
Whistling to the air; which, but for vacancy,
Had gone to gaze on Cleopatra too,
And made a gap in nature.

—Antony and Cleopatra, ii., 2.

TONE OF ARGUMENT.
(See Tone Drill No. 21.)

[The tone of Argument indicates that the speaker is in discussion with some person, real or imaginary, whom he is seeking to convince. This tone is closely allied to Assertion, and at times runs into Indignation, Contempt, Interrogation and Concession.]

The Present Age.

CHARLES DICKENS.

I confess, standing here in this responsible situation, I do not understand this much-used and much-abused phrase—the "material age." I cannot comprehend—if anybody can I very much doubt—its logical signification. For instance, has electricity become more material in the mind of any

sane or moderately insane man, woman, or child, because of
the discovery that in the good providence of God it could be
made available for the service and use of man to an immeasurably greater extent than for his destruction? Do I make
a more material journey to the bedside of my dying parent
or my dying child when I travel there at the rate of sixty
miles an hour, than when I went thither at the rate of six?
Rather, in the swiftest case, does not my agonized heart become over-fraught with gratitude to that Supreme Beneficence
from whom alone could have proceeded the wonderful means
of shortening my suspense?

What is the materiality of the cable or the wire compared
with the materiality of the spark? What is the materiality
of certain chemical substances that we can weigh or measure,
imprison or release, compared with the materiality of their
appointed affinities and repulsion present in them from
the instant of their creation to the day of judgment? When
did this so-called material age begin? With the use of cloth-
ing; with the discovery of the compass; with the invention
of the art of printing? Surely it has been a long time about.
And which is the more material object—the farthing tallow
candle that will not give me light, or that flame of gas which
will?

No, ladies and gentlemen, do not let us be discouraged or
deceived by any fine, vapid, empty words. The true material
age is the stupid Chinese age, in which no new or grand
revelations of nature are granted, because they are ignorantly
and insolently repelled, instead of being diligently and humbly
sought.

On the Being of a God.

EDWARD YOUNG.

Retire;—the world shut out;—thy thoughts call home;—
Imagination's airy wing repress;—

Lock up thy senses;—let no passions stir;—
Wake all to Reason—let her reign alone;—
Then, in thy soul's deep silence, and the depth
Of Nature's silence, midnight, thus inquire:
What am I? and from whence? I nothing know
But that I am; and, since I am, conclude
Something eternal; had there e'er been nought,
Nought still had been; Eternal there must be—
But what eternal? Why not human race,
And Adam's ancestors without an end?—
That's hard to be conceived; since ev'ry link
Of that long chain's succession is so frail:
Can every part depend, and not the whole?
Yet grant it true; new difficulties rise;
I'm still quite out at sea; nor see the shore.
Whence earth, and these bright orbs?—Eternal too?
Grant matter was eternal; still these orbs
Would want some other Father—much design
Is seen in all their motions, all their makes.
Design implies intelligence and art,
That can't be from themselves—or man; that art
Man scarce can comprehend could man bestow?
And nothing greater yet allow'd than man.—
Who motion, foreign to the smallest grain,
Shot through vast masses of enormous weight?
Who bid brute matter's restive lump assume
Such various forms, and gave it wings to fly?
Has matter innate motion? Then each atom,
Asserting its indisputable right
To dance, would form a universe of dust.
Has matter none? Then whence these glorious forms
And boundless flights, from shapeless and reposed?
Has matter more than motion? Has it thought,
Judgment, and genius? Is it deeply learn'd

In mathematics? Has it framed such laws,
Which, but to guess, a Newton made immortal?—
If art to form, and counsel to conduct,
And that with greater far than human skill,
Reside not in each block;—a God-head reigns;—
And, if a God there is, that God how great!

Belial's Address.

JOHN MILTON.

  I should be much for open war, O Peers,
As not behind in hate, if what was urged
Main reason to persuade immediate war,
Did not dissuade me most, and seem to cast
Ominous conjecture on the whole success;—
When he, who most excels in fact of arms,
In what he counsels, and in what excels,
Mistrustful, grounds his courage on despair
And utter dissolution, as the scope
Of all his aim, after some dire revenge!—
First, what revenge?—The towers of Heaven are filled
With arméd watch, that render all access
Impregnable: oft on the bordering deep
Encamp their legions; or, with obscure wing,
Scout far and wide into the realm of night,
Scorning surprise.—Or, could we break our way
By force, and, at our heels, all hell should rise,
With blackest insurrection, to confound
Heaven's purest light; yet our great Enemy,
All incorruptible, would, on His throne,
Sit unpolluted; and the ethereal mould,
Incapable of stain, would soon expel
Her mischief, and purge off the baser fire,
Victorious.

Thus repulsed, our final hope
Is flat despair: we must exasperate
The Almighty Victor to spend all His rage,
And that must end us; that must be our cure,—
To be no more.—Sad cure!—for who would lose,
Though full of pain, this intellectual being,
Those thoughts that wander through eternity,—
To perish rather, swallowed up and lost
In the wide womb of uncreated night,
Devoid of sense and motion?—And who knows,
Let this be good, whether our angry Foe
Can give it, or will ever? How He can,
Is doubtful; that He never will, is sure.
Will He, so wise, let loose at once His ire,
Belike through impotence, or unaware,
To give His enemies their wish, and end
Them in His anger, whom His anger saves
To punish endless?—"Wherefore cease we, then?"
Say they, who counsel war: "We are decreed,
Reserved, and destined to eternal woe:
Whatever doing, what can we suffer more,
What can we suffer worse?" Is this, then, worst,
Thus sitting, thus consulting, thus in arms?
What! when we fled amain, pursued and struck
With Heaven's afflicting thunder, and besought
The deep to shelter us? this hell then seemed
A refuge from those wounds! or when we lay
Chained on the burning lake? that sure was worse.
What if the breath that kindled those grim fires,
Awaked, should blow them into seven-fold rage,
And plunge us in the flames? or, from above,
Should intermitted vengeance arm again
His red right hand to plague us? what, if all
Her stores were opened, and this firmament

Of hell should spout her cataracts of fire,
Impendent horrors, threatening hideous fall
One day upon our heads? while we, perhaps
Designing or exhorting glorious war,
Caught in a fiery tempest, shall be hurled,
Each on his rock transfixed, the sport and prey
Of racking whirlwinds; or forever sunk
Under yon boiling ocean, wrapped in chains;
There to converse with everlasting groans,
Unrespited, unpitied, unreprieved,
Ages of hopeless end?—this would be worse.
War, therefore, open or concealed, alike
My voice dissuades.   —Paradise Lost, Book II.

TONE OF AFFECTION.
(See Tone Drill No. 5.)

[The tone of Affection is akin to that of Love, but has not the
same intensity and abandon. It is more under control, and usually
has the approval of the judgment.]

The Star Spangled Banner.
HENRY WATTERSON.

The Star-Spangled Banner! Was ever flag so beautiful?
Did ever flag so fill the soul of man? The love of woman;
the sense of duty; the thirst for glory; the heart throbbing
that impels the humblest American to stand by his colors
fearless in the defence of his native land, and holding it sweet
to die for it—the yearning which draws him to it when exiled
from it—its free institutions and its blessed memories, all
are embodied and symbolized by the broad stripes and bright
stars of the nation's emblem. All live again in the lines
and tones of Key's anthem.

Two or three began the song, millions joined the chorus.
They are singing it in Porto Rican trenches and on the ram-

parts of Santiago, and its echoes, borne upon the wings of morning, come rolling back from far-away Manila; the soldier's message to the soldier; the hero's shibboleth in battle; the patriot's solace in death! Even to the lazy sons of peace who lag at home—the pleasure seekers whose merry-making turns the night into day—those stirring strains come as a sudden trumpet-call, and above the sounds of revelry, subjugate for the moment to the stronger power, rises wave upon wave of melodious resonance, the idler's aimless but heartfelt tribute to his country and his country's flag

"'Tis the Star-Spangled Banner, O, long may it wave
O'er the land of the free and the home of the brave!"

Home.

T. DE WITT TALMAGE.

Home! Upon that word there drop the sunshine of boyhood and the shadow of tender sorrows and the reflection of ten thousand fond memories. Home! When I see it in book or newspaper, that word seems to rise and sparkle and leap and thrill and whisper and chant and pray and weep. It glitters like a shield. It springs up like a fountain. It trills like a song. It twinkles like a star. It leaps like a flame. It glows like a sunset. It sings like an angel. And if some lexicographer, urged on by a spirit from beneath, should seek to cast forth that word from the language, the children would come forth and hide it under garlands of wild flowers, and the wealthy would come forth to cover it up with their diamonds and pearls; and kings would hide it under their crowns, and after Herod had hunted its life from Bethlehem to Egypt, and utterly given up the search, some bright, warm day it would flash from among the gems, and breathe from among the coronets, and the world would read it bright and fair, and beautiful, and resonant, as before,—Home! Home! Home!

John Anderson, My Jo.

ROBERT BURNS.

John Anderson, my jo, John,
When we were first acquent,
Your locks were like the raven,
Your bonnie brow was brent;
But now your brow is beld, John,
Your locks are like the snaw;
But blessings on your frosty pow,
John Anderson, my jo.

John Anderson, my jo, John,
We clamb the hill thegither;
And monie a canty day, John,
We've had wi' ane anither:
Now we maun totter down, John,
But hand in hand we'll go,
And sleep thegither at the foot,
John Anderson, my jo.

The Bells of Shandon.

FRANCIS MAHONEY.

With deep affection and recollection,
  I often think of those Shandon bells,
Whose sound so wild would, in the days of childhood,
  Fling round my cradle their magic spells.

On this I ponder where'er I wander,
  And thus grow fonder, sweet Cork, of thee,—
With thy bells of Shandon, that sound so grand, on
  The pleasant waters of the river Lee.

I've heard bells chiming full many a clime in,
  Tolling sublime in cathedral shrine;
While at a glib rate, brass tongues would vibrate;
  But all their music spoke naught like thine.

For memory dwelling, on each proud swelling
  Of thy belfry, knelling its bold notes free,
Made the bells of Shandon sound far more grand, on
  The pleasant waters of the river Lee.

I've heard bells tolling old Adrian's Mole in,
  Their thunder rolling from the Vatican;
And cymbals glorious swinging uproarious
  In the gorgeous turret of Notre Dame;

But thy sounds were sweeter than the dome of Peter
  Flings o'er the Tiber, pealing solemnly.
Oh! the bells of Shandon sound far more grand, on
  The pleasant waters of the river Lee . . .

TONE OF COMMAND.
(See Tone Drills No. 46 and 26.)

[The tone of Command manifests authority. It indicates finality. It says, "Ask no questions, but do."]

The Bended Bow.

FELICIA HEMANS.

There was heard the sound of the coming foe, there was sent through the land a Bended Bow; and a Voice was poured on the free winds far, as the land rose up at the sign of war.

"Heard ye not the battle horn? Reaper! leave thy golden corn! leave it for the birds of heaven,—swords must flash, and shields be riven! leave it for the winds to shed:—arm!

ere stone and turf grow red!" And the Reaper armed like a foeman's son,—and the Bended Bow and the Voice passed on!

"Hunter! leave the mountain chase; take the falchion from its place; let the wolf go free to-day, leave him for a nobler prey! let the deer ungalled sweep by:—arm thee! freedom's foes are nigh!" And the Hunter armed ere his chase was done,—and the Bended Bow and the Voice passed on!

"Chieftain! quit the joyous feast,—stay not till the song hath ceased! though the mead be foaming bright, though the fires give ruddy light, leave the hearth and leave the hall:—arm thee! freedom's foes must fall." And the Chieftain armed, and the horn was blown, and the Bended Bow and the Voice passed on!

"Prince! thy father's deeds are told in the bower, and in the hold! where the goat-herd's lay is sung, where the minstrel's harp is strung! foes are on thy native sea—give our bards a tale of thee!" And the Prince came armed like a leader's son,—and the Bended Bow and the Voice passed on!

"Mother! stay thou not thy boy! he must learn the battle's joy; Sister! bring the sword and spear, give thy brother words of cheer; Maiden! bid thy lover part, freedom calls the strong in heart!" And the Bended Bow and the Voice passed on,—and the bards made song for a battle won!

TONE OF CALMNESS, QUIETUDE.
(See Tone Drill No. 36.)

[The tone of Calmness manifests serenity, poise, and restfulness. It is akin to Solemnity, and there is, at times, a tinge of Awe.]

Evening.

ARCHIBALD ALLISON.

There is an even-tide in the day,—an hour when the sun retires, and the shadows fall, and when nature assumes the appearance of soberness and silence. It is an hour from which everywhere the thoughtless fly, as peopled only in their imagination with images of gloom:—it is the hour, on the other hand, which, in every age, the wise have loved, as bringing with it sentiments and affections more valuable than all the splendors of the day.

Its first impression is to still all the turbulence of thought or passion which the day may have brought forth. We follow, with our eye, the descending sun,—we listen to the decaying sounds of labor and of toil,—and, when all the fields are silent around us, we feel a kindred stillness to breathe upon our souls, and to calm them from the agitations of society.

From this first impression, there is a second which naturally follows it;—in the day we are living with men,—in the eventide we begin to live with nature;—we see the world withdrawn from us,—the shades of night darken over the habitations of men; and we feel ourselves alone. It is an hour fitted, as it would seem, by Him who made us, to still, but with gentle hand, the throb of every unruly passion, and the ardor of every impure desire; and while it veils for a time the world that misleads us, to awaken in our hearts those legitimate affections which the heat of the day may have dissolved.

The Day of Rest.

JAMES GRAHAME.

How still the morning of the hallowed day!
Mute is the voice of rural labour, hushed
The ploughboy's whistle and the milkmaid's song.
The scythe lies glittering in the dewy wreath
Of tedded grass, mingled with faded flowers,
That yester morn bloomed waving in the breeze;
Sounds the most faint attract the ear,—the hum
Of early bee, the trickling of the dew,

The distant bleating midway up the hill.
Calmness sits throned on yon unmoving cloud.
To him who wanders o'er the upland leas
The blackbird's note comes mellow from the dale,
And sweeter from the sky the gladsome lark
Warbles his heaven-tuned song; the lulling brook
Murmurs more gently down the deep-worn glen;
While from yon lowly roof, whose curling smoke
O'ermounts the mist, is heard at intervals
The voice of psalms, the simple song of praise.
With dovelike wings peace o'er yon village broods;
The dizzying mill-wheel rests; the anvil's din
Hath ceased; all, all around is quietness.

TONE OF APPEAL.
(See Tone Drill No. 16.)

[The tone of Appeal is objective and personal. Its characteristic is a desire to persuade or dissuade. It does not demand. It asks and hopes.]

An Appeal for the Cause of Liberty.
JOHN HARRINGTON.

I do not say, elect this candidate or that candidate. I am not canvassing for any candidate. I am canvassing for the cause of liberty against slavery, I am defending the reputation of Union against the slanderous attack of Disunion, against the fearful peril of secession. I appeal to you, as you are men, to act as men in this great crisis; to put your strong hands together and avert the overwhelming disaster that threatens us; to stand side by side, as brothers.

I appeal from license to law, from division to harmony, from the raging turmoil of angry and devouring passion without, to the calm serenity which reigns within these walls. As we turn in horror and loathing from the unbridled fury of human beings, changed almost to beasts, so let us turn in hope and security to those things we can honor and respect, to the dignity of truth, to the unbending strength of unquestioned right.

I appeal to you to make this day the greatest in your lives, the most memorable in our history as a nation. Lay aside this day the memories of the past, and look forward to the brightness of the future. Throw down the weapons of petty and murderous strife, and join together in perfect harmony of mutual trust. Be neither Republicans, nor Democrats, nor Independents. Be what it is your greatest privilege to be —American citizens. Cast parties to the winds and uphold the State. Trample under your freeborn feet the badges of party bondage, the ignoble chains of party slavery, the wretched hopes of preferment;

> "Yes, by the blood our fathers shed,
> O Union, in thy sacred cause,
> Whilst streaming from the gallant dead,
> It sealed and sanctified thy laws."

Choose, then, of your own heart and will, a man, to be our President and our leader. Elect him with one accord, and, as you give your voices in his choice, stand here together, knee to knee, shoulder to shoulder, hand to hand, and let the mighty oath go thundering up to Heaven, "This Union shall not be broken."

Patriotic Appeal.

J. M'DOWELL.

Give us but a part of that devotion which glowed in the heart of the younger Pitt, and of our own elder Adams, who, in the midst of their agonies, forgot not the countries they had lived for, but mingled with the spasms of their dying hour a last and imploring appeal to the Parent of all Mercies that he would remember, in eternal blessings, the land of their birth: give us their devotion, give us that of the young enthusiast of Paris, who listening to Mirabeau in one of his surpassing vindications of human right, and seeing him fall from his stand, dying, as a physician proclaimed, for the want of blood, rushed to the spot, and as he bent over the expiring man, bared his arm for the lancet, and cried again, and again, with impassioned voice—"Here, take it—take it —oh! take it from *me, let me* die, so that Mirabeau and the liberties of my country may not perish!" Give us something only of such a spirit as this—something only of such a love of country, and we are safe, forever safe: the troubles which shadow over and oppress us now, will pass away as a summer cloud. No measure of unalienable wrong, no measure of unconquerable disagreement, will be pressed upon us here. The fatal element of all our discord will be taken from amongst us.

Let gentlemen be entreated to remove it as the one only and solitary obstacle to our perfect peace. Let them be adjured by the weal of this and coming ages—by our own and our children's good—by all that we love or that we look for in the progress and the glories of our land, to leave the entire subject of slavery, with every accountability it may impose, every remedy it may require, every accumulation of difficulty or pressure it may reach; to leave it all to the interest, to the wisdom, and to the conscience of those upon whom the providence of God and the Constitution of their country have cast it. Leave it to them *now and forever,* and stop, whilst it is yet possible to stop, the furious and blind headway of that wild and mad philanthropy, which is lighting up for the nation itself the fires of the stake, and which is rushing on, stride after stride, to an intestine struggle that may bring us all under a harder, and wickeder and more incurable slavery, than any it would extinguish.

Arthur's Appeal.

WILLIAM SHAKESPEARE.

O, save me Hubert, save me! my eyes are out
Even with the fierce looks of these bloody men.
For heaven sake, Hubert, let me not be bound!
Nay, hear me, Hubert, drive these men away,
And I will sit as quiet as a lamb;
I will not stir, nor wince, nor speak a word,
Nor look upon the iron angerly:
Thrust but these men away, and I 'll forgive you,
Whatever torment you do put me to.
Is there no remedy? . . .
O heaven, that there were but a mote in yours,
A grain, a dust, a gnat, a wandering hair,
Any annoyance in that precious sense!·
Then, feeling what small things are boisterous there,
Your vile intent must needs seem horrible.
Let me not hold my tongue, let me not, Hubert;
Or, Hubert, if you will, cut out my tongue,
So I may keep mine eyes: O, spare mine eyes,
Though to no use but still to look on you!
Lo, by my troth, the instrument is cold
And would not harm me.

King John iv., 1.

Katherine's Appeal.

WILLIAM SHAKESPEARE.

Sir, I desire you do me right and justice,
And to bestow your pity on me; for
I am a most poor woman, and a stranger,
Born out of your dominions; having here
No judge indifferent, nor no more assurance

Of equal friendship and proceeding. Alas, sir,
In what have I offended you? what cause
Hath my behaviour given to your displeasure,
That thus you should proceed to put me off,
And take your good grace from me? Heaven witness,
I have been to you a true and humble wife,
At all times to your will conformable,
Ever in fear to kindle your dislike,
Yea, subject to your countenance, glad or sorry
As I saw it inclined: when was the hour
I ever contradicted your desire,
Or made it not mine too? Or which of your friends
Have I not strove to love, although I knew
He were mine enemy? what friend of mine
That had to him derived your anger, did I
Continue in my liking? nay, gave notice
He was from thence discharged? Sir, call to mind
That I have been your wife, in this obedience,
Upward of twenty years, and have been blest
With many children by you: if in the course
And process of this time you can report,
And prove it too, against mine honour aught,
My bond to wedlock or my love and duty,
Against your sacred person, in God's name,
Turn me away, and let the foul'st contempt
Shut door upon me, and so give me up
To the sharp'st kind of justice. . . .
                    I humbly
Beseech you, sir, to spare me, till I may
Be by my friends in Spain advised, whose counsel
I will implore: if not, i' the name of God,
Your pleasure be fulfill'd!

                              Henry VIII ii., 4.

TONE OF AWE.
(See Tone Drill No. 28.)

[The tone of Awe indicates that the speaker is deeply impressed. There is implied reverential fear, sometimes a mild horror. Awe borders on Solemnity and Sublimity.]

The Burning of Moscow.

J. T. HEADLEY.

When night again descended on the city, it presented a spectacle, the like of which was never seen before, and which baffles all description. The streets were streets of fire, the heavens a canopy of fire, and the entire body of the city a mass of fire, fed by a hurricane that sped the blazing fragments in a constant stream through the air. Incessant explosions, from the blowing up of stores of oil, and tar, and spirits, shook the very foundations of the city, and sent vast volumes of smoke rolling furiously toward the sky. Huge sheets of canvas on fire came floating like messengers of death through the flames; the towers and domes of the churches and palaces glowing with a red-hot heat over the wild sea below, then tottering a moment on their bases, were hurled by the tempest into the common ruin.

Thousands of wretches, before unseen, were driven by the heat from the cellars and hovels, and streamed in an incessant throng through the streets. Children were seen carrying their parents; the strong, the weak. O, it was a scene of woe and fear inconceivable and indescribable! A mighty and close-packed city of houses, and churches, and palaces, wrapped from limit to limit in flames!

Huge domes and towers, throwing off sparks like blazing firebrands, now disappeared in their maddening flow, as they rushed and broke high over their tops, scattering their spray of fire against the clouds. The heavens themselves seemed to have caught the conflagration, and the angry masses that

swept it rolled over a bosom of fire. Columns of flame would
rise and sink along the surface of this sea, and huge volumes
of black smoke suddenly shoot into the air, as if volcanoes
were working below. The black form of the Kremlin alone
towered above the chaos, now wrapped in flame and smoke,
again emerging into view, standing amid this scene of desolation and terror, like Virtue in the midst of a burning world,
enveloped but unscathed by the devouring elements.

Said Napoleon years afterward: "It was a spectacle of a
sea and billows of fire, a sky and clouds of flame, mountains
of red rolling flames, like immense waves of the sea, alternately bursting forth and elevating themselves to skies
of flame above. O, it was the most grand, the most sublime,
and the most terrific sight the world ever beheld."

Darkness.

LORD BYRON.

I had a dream which was not all a dream:
The bright sun was extinguish'd, and the stars
Did wander, darkling, in the eternal space,
Rayless and pathless; and the icy earth
Swung blind and black'ning in the moonless air.
Morn came and went—and came, and brought no day;
And men forgot their passions in the dread
Of this their desolation; and all hearts
Were chill'd into a selfish prayer for light.
And they did live by watch-fires; and the thrones,
The palaces of crownèd kings, the huts,
The habitations of all things which dwell,
Were burned for beacons: cities were consumed,
And men were gather'd round their blazing homes
To look once more into each other's face.   .   .   .
A fearful hope was all the world contained.

Forests were set on fire; but hour by hour
They fell and faded, and the crackling trunks
Extinguished with a crash, and all was black. . .
The world was void;
The populous and the powerful was a lump—
Seasonless, herbless, treeless, manless, lifeless—
A lump of death, a chaos of hard clay.
The rivers, lakes, and ocean all stood still,
And nothing stirred within their silent depths.
Ships sailorless lay rotting on the sea,
And their masts fell down piecemeal; as they dropp'd
They slept on the abyss without a surge.
The waves were dead; the tides were in their grave;
The moon, their mistress, had expired before;
The winds were withered in the stagnant air,
And the clouds perished. Darkness hath no need
Of aid from them. She was the universe.

TONE OF REPROOF.
(See Tone Drill No. 174.)

[The tone of Reproof denotes dignified dissatisfaction and correction. It is tinged with authority and sometimes with reproach.]

Reproof of the Duke of Bedford.
JUNIUS.

Compare the natural dignity and importance of the richest peer of England; the noble independence, which he might have maintained in parliament, and the real interest and respect, which he might have acquired, not only in parliament, but through the whole kingdom; compare these glorious distinctions with the ambition of holding a share in government, the emoluments of a place, the sale of a borough, or the purchase of a corporation; and, though you may not regret the virtues which create respect, you may see, with anguish, how much real importance and authority you have lost. Consider the character of an independent, virtuous Duke of Bedford; imagine what he *might* be in this country.

He would never prostitute his dignity in parliament by an indecent violence either in opposing or defending a minister. He would not at one moment rancorously persecute, at another basely cringe to the favorite of his sovereign. After outraging the royal dignity with peremptory conditions, little short of menace and hostility, he would never descend to the humility of soliciting an interview with the favorite, and of offering to recover, at any price, the honor of his friendship. Though deceived, perhaps, in his youth, he would not, through the course of a long life, have invariably chosen his friends from among the most profligate of mankind.

His own honor would have forbidden him from mixing his private pleasures or conversation with jockeys, gamesters, blasphemers, gladiators, or buffoons. He would then have never felt, much less would he have submitted to the humiliating, dishonest necessity of engaging in the interest and intrigues of his dependents, of supplying their vices, or relieving their beggary, at the expense of his country. He would not have betrayed such ignorance, or such contempt of the constitution, as openly to avow, in a court of justice, the purchase and sale of a borough. He would not have thought it consistent with his rank in the state, or even with his personal importance, to be the little tyrant of a little corporation.

Henry IV to His Son.

WILLIAM SHAKESPEARE.

Thou dost, in thy passages of life,
Make me believe, that thou art only mark'd
For the hot vengeance and the rod of heaven,
To punish my mistreadings. Tell me else,

Could such inordinate, and low desires,
Such poor, such bare, such lewd, such mean attempts,
Such barren pleasures, rude society,
As thou art match'd withal, and grafted to,
Accompany the greatness of thy blood,
And hold their level with thy princely heart?
God pardon thee!—yet let me wonder, Harry,
At thy affections, which do hold a wing
Quite from the flight of all thy ancestors.
Thy place in council thou hast rudely lost,
Which by thy younger brother is supplied;
And art almost an alien to the hearts
Of all the court, and princes of my blood:
The hope and expectation of thy time
Is ruin'd; and the soul of every man
Prophetically doth fore-think thy fall.
For thou hast lost thy princely privilege,
With vile participation: not an eye
But is a-weary of thy common sight,
Save mine, which hath desir'd to see thee more;
Why, Harry, do I tell thee of my foes,
Which art my nearest and dearest enemy!
Thou art like enough, through vassal fear,
Base inclination, and the start of spleen,
To fight against me under Percy's pay,
To dog his heels and curtsy at his frowns,
To show how much thou art degenerate.

                              Henry IV, Pt. I, iii., 2.

COMPARISON AND CONTRAST.

(See Tone Drills Nos. 14 and 45.)

[These styles of expression have no distinct tone. They usually demand Assertion tinged with Admiration or Depreciation. Some times Comparison calls for the tone of Concession.]

Conservatism and Reform.

RALPH WALDO EMERSON.

Conservatism stands on man's incontestable limitations; Reform on his indisputable infinitude; Conservatism on circumstance; Liberalism on power; one goes to make an adroit member of the social frame; the other to postpone all things to the man himself; Conservatism is debonair and social; Reform is individual and imperious. We are reformers in spring and summer; in autumn and winter we stand by the old; reformers in the morning, conservers at night. Reform is affirmative, Conservatism negative; Conservatism goes for comfort, Reform for truth. Conservatism is more candid to behold another's worth; Reform more disposed to maintain and increase its own. Conservatism makes no poetry, breathes no prayer, has no invention; it is all memory. Reform has no gratitude, no prudence, no husbandry.

It makes a great difference to your figure and to your thought, whether your foot is advancing or receding. Conservatism never puts the foot forward; in the hour when it does that, it is no establishment, but Reform. Conservatism tends to universal seeming, and treachery, believes a negative fate; believes that men's temper governs them; that for me, it avails not to trust in principles; they will fail me; I must bend a little; it distrusts nature; it thinks that there is a general law without a particular application—law for all that does not include anyone. Reform in its antagonism inclines to asinine resistance, to kick with hoofs; it runs to egotism and bloated self-conceit; it runs to a bodiless pretension, to unnatural refining and elevation, which ends in hypocrisy and sensual reaction.

And so whilst we do not go beyond general statements, it may be safely affirmed of these two metaphysical antagonists, that each is a good half, but an impossible whole. Each exposes the abuses of the other, but in a true society, in a true man, both must combine. Nature does not give the crown of its approbation, namely, Beauty, to any action, or emblem, or actor, but to one which combines both these elements; not to the rock which resists the waves from age to age, nor to the wave which lashes incessantly the rock; but the superior beauty is with the oak, which stands with its hundred arms against the storms of a century, and grows every year like a sapling; or the river which, ever flowing, yet is found in the same bed from age to age; or, greatest of all, the man who has subsisted for years amid the changes of nature, yet has distanced himself so that when you remember what he was, and see what he is, you say, What strides!

Anglo-Saxon and American Civilizations.

WILLIAM JENNINGS BRYAN.

Civil and religious liberty, universal education and right to participate directly or through representatives chosen by himself, in all the affairs of government—these give to the American citizen an opportunity and an inspiration which can be found nowhere else. Standing upon the vantage ground already gained, the American people can aspire to a grander destiny than has opened before any other race.

Anglo-Saxon civilization has taught the individual to take care of himself; American civilization, proclaiming the equality of all before the law, will teach him that his own highest good requires the observance of the commandment: "Thou shalt love thy neighbor as thyself." Anglo-Saxon civilization has, by force of arms, applied the art of government to other races for the benefit of the Anglo-Saxons; American civilization will, by the influence of example, excite in other races a desire for self-government and a determination to secure it. Anglo-Saxon civilization has carried its flag to every clime and defended it with forts and garrisons; American civilization will imprint its flag upon the hearts of all who long for freedom. To American civilization, all hail!

"Time's noblest offspring is the last."

Shylock on Tubal's News.

WILLIAM SHAKESPEARE.

Shy. How now, Tubal! what news from Genoa? hast thou found my daughter?

Tub. I often came where I did hear of her, but cannot find her.

Shy. Why, there, there, there, there! a diamond gone, cost me two thousand ducats in Frankfort! The curse never fell upon our nation till now; I never felt it till now: two thousand ducats in that; and other precious, precious jewels. I would my daughter were dead at my foot, and the jewels in her ear! would she were hearsed at my foot, and the ducats in her coffin! No news of them? Why, so:—and I know not what's spent in the search: why, thou loss upon loss! the thief gone with so much, and so much to find the thief; and no satisfaction, no revenge: nor no ill luck stirring but what lights on my shoulders; no sighs but of my breathing; no tears but of my shedding.

Tub. Yes, other men have ill luck too: Antonio, as I heard in Genoa,—

Shy What, what, what? ill luck, ill luck?

Tub. Hath an argosy cast away, coming from Tripolis.

Shy. I thank God, I thank God! Is't true, is't true?

Tub. I spoke with some of the sailors that escaped the wreck

Shy. I thank thee, good Tubal: good news, good news! ha, ha! where? in Genoa?

Tub. Your daughter spent in Genoa, as I heard, in one night fourscore ducats.

Shy. Thou stick'st a dagger in me: I shall never see my gold again: fourscore ducats at a sitting! fourscore ducats!

Tub. There came divers of Antonio's creditors in my company to Venice, that swear he cannot choose but break.

Shy. I am very glad of it; I'll plague him; I'll torture him: I am glad of it.

Tub. One of them showed me a ring that he had of your daughter for a monkey.

Shy. Out upon her! Thou torturest me, Tubal: it was my turquoise; I had it of Leah when I was a bachelor: I would not have given it for a wilderness of monkeys.

Tub. But Antonio is certainly undone.

Shy. Nay, that's true, that's very true: Go, Tubal, fee me an officer, bespeak him a fortnight before. I will have the heart of him, if he forfeit; for were he out of Venice, I can make what merchandise I will. Go, go, Tubal, and meet me at our synagogue; go, good Tubal; at our synagogue, Tubal.   —Merchant of Venice, iii., 1.

TONE OF CHALLENGE.
(See Tone Drill No. 40.)

[The tone of Challenge manifests an aggressive self-confidence. It says, "I am not afraid to cope with you. Come on."]

Matches and Over-matches.
DANIEL WEBSTER.

Matches and over-matches! Those terms are more applicable elsewhere than here, and fitter for other assemblies than this. Sir, the gentleman seems to forget where and what we are. This is a Senate; a Senate of equals; of men of individual honor and personal character, and of absolute independence. We know no masters; we acknowledge no dictators. This is a Hall for mutual consultation and discussion, not an arena for the exhibition of champions. I offer myself, Sir, as a match for no man; I throw the challenge of debate at no man's feet.

But, then, Sir, since the honorable member has put the question, in a manner that calls for an answer, I will give him an answer; and I tell him, that, holding myself to be the humblest of the members here, I yet know nothing in the arm of his friend from Missouri, either alone, or when aided by the arm of his friend from South Carolina, that need deter even me from espousing whatever opinions I may choose to espouse, from debating whenever I may choose to debate, or from speaking whatever I may see fit to say, on the floor of the Senate.

Sir, when uttered as matter of commendation or compliment, I should dissent from nothing which the honorable member might say of his friend. Still less do I put forth any pretensions of my own. But, when put to me as matter of taunt, I throw it back, and say to the gentleman that he could possibly say nothing less likely than such a comparison to wound my pride of personal character. The anger of its tone rescued the remark from intentional irony, which, otherwise, probably, would have been its general acceptation.

But, Sir, if it be imagined that, by this mutual quotation and commendation; if it be supposed that by casting the characters of the drama, assigning to each his part,—to one, the attack; to another, the cry of onset;—or, if it be thought that, by a loud and empty vaunt of anticipated victory, any laurels are to be won here; if it be imagined, especially, that any or all these things shall shake any purpose of mine,—

I can tell the honorable member, once for all, that he is greatly mistaken, and that he is dealing with one of whose temper and character he has yet much to learn.

Sir, I shall not allow myself, on this occasion,—I hope on no occasion,—to be betrayed into any loss of temper; but if provoked, as I trust I never shall allow myself to be, into crimination and recrimination, the honorable member may, perhaps, find that in that contest there will be blows to take, as well as blows to give; that others can state comparisons as significant, at least, as his own; and that his impunity may, perhaps, demand of him whatever powers of taunt and sarcasm he may possess. I commend him to a prudent husbandry of his resources.

TONE OF MODESTY.
(See Tone Drill No. 139.)

[This tone indicates a self-depreciation compatible with no loss of self-respect.]

The Saviors of the Nation.

ULYSSES S. GRANT.

I share with you all the pleasure and gratitude which Americans so far away from home should feel on this anniversary. But I must dissent from one remark of our consul to the effect that I saved the country during the war. If our country could be saved or ruined by the efforts of any one man, we should not have a country and we should not be celebrating our Fourth of July. There are many men who would have done far better than I did, under the circumstances in which I found myself during the war. If I had never held command, if I had fallen, if all our generals had fallen, there were ten thousand behind us who would have done our work just as well, who would have followed the contest to the end, and never surrendered the Union.

Therefore, it is a mistake and a reflection upon the people to attribute to me, or to any number of us, who hold high commands, the salvation of the Union. We did our work as well as we could, and so did hundreds of thousands of others. We demand no credit for it, for we should have been unworthy of our country, and of the American name, if we had not made every sacrifice to save the Union.

What saved the Union was the coming forward of the young men of the nation. They came from their homes and fields, as they did in the time of the Revolution, giving everything to the country. To their devotion we owe the salvation of the Union. The humblest soldier who carried a musket is entitled to as much credit for the results of the war as those who were in command. So long as our young men are animated by this spirit, there will be no fear for the Union.

TONE OF BOLDNESS.

(See Tone Drill No. 33.)

[The tone of Boldness manifests fearlessness. It says to the listener, ''I dare to do.'']

Lochinvar.

SIR WALTER SCOTT.

O young Lochinvar is come out of the West,—
Through all the wide Border his steed was the best!
And, save his good broadsword, he weapon had none,—
He rode all unarmed, and he rode all alone.
So faithful in love, and so dauntless in war,
There never was knight like the young Lochinvar.

He stayed not for brake, and he stopped not for stone,
He swam the Eske River where ford there was none;
But, ere he alighted at Netherby gate,

The bride had consented, the gallant came late:
For a laggard in love, and a dastard in war,
Was to wed the fair Ellen of brave Lochinvar.

So boldly he entered the Netherby hall,
'Mong bridesmen, and kinsmen, and brothers, and all:
Then spoke the bride's father, his hand on his sword
(For the poor craven bridegroom said never a word),
"O, come ye in peace here, or come ye in war,
Or to dance at our bridal, young Lord Lochinvar?"

"I long wooed your daughter,—my suit you denied;—
Love swells like the Solway, but ebbs like its tide;
And now am I come, with this lost love of mine
To lead but one measure, drink one cup of wine.
There are maidens in Scotland more lovely by far,
That would gladly be bride to the young Lochinvar."

The bride kissed the goblet; the knight took it up,
He quaffed off the wine, and he threw down the cup.
She looked down to blush, and she looked up to sigh,
With a smile on her lips and a tear in her eye
He took her soft hand, ere her mother could bar,—
"Now tread we a measure!" said young Lochinvar.

So stately his form, and so lovely her face,
That never a hall such a galliard did grace;
While her mother did fret, and her father did fume,
And the bridegroom stood dangling his bonnet and plume;
And the bride-maidens whispered, " 'T were better by far
To have matched our fair cousin with young Lochinvar."

One touch to her hand, and one word in her ear,
When they reached the hall-door, and the charger stood
        near;

So light to the croup the fair lady he swung,
So light to the saddle before her he sprung.
"She is won! we are gone! over bank, bush, and scar;
They'll have fleet steeds that follow," quoth young Loch-
  invar.

There was mounting 'mong Græmes of the Netherby clan;
Forsters, Fenwicks, and Musgraves, they rode and they ran;
There was racing and chasing on Cannobie Lee,
But the lost bride of Netherby ne'er did they see.
So daring in love, and so dauntless in war,
Have ye e'er heard of gallant like young Lochinvar?

TONE OF DETERMINATION.

(See Tone Drill No. 69.)

[The tone of Determination is closely allied to that of Assertion, and says, "My mind is made up." "This shall be so." "I will not yield.]

Webster's Determination.

DANIEL WEBSTER.

For myself, I propose, sir, to abide by the principles and purposes which I have avowed. I shall stand by the Union, and by all who stand by it. I shall do justice to the whole country, according to the best of my ability, in all I say, and act for the good of the whole country in all I do. I mean to stand upon the Constitution. I need no other platform. I shall know but one country. The ends I aim at shall be my country's, my God's, and truth's.

I was born an American, I will live an American, I shall die an American, and I intend to perform the duties incumbent upon me in that character to the end of my career.

I mean to do this with absolute disregard of personal consequences. What are personal consequences? What is the individual man, with all the good or evil that may betide him,
in comparison with the good or evil which may befall a great
country in a crisis like this, and in the midst of great trans-
actions which concern that country's fate? Let the consequences be what they may, I am careless. No man can suffer
too much, and no man can fall too soon, if he suffer, or if
he fall, in defence of the liberties and constitution of his
country.

On a Motion to Censure the Ministry.

WILLIAM PITT.

The triumphs of party, sir, shall never seduce me to any
inconsistency which the busiest suspicion shall presume to
glance at. I will never engage in political enmities without
a public cause. I will never forego such enmities without the
public approbation; nor will I be questioned and cast off in
the face of the House, by one virtuous and dissatisfied friend.
These, sir, the sober and durable triumphs of reason over the
weak and profligate inconsistencies of party violence,—these,
sir, the steady triumphs of virtue over success itself,—shall
be mine not only in my present condition, but through every
future condition of my life; triumphs which no length of
time shall diminish, which no change of principles shall ever
sully.

It is impossible to deprive me of those feelings, which must
always spring from the sincerity of my endeavors to fulfill
with integrity every official engagement. You may take from
me, sir, the privileges and emoluments of place; but you
cannot, and you shall not, take from me those habitual and
warm regards for the prosperity of my country, which constitute the honor, the happiness, the pride of my life; and
which I trust death alone can extinguish.

Prince Henry's Purpose.

WILLIAM SHAKESPEARE.

God forgive them that so much have sway'd
Your majesty's good thoughts away from me!
I will redeem all this on Percy's head,
And in the closing of some glorious day
Be bold to tell you that I am your son;
When I will wear a garment all of blood,
And stain my favours in a bloody mask,
Which, wash'd away, shall scour my shame with it:
And that shall be the day, whene'er it lights,
That this same child of honour and renown,
This gallant Hotspur, this all-praised knight,
And your unthought-of Harry chance to meet,
For every honour sitting on his helm,
Would they were multitudes, and on my head
My shames redoubled! for the time will come,
That I shall make this northern youth exchange
His glorious deeds for my indignities.
Percy is but my factor, good my lord,
To engross up glorious deeds on my behalf;
And I will call him to so strict account,
That he shall render every glory up,
Yea, even the slightest worship of his time,
Or I will tear the reckoning from his heart.
This, in the name of God, I promise here:
The which if He be pleased I shall perform,
I do beseech your majesty may salve
The long-grown wounds of my intemperance:
If not, the end of life cancels all bands;
And I will die a hundred thousand deaths
Ere break the smallest parcel of this vow.

—Henry IV, Pt. I, iii., 2.

TONE OF ENCOURAGEMENT.

(See Tone Drill No. 85.)

[The tone of Encouragement manifests an urging tinged with assurance and confidence.]

The Onset.

BARRY CORNWALL.

Sound an alarum! The foe is come!
I hear the tramp,—the neigh,—the hum,
The cry, and the blow of his daring drum:
   Huzzah!
Sound! The blast of our trumpet blown
Shall carry dismay into hearts of stone:
What! shall we shake at a foe unknown?
   Huzzah!—Huzzah!

Have we not sinews as strong as they?
Have we not hearts that ne'er gave way?
Have we not God on our side to-day?
   Huzzah!
Look! They are staggered on yon black heath!
Steady awhile, and hold your breath!
Now is your time, men,—Down like Death!
   Huzzah!—Huzzah!

Stand by each other, and front your foes!
Fight, whilst a drop of the red blood flows!
Fight, as ye fought for the old red rose!
   Huzzah!
Sound! Bid your terrible trumpets bray!
Blow, till their brazen throats give way!
Sound to the battle! Sound, I say!
   Huzzah!—Huzzah!

Henry V Before Harfleur.

WILLIAM SHAKESPEARE.

Once more unto the breach, dear friends, once more;
Or close the wall up with our English dead.
In peace there's nothing so becomes a man
As modest stillness and humility;
But when the blast of war blows in our ears,
Then imitate the action of the tiger;
Stiffen the sinews, summon up the blood,
Disguise fair nature with hard-favour'd rage;
Then lend the eye a terrible aspect;
Let it pry through the portage of the head
Like the brass cannon; let the brow o'erwhelm it
As fearfully as doth a galled rock
O'erhang and jutty his confounded base,
Swill'd with the wild and wasteful ocean.
Now set the teeth and stretch the nostril wide,
Hold hard the breath and bend up every spirit
To his full height. On, on, you noblest English,
Whose blood is fet from fathers of war-proof!
Fathers that, like so many Alexanders,
Have in these parts from morn till even fought,
And sheathed their swords for lack of argument:
Dishonour not your mothers; now attest
That those whom you call'd fathers did beget you.
Be copy now to men of grosser blood,
And teach them how to war. And you, good yeomen,
Whose limbs were made in England, show us here
The mettle of your pasture; let us swear
That you are worth your breeding; which I doubt not;
For there is none of you so mean and base,
That hath not noble lustre in your eyes.
I see you stand like greyhounds in the slips,

Straining upon the start. The game's afoot:
Follow your spirit, and upon this charge
Cry "God for Harry, England, and Saint George!"

       —Henry V, iii., 1.

THE TONE OF ADVICE.
(See Tone Drill No. 4.)

[The tone of Advice has in it something of command, but lacks the insistence of the latter. Sometimes there is a suggestion of deference.]

Free Speech.

JOHN JAY CHAPMAN.

When I was asked to make this address, I wondered what I had to say to you who are graduating. And I think I have one thing to say. If you wish to be useful, never take a course that will silence you. Refuse to learn anything that you cannot proclaim. Refuse to accept anything that implies collusion, whether it be a clerkship or a curacy, a legal fee or a post in a university. Retain the power of speech, no matter what other power you lose. If you can, take this course, and in so far as you take it, you will bless this country. In so far as you depart from this course, you become dampers, mutes, and hooded executioners.

As for your own private character, it will be preserved by such a course. Crime you cannot commit, for crime gags you   Collusion gags you. As a practical matter, a mere failure to speak out upon occasions where no opinion is asked or expected of you, and when the utterance of an uncalled for suspicion is odious, will often hold you to a concurrence in palpable iniquity. It will bind and gag you and lay you dumb and in shackles like the veriest serf in Russia. I give you this one rule of conduct. Do what you will, but speak out always. Be shunned, be hated, be ridiculed, be scared, be in doubt, but don't be gagged.

Polonius's Advice to Laertes.

WILLIAM SHAKESPEARE.

These few precepts in thy memory
Look thou character. Give thy thoughts no tongue,
Nor any unproportion'd thought his act.
Be thou familiar, but by no means vulgar.
Those friends thou hast, and their adoption tried,
Grapple them to thy soul with hoops of steel,
But do not dull thy palm with entertainment
Of each new-hatch'd unfledged comrade. Beware
Of entrance to a quarrel; but being in,
Bear 't, that the opposed may beware of thee.
Give every man thy ear, but few thy voice:
Take each man's censure, but reserve thy judgment.
Costly thy habit, as thy purse can buy,
But not express'd in fancy; rich, not gaudy:
For the apparel oft proclaims the man;
And they in France of the best rank and station
Are of a most select and generous chief in that.
Neither a borrower nor a lender be:
For loan oft loses both itself and friend,
And borrowing dulls the edge of husbandry.
This above all: to thine own self be true,
And it must follow, as the night the day,
Thou canst not then be false to any man.

—Hamlet, i., 3.

CLIMAX.

(See Tone Drill No. 41.)

[In its purest form Climax is a manifestation of increasing
intensity of feeling or of an increasing importance in the thought.
Climax has no distinct tone. It manifests itself in increasing degrees
of the particular tone demanded.]

Liberty Under Law.

(Abridged.)

GEORGE WILLIAM CURTIS.

The day we celebrate commemorates the introduction upon
this Continent of the master principle of its civilization. I
do not forget that we are a nation of many nationalities. I
remember the forget-me-nots of Germany; I recall the delicate shamrock; I remember, surely, sir, the lily of France,
and the thistle of Scotland; I recall the daisy and the rose
of England; and, sir, in Switzerland, high upon the Alps,
on the very edge of the glacier, the highest flower that grows
in Europe, is the rare edelweiss. And here in America,
higher than the shamrock or thistle, higher than rose, lily or
daisy, higher than the highest, blooms the perennial Mayflower. For, sir and gentlemen, it is the English-speaking
race that has moulded the destiny of this Continent; and the
Puritan influence is the strongest influence that has acted
upon it.

I am surely not here to assert that the men who have rep-
resented that influence have always been men whose spirit
was blended of sweetness and light. I confess truly their
hardness, their prejudice, their narrowness. All this I know.
But, sir, we estimate the cause beyond the man. If we
would see the actual force, the creative power of the Pilgrim
principle, we are not to look at the company who came over
in the cabin of the "Mayflower;" we are to look upon the
forty millions who fill this Continent from sea to sea. The

"Mayflower," sir, brought seed and not a harvest. In a century and a half the religious restrictions of the Puritans had grown into absolute religious liberty, and in two centuries it had burst beyond the limits of New England, and John Carver of the "Mayflower" had ripened into Abraham Lincoln of the Illinois prairie.

Do you ask me then what is this Puritan principle? Do you ask me whether it is as good for today as for yesterday; whether it is good for every national emergency; whether it is good for the situation of this hour? I think we need neither doubt nor fear. The Puritan principle in its essence is simply individual freedom. From that spring religious liberty and political equality. The free State, the free Church, the free School—these are the triple armor of American nationality, of American security. But the Pilgrims, while they have stood above all men for their idea of liberty, have always asserted liberty under law, and never separated it from law. They knew that the will of the people alone is but a gale smiting a rudderless and sailless ship, and hurling it a mass of wreck upon the rocks. But the will of the people, subject to law, is the same gale filling the trim canvas of a ship that minds the helm, bearing it over awful and yawning abysses of ocean safely to port.

Now, gentlemen, in this country, the Puritan principle in its development has advanced to this point, that it provides us a lawful remedy for every emergency that may arise. I stand here as a son of New England. In every fibre of my being am I a child of the Pilgrims. The most knightly of all the gentlemen at Elizabeth's court said to the young poet when he would write an immortal song, "Look into your own heart and write." And I, sir and brothers, if, looking into my own heart at this moment, I might dare to think that what I find written there is also written upon the heart of my mother, clad in her snows at home, her voice at this hour would be a message spoken from the land of the Pilgrims to the capital of this nation—a message like that which Patrick Henry sent from Virginia to Massachusetts when he heard of Concord and Lexington: "I am not a Virginian—I am an American." And so, gentlemen, at this hour we are not Republicans, we are not Democrats—we are Americans.

The voice of New England, I believe, going to the capital, would be this, that neither is the Republican Senate to insist upon its exclusive partisan way, nor is the Democratic House to insist upon its exclusive partisan way, but Senate and House, representing the American people and the American people only, in the light of the Constitution and by the authority of the law, are to provide a way over which a President, be he Republican or be he Democrat, shall pass unchallenged to his chair. Ah! gentlemen, think not, Mr. President, that I am forgetting the occasion or its amenities. I am remembering the Puritans; I am remembering Plymouth Rock, and the virtues that made it illustrious. But we, gentlemen, are to imitate those virtues, as our toast says, only by being greater than the men who stood upon that rock.

Sons of the Pilgrims, you are not to level forests, you are not to war with savage men and savage beasts, you are not to tame a continent, nor even found a State,—that was their task. Our task is nobler, is diviner. Our task, sir, is to reconcile a nation. It is to curb the fury of party spirit. It is to introduce a loftier and manlier tone everywhere into our political life. It is to educate every boy and every girl and then leave them perfectly free to go from any schoolhouse to any church. Above all, sir, it is to protect absolutely the equal rights of the poorest and the richest, of the most ignorant and the most intelligent citizen, and it is to stand forth, brethren, as a triple wall of brass around our native land against the mad blows of violence or the fatal dry-rot of fraud. At this moment, sir, the grave and august shades of the forefathers whom we invoke bend over us in benediction as they call us to this sublime task. This, brothers and friends, this is to imitate the virtues of our forefathers; this is to make our day as glorious as theirs.

The Irish Aliens.

RICHARD L. SHIEL.

The Duke of Wellington is not a man of an excitable temperament. His mind is of a cast too martial to be easily moved; but, notwithstanding his habitual inflexibility, I cannot help thinking that, when he heard his Roman Catholic countrymen (for we are his countrymen) designated by a phrase as offensive as the abundant vocabulary of his eloquent confederate could supply,—I cannot help thinking that he ought to have recollected the many fields of fight in which we have been contributors to his renown. "The battles, sieges, fortunes that he has passed," ought to have come back upon him. He ought to have remembered that, from the earliest achievement in which he displayed that military genius which has placed him foremost in the annals of modern warfare, down to that last and surpassing combat which has made his name imperishable,—from Assaye to Waterloo—the Irish soldiers, with whom your armies are filled, were the inseparable auxiliaries to the glory with which his unparalleled successes have been crowned.

Whose were the arms that drove your bayonets at Vimiéra through the phalanxes that never reeled in the shock of war before? What desperate valor climbed the steeps and filled the moats at Badajos? All his victories should have rushed and crowded back upon his memory,—Vimiéra, Badajos, Salamanca, Albuéra, Toulouse, and last of all, the greatest——. Tell me,—for you were there,—I appeal to the gallant soldier before me (Sir Henry Hardinge), from whose opinions I differ, but who bears, I know, a generous heart in an

intrepid breast;—tell me,—for you must needs remember,—
on that day when the destinies of mankind were trembling in
the balance, while death fell in showers, when the artillery of
France was levelled with a precision of the most deadly
science,—when her legions, incited by the voice and inspired
by the example of their mighty leader, rushed again and again
to the onset,—tell me if, for an instant, when to hesitate for
an instant was to be lost, the "aliens" blenched?

And when, at length, the moment for the last and decided
movement had arrived, and the valor which had so long been
wisely checked was, at last, let loose,—when, with words
familiar, but immortal, the great captain commanded the
great assault,—tell me if Catholic Ireland with less heroic
valor than the natives of this your own glorious country pre-
cipitated herself upon the foe? The blood of England, Scotland, and of Ireland, flowed in the same stream, and drenched
the same field. When the chill morning dawned, their dead
lay cold and stark together;—in the same deep pit their bodies
were deposited; the green corn of spring is now breaking
from their commingled dust; the dew falls from Heaven
upon their union in the grave. Partakers in every peril, in
the glory shall we not be permitted to participate; and shall
we be told, as a requital, that we are estranged from the noble
country for whose salvation our life-blood was poured out?

Marullus to the People.

WILLIAM SHAKESPEARE.

Wherefore rejoice? What conquest brings he home?
What tributaries follow him to Rome,
To grace in captive bonds his chariot-wheels?
You blocks, you stones, you worse than senseless things!
O you hard hearts, you cruel men of Rome,
Knew you not Pompey? Many a time and oft
Have you climb'd up to walls and battlements,

To towers and windows, yea, to chimney-tops,
Your infants in your arms, and there have sat
The live-long day with patient expectation
To see great Pompey pass the streets of Rome:
And when you saw his chariot but appear,
Have you not made an universal shout,
That Tiber trembled underneath her banks
To hear the replication of your sounds
Made in her concave shores?
And do you now put on your best attire?
And do you now cull out a holiday?
And do you now strew flowers in his way
That comes in triumph over Pompey's blood?
Be gone!
Run to your houses, fall upon your knees,
Pray to the gods to intermit the plague
That needs must light on this ingratitude.

—Julius Cæsar, i., 1.

TONE OF FRANKNESS.
(See Tone Drill No. 104.)

[The tone of Frankness indicates that the speaker is withholding or coloring nothing; that there is a sincere desire to show things exactly as they are.]

Portia to Bassanio.
WILLIAM SHAKESPEARE.

You see me, Lord Bassanio, where I stand,
Such as I am: though for myself alone
I would not be ambitious in my wish,
To wish myself much better; yet for you
I would be trebled twenty times myself;
A thousand times more fair, ten thousand
        times more rich;
That only to stand high in your account,

I might in virtues, beauties, livings, friends,
Exceed account; but the full sum of me
Is sum of something; which, to term in gross,
Is an unlesson'd girl, unschool'd, unpractis'd:
Happy in this, she is not yet so old
But she may learn; happier than this,
She is not bred so dull but she can learn;
Happiest of all is, that her gentle spirit
Commits itself to yours to be directed,
As from her lord, her governor, her king.
Myself, and what is mine, to you, and yours,
Is now converted; but now I was the lord
Of this fair mansion, master of my servants,
Queen o'er myself; and even now, but now,
This house, these servants, and this same myself,
Are yours, my lord. I give them with this ring,
Which when you part from, lose, or give away,
Let it presage the ruin of your love,
And be my vantage to exclaim on you.

—Merchant of Venice, iii., 2.

TONE OF EXCITEMENT.
(See Tone Drill No. 88.)

[This tone is always found with some other tone. It denotes
that the speaker is roused from his normal state. Every nerve is
alive to the spirit of the thing he is telling. The tone finds natural
expression in events of stirring action—great uprisings, contests,
calamities.]

The Revolutionary Alarm.
GEORGE BANCROFT.

Darkness closed upon the country and upon the town, but
it was no night for sleep. Heralds on swift relays of horses
transmitted the war message from hand to hand, till village
repeated it to village, the sea to the backwoods, the plains to
the highlands, and it was never suffered to droop till it had

been borne North and South and East and West, throughout the land. It spread over the bays that receive the Saco and the Penobscot; its loud reveille broke the rest of the trappers of New Hampshire, and, ringing like bugle notes from peak to peak, overleapt the Green Mountains, swept onward to Montreal, and descended the ocean-river till the responses were echoed from the cliffs at Quebec.

The hills along the Hudson told one another the tale. As the summons hurried to the South, it was one day at New York, in one more at Philadelphia, the next it lighted a watch-fire at Baltimore, thence it waked an answer at Annapolis. Crossing the Potomac near Mt. Vernon, it was sent forward without a halt to Williamsburg. It traversed the Dismal Swamp to Nansemond, along the route of the first emigrants to North Carolina. It moved onward and still onward, through boundless groves of evergreen to Newbern and to Wilmington.

"For God's sake, forward it by night and day," wrote Cornelius Harnett, by the express, which sped for Brunswick. Patriots of South Carolina caught up its tones at the border and despatched it to Charleston, and, through pines and palmettos and moss-clad live-oaks, farther to the South, till it resounded among the New England settlements beyond the Savannah. The Blue Ridge took up the voice and made it heard from one end to the other of the valley of Virginia. The Alleghanies, as they listened, opened their barriers that the "loud call" might pass through to the hardy riflemen on the Holston, the Watauga and the French Broad. Ever renewing its strength, powerful enough even to create a commonwealth, it breathed its inspiring word to the first settlers of Kentucky, so that hunters who made their halt in the valley of the Elkhorn commemorated the nineteenth day of April, 1776, by naming their encampment "Lexington." With one impulse the Colonies sprang to arms; with

one spirit they pledged themselves to each other, "to be ready
for the extreme event." With one heart the Continent cried,
"Liberty or death!"

The Ride to Aix.

ROBERT BROWNING.

I sprang to the stirrup, and Joris, and he;
I galloped, Dirck galloped, we galloped all three.
"Good speed!" cried the watch as the gate-bolts undrew;
"Speed!" echoed the wall to us galloping through.
Behind shut the postern, the lights sank to rest,
And into the midnight we galloped abreast.

Not a word to each other; we kept the great pace—
Neck by neck, stride by stride, never changing our place;
I turned in my saddle and made its girths tight,
Then shortened each stirrup, and set the pique right,
Rebuckled the check-strap, chained slacker the bit,
Nor galloped less steadily Roland a whit. . . .

By Hasselt Dirck groaned; and cried Joris, "Stay spur!
Your Roos galloped bravely, the fault's not in her,
We'll remember at Aix;" for one heard the quick wheeze
Of her chest, saw the stretched neck and staggering knees
And sunk tail, and horrible heave of the flank,
As down on her haunches she shuddered and sank.

So we were left galloping, Joris and I,
Past Looz and past Tongres, no cloud in the sky;
The broad sun above laughed a pitiless laugh,
'Neath our feet broke the brittle bright stubble like chaff;
Till over by Dalheim a dome-spire sprang white,
And "Gallop," gasped Joris, "for Aix is in sight!"

"How they'll greet us!"—and all in a moment his roan
Rolled neck and croup over, lay dead as a stone;

And there was my Roland to bear the whole weight
Of the news which alone could save Aix from her fate,
With his nostrils like pits full of blood to the brim,
And with circles of red for his eye-sockets' rim.

Then I cast loose my buffcoat, each holster let fall,
Shook off both my jack-boots, let go belt and all;
Stood up in the stirrup, leaned, patted his ear,
Called my Roland his pet-name, my horse without peer;
Clapped my hands, laughed and sang, any noise, bad or good,
Till at length into Aix Roland galloped and stood.

And all I remember is friends flocking round
As I sat with his head 'twixt my knees on the ground;
And no voice but was praising this Roland of mine
As I poured down his throat our last measure of wine,
Which (the burgesses voted by common consent)
Was no more than his due who brought good news from
    Ghent.

TONE OF INDIFFERENCE.

(See Tone Drill No. 120.)

[The tone of Indifference manifests personal unconcern. It is
allied to Belittling. It says, "It matters nothing to me."]

What Care I?

GEORGE WITHER.

Shall I, wasting in despair,
Die because a woman's fair?
Or make pale my cheeks with care
'Cause another's rosy are?
Be she fairer than the day,
Or the flow'ry meads in May,
    If she be not so to me,
    What care I how fair she be?

Should my heart be grieved or pined
'Cause I see a woman kind?
Or a well disposèd nature
Joinèd with a lovely feature?
Be she meeker, kinder than
Turtle-dove or pelican,
   If she be not so to me,
   What care I how kind she be?

Shall a woman's virtues move
Me to perish for her love?
Or her well-deservings, known,
Make me quite forget my own?
Be she with that goodness blest
Which may gain her name of best,
   If she be not so to me,
   What care I how good she be?

'Cause her fortune seem too high,
Shall I play the fool and die?
Those that bear a noble mind,
Where they want of riches find,
Think what with them they would do,
That without them dare to woo;
   And unless that mind I see,
   What care I how great she be?

Great or good, or kind, or fair,
I will ne'er the more despair:
If she love me, this believe,
I will die e'er she shall grieve:
If she slight me when I woo,
I can scorn and let her go;
   For if she be not for me
   What care I for whom she be?

THE TONE OF LOVE.

(See Tone Drill No. 132.)

[The tone of Love manifests the most intense regard. It is more impulsive than Affection, in its strongest forms showing a reckless abandon. There is usually in it a tinge of cooing and coaxing.]

Love's Welcome.

THOMAS DAVIS.

Come in the evening, or come in the morning;
Come when you're looked for, or come without warning;
Kisses and welcome you'll find here before you,
And the oftener you come here the more I'll adore you!
Light is my heart since the day we were plighted;
Red is my cheek that they told me was blighted;
The green of the trees looks far greener than ever,
And the linnets are singing, "True lovers don't sever!"

I'll pull you sweet flowers to wear if you choose them,
Or, after you've kissed them, they'll lie on my bosom;
I'll fetch from the mountain its breeze to inspire you;
I'll fetch from my fancy a tale that won't tire you.
Oh! your step's like the rain to the summer-vexed farmer,
Or sabre and shield to a knight without armor;
I'll sing you sweet songs till the stars rise above me,
Then, wandering, I'll wish you in silence to love me.

We'll look through the trees at the cliff and the eyrie;
We'll tread round the rath on the track of the fairy;
We'll look on the stars and we'll list to the river,
Till you ask of your darling what gift you can give her.
Oh! she'll whisper you,—"Love as unchangeably beaming,
And trust, when in secret most tunefully streaming
Till the starlight of heaven above us shall quiver,
As our souls flow in one down eternity's river."

So come in the evening, or come in the morning;
Come when you're looked for, or come without warning;
Kisses and welcome you'll find here before you,
And the oftener you come the more I'll adore you!
Light is my heart since the day we were plighted;
Red is my cheek that they told me was blighted;
The green of the trees looks far greener than ever,
And the linnets are singing, "True lovers don't sever!"

Two Lovers.

GEORGE ELIOT.

Two lovers by a moss-grown spring:
    They leaned soft cheeks together there,
    Mingled the dark and sunny hair,
And heard the wooing thrushes sing.
        O budding time!
        O love's blest prime!

Two wedded from the portal stept;
    The bells made happy carollings,
    The air was soft as fanning wings,
White petals on the pathway slept.
        O pure-eyed bride!
        O tender pride!

Two faces o'er a cradle bent:
    Two hands above the head were locked;
    These pressed each other while they rocked,
Those watched a life that love had sent.
        O solemn hour!
        O hidden power!

Two parents by the evening fire:
    The red light fell about their knees
    On heads that rose by slow degrees

Like buds upon the lily spire.
O patient life!
O tender strife!

The two still sat together there,
The red light shone about their knees;
But all the heads by slow degrees
Had gone and left that lonely pair.
O voyage fast!
O vanished past!

The red light shone upon the floor
And made the space between them wide;
They drew their chairs up side by side,
Their pale cheeks joined, and said, "Once more!"
O memories!
O past that is!

Romeo to Juliet.

WILLIAM SHAKESPEARE.

Soft! what light through yonder window breaks!
It is the east, and Juliet is the sun!
Arise, fair sun, and kill the envious moon,
Who is already sick and pale with grief,　　.
That thou her maid are far more fair than she:
It is my lady; O, it is my love!
O, that she knew she were!
She speaks, yet she says nothing: what of that?
Her eye discourses, I will answer it.
I am too bold, 'tis not to me she speaks:
Two of the fairest stars in all the heaven,
Having some business, do intreat her eyes
To twinkle in their spheres till they return.

What if her eyes were there, they in her head?
The brightness of her cheek would shame those stars,
As daylight doth a lamp; her eyes in heaven
Would through the airy region stream so bright
That birds would sing and think it were not night.
See, how she leans her cheek upon her hand!
O, that I were a glove upon that hand,
That I might touch that cheek!

She speaks:

O, speak again, bright angel! for thou art
As glorious to this night, being o'er my head,
As is a winged messenger of heaven
Unto the white-upturned wondering eyes
Of mortals that fall back to gaze on him,
When he bestrides the lazy-pacing clouds
And sails upon the bosom of the air.

Romeo and Juliet, ii., 2.

TONE OF CONTEMPT.
(See Tone Drill No. 54.)

[The tone of Contempt denotes that the person or thing is felt to be unworthy. It says, "You are beneath me," "I scorn you," "It disgusts." In its mildest form it is linked with indifference, in the more intense forms it partakes of loathing.]

The Coalition.

DANIEL WEBSTER.

The coalition! The coalition! Ay, "the murdered coalition!" The gentleman asks if I were led or frighted into this debate by the spectre of the coalition. "Was it the ghost of the murdered coalition," he exclaims, "which haunted the member from Massachusetts, and which, like the ghost of Banquo, would never down?" "The murdered coalition!"

Sir, this charge of a coalition, in reference to the late administration, is not original with the honorable member. It did not spring up in the Senate. Whether as a fact, as an argument, or as an embellishment, it is all borrowed. He adopts it, indeed, from a very low origin, and a still lower present condition. It is one of the thousand calumnies with which the press teemed during an excited political canvass. It was a charge of which there was not only no proof or probability, but which was, in itself, wholly impossible to be true. No man of common information ever believed a syllable of it.

Yet it was of that class of falsehoods which, by continued repetition through all the organs of detraction and abuse, are capable of misleading those who are already far misled, and of further fanning passion already kindling into flame. Doubtless it served its day, and in a greater or less degree, the end designed by it. Having done that it has sunk into the general mass of stale and loathed calumnies. It is the very cast-off slough of a polluted and shameless press. Incapable of further mischief, it lies in the sewer, lifeless and despised. It is not now, sir, in the power of the honorable member to give it dignity or decency, by attempting to elevate it, and to introduce it into the Senate. He cannot change it from what it is—an object of general disgust and scorn. On the contrary, the contact, if he chooses to touch it, is more likely to drag him down, down to the place where it lies itself.

Richard III to His Soldiers.

WILLIAM SHAKESPEARE.

What shall I say more than I have inferr'd?
Remember whom you are to cope withal;
A sort of vagabonds, rascals, and runaways,
A scum of Bretons, and base lackey peasants,

Whom their o'er-cloyed country vomits forth
To desperate ventures and assured destruction.
You sleeping safe, they bring to you unrest;
You having lands and blest with beauteous wives,
They would restrain the one, distain the other.
And who doth lead them but a paltry fellow,
Long kept in Bretagne at our mother's cost?
A milk-sop, one that never in his life
Felt so much cold as over shoes in snow?
Let's whip these stragglers o'er the seas again,
Lash hence these overweening rags of France,
These famish'd beggars, weary of their lives,
Who, but for dreaming on this fond exploit,
For want of means, poor rats, had hang'd themselves:
If we be conquer'd, let men conquer us,
And not these Bretons, whom our fathers
Have in their own land beaten, bobb'd, and thump'd,
And in record left them the heirs of shame.

—Richard III, v., 3.

TONE OF PITY.
(See Tone Drill No. 150.)

[The tone of Pity denotes a deep and serious feeling for or with another. It says, "I am sorry for you. I feel with you, or for you; your sorrow is my sorrow."]

The Martyr President.

HENRY WARD BEECHER.

There is no historic figure more noble than that of the Jewish law-giver. After so many thousand years the figure of Moses is not diminished, but stands up against the background of early days, distinct and individual, as if he had lived but yesterday. There is scarcely another event in history more touching than his death. He had borne the great burdens of state for forty years, shaped the Jews to a nation, administered their laws, guided their steps, or dwelt with them in all their journeyings in the wilderness; had mourned in their punishment, kept step with their march, and led them in wars, until the end of their labors drew nigh. The last stage was reached. Jordan, only, lay between them and the promised land.

The promised land!—oh, what yearnings had heaved his breast for that divinely promised place! He had dreamed of it by night, and mused by day. It was holy and endeared as God's favored spot. It was to be the cradle of an illustrious history. All his long, laborious, and now weary life, he had aimed at this as the consummation of every desire, the reward of every toil and pain. Then came the word of the Lord to him, "Thou mayest not go over: Get thee up into the mountain, look upon it, and die."

From that silent summit, the hoary leader gazed to the north, to the south, to the west, with hungry eyes. There lay God's promise fulfilled. There was the seat of the coming Jerusalem; there the city of Judah's King; the sphere of judges and prophets; the mount of sorrow and salvation; the nest whence were to fly blessings innumerable to all mankind. Joy chased sadness from every feature, and the prophet laid him down and died.

Again a great leader of the people has passed through toil, sorrow, battle, and war, and come near to the promised land of peace, into which he might not pass over. Who shall recount our martyr's sufferings for this people? Since the November of 1860, his horizon has been black with storms. By day and by night he trod a way of danger and darkness. On his shoulders rested a government dearer to him than his own life. At its integrity millions of men were striking at home. Upon this government foreign eyes lowered.

It stood like a lone island in a sea full of storms; and every tide and wave seemed eager to devour it. Upon thousands of hearts great sorrows and anxieties have rested, but on none such, and in such measure, as upon that simple, truthful, noble soul, our faithful and sainted Lincoln. He wrestled ceaselessly, through four black and dreadful purgatorial years, wherein God was cleansing the sin of his people as by fire.

At last the watcher beheld the gray dawn for the country. The East came rushing towards us with arms full of joy for all our sorrows. Then it was for him to be glad exceedingly, that had sorrowed immeasurably. Peace could bring to no other heart such joy, such rest, such honor, such trust, such gratitude. But he looked upon it as Moses looked upon the promised land. Then the wail of a nation proclaimed that he had gone from among us.

In one hour joy lay without a pulse, without a gleam, or breath. A sorrow came that swept through the land as huge storms sweep through the forest and field, rolling thunder along the sky, dishevelling the flowers, daunting every singer in thicket or forest, and pouring blackness and darkness across the land and up the mountains. Did ever so many hearts in so brief a time touch two such boundless feelings? It was the uttermost of joy; it was the uttermost of sorrow—noon and midnight, without a space between.

And now the martyr is moving in triumphal march, mightier than when alive. The nation rises up at every stage of his coming. Cities and states are his pall-bearers, and the cannon beats the hours with solemn progression. Dead, he yet speaketh! Is Washington dead? Is Hampden dead? Is David dead? Is any man that ever was fit to live dead? Disenthralled of flesh, and risen in the unobstructed sphere where passion never comes he begins his illimitable work. His life now is grafted upon the infinite, and will be fruitful as no earthly life can be. Your sorrows, oh

people, are his peace! Your bells, and bands and muffled
drums, sound triumph in his ear. Wail and weep here; God
makes it echo joy and triumph there.

The Return of Enoch Arden.

ALFRED TENNYSON.

Enoch yearned to see her face again;
"If I might look on her sweet face again
And know that she is happy." So the thought
Haunted and harass'd him, and drove him forth,
At evening when the dull November day
Was growing duller twilight, to the hill.
There he sat down gazing on all below;
There did a thousand memories roll upon him,
Unspeakable for sadness. By and by
The ruddy square of comfortable light,
Far-blazing from the rear of Philip's house,
Allured him, as the beacon-blaze allures
The bird of passage, till he madly strikes
Against it, and beats out his weary life. . . .

Enoch shunn'd the middle walk and stole
Up by the wall, behind the yew; and thence
That which he better might have shunn'd, if griefs
Like his have worse or better, Enoch saw.

Now when the dead man come to life beheld
His wife his wife no more, and saw the babe
Hers, yet not his, upon the father's knee,
And all the warmth, the peace, the happiness,
And his own children tall and beautiful,
And him, that other, reigning in his place,
Lord of his rights and of his children's love,—

Then he, tho' Miriam Lane had told him all,
Because things seen are mightier than things heard,
Stagger'd and shook, holding the branch, and fear'd
To send abroad a shrill and terrible cry,
Which in one moment, like the blast of doom,
Would shatter all the happiness of the hearth.

He therefore turning softly like a thief,
Lest the harsh shingle should grate underfoot,
And feeling all along the garden wall,
Lest he should swoon and tumble and be found,
Crept to the gate, and open'd it, and closed,
As lightly as a sick man's chamber-door,
Behind him, and came out upon the waste.

And there he would have knelt, but that his knees
Were feeble, so that falling prone he dug
His fingers into the wet earth, and pray'd.

"Too hard to bear! why did they take me thence?
O God Almighty, blessed Saviour, Thou
That didst uphold me on my lonely isle,
Uphold me, Father, in my loneliness
A little longer! aid me, give me strength
Not to tell her, never to let her know.
Help me not to break in upon her peace.
My children too! must I not speak to these?
They know me not. I should betray myself.
Never: no father's kiss for me—the girl
So like her mother, and the boy, my son."

There speech and thought and nature fail'd a little
And he lay tranced; but when he rose and paced
Back toward his solitary home again,
All down the long and narrow street he went

Beating it in upon his weary brain,
As tho' it were the burthen of a song,
"Not to tell her, never to let her know."

TONE OF RIDICULE.

(See Tone Drill No. 180.)

[The tone of Ridicule indicates an "amused contempt" or "mocking merriment." It says, "Look at the absurdity in this thing and laugh at it."]

The Evidence of Mr. O'Brien.

JOHN P. CURRAN.

What is the evidence of O'Brien? What has he stated? How does Mr. O'Brien's tale hang together? Look to its commencement. He walks along Thomas street, in the open day (a street not the least populous in the city), and is accosted by a man, who, without any preface, tells him, he'll be murdered before he goes half the street, unless he becomes a United Irishman! Do you think this is a probable story? Suppose any of you, gentlemen, be a United Irishman, or a freemason, or a friendly brother, and that you met me walking innocently along, just like Mr. O'Brien, and meaning no harm, would you say, "Stop, sir, don't go further, you'll be murdered before you go half the street, if you do not become a United Irishman, a freemason, or a friendly brother?"

Did you ever hear so coaxing an invitation to felony as this? "Sweet Mr. James O'Brien, come in and save your precious life; come in and take an oath, or you'll be murdered before you go half the street! Do, sweetest, dearest Mr. James O'Brien, come in and do not risk your valuable existence." What a loss had he been to his king, whom he loves so marvellously!

Well, what does poor Mr. O'Brien do? Poor, dear man, he stands petrified with the magnitude of his danger—all his members refuse their office—he can neither run from the danger, nor call for assistance; his tongue cleaves to his mouth! and his feet incorporate with the paving stones—it is in vain that his expressive eye silently implores protection of the passenger; he yields at length, as greater men have done, and resignedly submits to his fate: he enters the house, and being led into a room, a parcel of men *make faces* at him: but mark the metamorphosis—well may it be said, that "miracles will never cease,"—he who feared to resist in the open air, and in the face of the public, becomes a bravo, when pent up in a room, and environed by sixteen men; and one is obliged to bar the door while another swears him; which, after some resistance, is accordingly done, and poor Mr. O'Brien becomes a United Irishman, for no earthly purpose whatever, but merely to save his sweet life!

TONE OF GRIEF.
(See Tone Drill No. 110.)

[The tone of Grief manifests a deep personal suffering. It is more poignant than sadness, but less so than agony. Sometimes there is the note of despair.]

Ivan the Czar.

FELICIA HEMANS.

He sat in silence on the ground,
　　The old and haughty Czar,
Lonely, though princes girt him round,
　　And leaders of the war;
He had cast his jewelled sabre,
　　That many a field had won,
To the earth beside his youthful dead—
　　His fair and first-born son.　.　.　.

"There is no crimson on thy cheek,
　　And on thy lip no breath;

I call thee, and thou dost not speak:
    They tell me this is death!
And fearful things are whispering
    That I the deed have done!
For the honour of thy father's name,
    Look up, look up, my son!

"Well might I know death's hue and mien;
    But on *thine* aspect, boy,
What, till this moment, have I seen
    Save pride and tameless joy?
Swiftest thou wert to battle,
    And bravest there of all;
How could I think a warrior's frame
    Thus like a flower should fall?

"I will not bear that still cold look—
    Rise up, thou fierce and free!
Wake as the storm wakes! I will brook
    All, save this calm, from thee.
Lift brightly up, and proudly,
    Once more thy kindling eyes:
Hath my word lost its power on earth?
    I say to thee, arise!

"Didst thou not know I loved thee well?
    Thou didst not! and art gone,
In bitterness of soul, to dwell
    Where man must dwell alone.
Come back, young fiery spirit!
    If but one hour, to learn
The secrets of the folded heart,
    That seemed to thee so stern.

"Thou wert the first, the first fair child
    That in mine arms I pressed;

Thou wert the bright one that hast smiled
  Like summer on my breast.
I reared thee as an eagle,
  To the chase thy steps I led,
I bore thee on my battle-horse,—
  I look upon thee—dead!

"Lay down my warlike banners here,
  Never again to wave,
And bury my red sword and spear,
  Chiefs, in my first-born's grave;
And leave me!—I have conquered,
  I have slain—my work is done!
Whom have I slain? Ye answer not;
  Thou too art mute, my son!"

And thus his wild lament was poured
  Through the dark resounding night,
And the battle knew no more his sword,
  Nor the foaming steed his might.
He heard strange voices moaning
  In every wind that sighed;
From the searching stars of heaven he shrank—
  Humbly the conqueror died.

Hamlet on His Mother's Marriage.

WILLIAM SHAKESPEARE.

O, that this too too solid flesh would melt,
Thaw and resolve itself into a dew!
Or that the Everlasting had not fix'd
His canon 'gainst self-slaughter! O God! God!
How weary, stale, flat and unprofitable
Seem to me all the uses of this world!
Fie on 't! o fie! 'tis an unweeded garden,

That grows to seed; things rank and gross in nature
Possess it merely.   That it should come to this!
But two months dead! nay, not so much, not two:
So excellent a king; that was, to this,
Hyperion to a satyr: so loving to my mother,
That he might not beteem the winds of heaven
Visit her face too roughly.   Heaven and earth!
Must I remember?   why, she would hang on him,
As if increase of appetite had grown
By what it fed on: and yet, within a month—
Let me not think on 't—Frailty, thy name is woman!—
A little month, or ere those shoes were old
With which she follow'd my poor father's body,
Like Niobe, all tears:—why she, even she,—
O God! a beast that wants discourse of reason
Would have mourn'd longer,—married with my uncle,
My father's brother, but no more like my father
Than I to Hercules: within a month;
Ere yet the salt of most unrighteous tears
Had left the flushing in her galled eyes,
She married!
It is not, nor it cannot come to good:
But break, my heart, for I must hold my tongue!

                                        —Hamlet, i., 2.

TONE OF SARCASM.
(See Tone Drill No. 182.)

[The tone of Sarcasm denotes a keen disrespect, bordering sometimes on cruelty.   The speaker seems to snarl and bite, and, at times,
to enjoy his verbal torture of the victim.]

Reply to Mr. Corry.
HENRY GRATTAN.

Has the gentleman done?   Has he completely done?   He
was unparliamentary from the beginning to the end of his

speech. There was scarce a word that he uttered that was not a violation of the privileges of the House. But I did not call him to order. Why? Because the limited talents of some men render it impossible for them to be severe without being unparliamentary. But before I sit down I shall show him how to be severe and parliamentary at the same time. On any other occasion, I should think myself justifiable in treating with silent contempt anything which might fall from that honorable member; but there are times when the insignificance of the accuser is lost in the magnitude of the accusation. I know the difficulty the honorable gentleman labored under when he attacked me, conscious that, on a comparative view of our characters, public and private, there is nothing he could say which would injure me. The public would not believe the charge. I despise the falsehood. If such a charge were made by an honest man, I would answer it in the manner I shall do before I sit down. But I shall first reply to it when not made by an honest man.

Reply to Mr. Walpole.

WILLIAM PITT.

The atrocious crime of being a young man, which the honourable gentleman has, with such spirit and decency, charged upon me, I shall neither attempt to palliate nor deny; but content myself with wishing that I may be one of those whose follies may cease with their youth, and not of those who continue ignorant in spite of age and experience.

Whether youth can be attributed to any man as a reproach, I will not, Sir, assume the province of determining; but surely, age may justly become contemptible, if the opportunities which it brings have passed away without improvement, and vice appear to prevail when the passions have subsided. The wretch who, after having seen the consequences of a thousand errors, continues still to blunder, and in whom age has only added obstinacy to stupidity, is surely the object either of abhorrence or contempt; and deserves not that his gray head should secure him from insults. Much more, Sir, is he to be abhorred who, as he has advanced in age, has receded from virtue, and become more wicked with less temptation; who prostitutes himself for money which he cannot enjoy, and spends the remainder of his life in the ruin of his country.

Shylock to Antonio.

WILLIAM SHAKESPEARE.

You come to me, and you say,
"Shylock, we would have moneys:" you say so;
You, that did void your rheum upon my beard,
And foot me as you spurn a stranger cur
Over your threshold: moneys is your suit.
What should I say to you? Should I not say
"Hath a dog money? is it possible
A cur can lend three thousand ducats?" or
Shall I bend low and in a bondman's key,
With bated breath and whispering humbleness,
Say this,—
"Fair sir, you spit on me on Wednesday last;
You spurn'd me such a day; another time
You call'd me dog; and for these courtesies
I'll lend you thus much moneys?"

　　　　　　　　　　—Merchant of Venice, i., 3.

TONE OF JOY.
(See Tone Drill No. 128.)

[The tone of Joy manifests brightness and happiness. It has less abandon than Gayety, being sweeter and richer.]

The Enjoyments of Spring.

T. DUNCAN.

This is truly the glad season of the year. Wherever we turn our eyes, Nature wears a smile of joy, as if, freed from the storms and the cold of winter, she revelled in the well enhanced luxury of spring. The lengthening day, the increasing warmth of the air, and the gradually deepening green of the awakened earth, excite in every breast a lively sense of gratitude, and pleasingly affect the imagination. A walk among the woods or fields, in a calm spring day, when the trees are bursting forth into beauty, and all the land is echoing with song, may well soothe the stormiest passions, and inspire that 'vernal delight,' which is 'able to drive away all sadness but despair.' The mind sympathizes with the joy of inanimate Nature, and rejoices to behold the reviving beauty of the earth, as if itself had escaped from a period of gloom, to bask in the sunshine of hope and enjoyment.

There is something in the flowery sweetness and genial warmth of spring that kindles in the rudest bosom feelings of gratitude and pleasure. The contrast to the cold and desolation of winter is so striking and agreeable, that every heart, unless it be hardened by the direst ignorance and crime, is melted to love and pious emotion; and breathings of deep-felt adoration escape from the most untutored lips. The carols of the ploughman, as he traverses the field, the live-long day, and turns up the fresh soil, seem to bespeak a light-some heart, and evince the joyousness of labor. The shepherd, as he sits upon the hill-side and surveys his quiet flock with its sportive companies of lambs,—those sweetest emblems of innocent mirth,—feels a joy and calm satisfaction, that is heightened by the recollection of the vanished snowstorms of recent winter, and of all the anxieties and toils attending his peculiar charge.

Even the hard-working mechanic of the village or town, shares the general gladness of the season. As he strolls in sweet relaxation into the glittering fields, or along the blossoming hedgerows and lanes, haply supporting with his hand the tottering footsteps of his child, or carrying the tender infant in his arms, he breathes the freshning air, treads the reviving turf beneath his feet, and inhales the first faint perfumes, and listens to the first melodies of the year, with an enjoyment that his untaught powers of expression cannot describe.

Voice of Spring.

FELICIA HEMANS.

I come, I come! ye have called me long,
I come o'er the mountains with light and song;
Ye may trace my step o'er the wakening earth,
By the winds which tell of the violet's birth,
By the primrose stars in the shadowy grass,
By the green leaves opening as I pass.

I have passed o'er the hills of the stormy north,
And the larch has hung all his tassels forth,
The fisher is out on the sunny sea,
And the reindeer bounds through the pasture free;
And the pine has a fringe of softer green,
And the moss looks bright where my step has been.

I have sent through the wood-paths a gentle sigh,
And called out each voice of the deep-blue sky,
From the night bird's lay through the starry time,

In the groves of the soft Hesperian clime,
To the swan's wild note by the Iceland lakes,
Where the dark fir-bough into verdure breaks.

From the streams and founts I have loosed the chain;
They are sweeping on to the silvery main,
They are flashing down from the mountain brows,
They are flinging spray on the forest boughs,
They are bursting fresh from their sparry caves,
And the earth resounds with the joy of waves.

Come forth, O ye children of gladness, come!
Where the violets lie may now be your home.
Ye of the rose cheek and dew-bright eye,
And the bounding footstep, to meet me fly;
With the lyre, and the wreath, and the joyous lay,
Come forth to the sunshine, I may not stay.   .   .   .

TONE OF GLOOM.
(See Tone Drill No. 136.)

[The tone of Gloom proclaims the dismal. It is tinged with melancholy, and sometimes there is a mild resentment.]

November.

THOMAS HOOD.

No sun—no moon!
No morn—no noon—
No dawn—no dusk—no proper time of day—
No sky—no earthly view—
No distance looking blue—
No road—no street—no "t'other side the way"—
No end to any Row—
No indications where the Crescents go—

No top to any steeple—
No recognitions of familiar people—
No courtesies for showing 'em—
No knowing 'em!
No traveling at all—no locomotion—
No inkling of the way—no notion—
"No go"—by land or ocean—

 . . . .   .

No warmth, no cheerfulness, no healthful ease,
No comfortable feel in any member—
No shade, no shine, no butterflies, no bees,
No fruits, no flowers, no leaves, no birds—
November.

TONE OF ASPIRATION.
(See Tone Drill No. 84.)

[As a rule the tone of aspiration suggests noble desire. It is allied to Ambition, Admiration, and is almost synonymous with Emulation.]

American Aspiration.

K. M. HUNTER.

I can conceive of nothing of which it is possible for human effort to obtain, greater than the destiny which we may reasonably hope to fulfill. If war has its dreams, dazzling in splendid pageantry, peace also has its visions of a more enduring form, of a higher and purer beauty. To solve by practical demonstration the grand problem of increasing social power consistent with personal freedom—to increase the efficiency of the human agent by enlarging individual liberty—to triumph over, not only the physical, but more difficult still, the moral difficulties which lie in the path of a man's progress, and to adorn that path with all that is rare and useful in art, and whatever is highest in civilization, are, in my opinion, the noblest achievements of which a nation is capable These are the ends to which our ambition should be directed.

If we reverse the old idea of the Deity who presides over our boundaries, let us see so far as we are concerned, that his movements are consistent with the peace of the world. The sword may be the occasional, but it is not the familiar weapon of our god Terminus. The axe and the hoe are his more appropriate emblems. Let him turn aside from the habitations of civilized man, his path is toward the wilderness, through whose silent solitudes, for more than two centuries, he has been rapidly and triumphantly advancing. Let him plunge still deeper into the forest, as the natural gravitation of the tide of population impels him onward. His progress in that direction is one of unmixed beneficence to the human race. The earth smiles beneath his feet, and a new creation arises as if by enchantment at his touch.

Household fires illuminate his line of march, and new-born lights, strange visitants to the night of primeval solitude, kindle on domestic altars erected to all the peaceful virtues and kindly affections which consecrate a hearth and endear a home. Victorious industry sacks the forest and mines the quarry, for materials for its stately cities, or spans the streams and saps the mountain to open the way for the advance of civilization still deeper into the pathless forest and neglected wild. The light of human thought pours in winged streams from sea to sea, and the lingering nomad may have but a moment's pause, to behold the flying car which comes to invade the haunts so long secured to savage life. These are the aspirations worthy of our name and race, and it is for the American people to decide whether a taste for peace or the habits of war are most consistent with such hopes. I trust that they may be guided by wisdom in their choice.

"Oh May I Join the Choir Invisible."

GEORGE ELIOT.

Oh may I join the choir invisible
Of those immortal dead who live again
In minds made better by their presence: live
In pulses stirred to generosity,
In deeds of daring rectitude, in scorn
For miserable aims that end with self,
In thoughts sublime that pierce the night like stars,
And with their mild persistence urge man's search
To vaster issues.

So to live is heaven ·
To make undying music in the world,
Breathing as beauteous order that controls
With growing sway the growing life of man.
So we inherit that sweet purity
For which we struggled, failed, and agonized
With widening retrospect that bred despair.
Rebellious flesh that would not be subdued,
A vicious parent shaming still its child
Poor anxious penitence, is quick dissolved;
Its discords, quenched by meeting harmonies,
Die in the large and charitable air.
And all our rarer, better, truer self,
That sobbed religiously in yearning song,
That watched to ease the burden of the world,
Laboriously tracing what must be,
And what may yet be better—saw within
A worthier image for the sanctuary,
And shaped it forth before the multitude
Divinely human, raising worship so
To higher reverence more mixed with love—

That better self shall live till human Time
Shall fold its eyelids, and the human sky
Be gathered like a scroll within the tomb
Unread forever.

This is life to come,
Which martyred men have made more glorious
For us who strive to follow. May I reach
That purest heaven, be to other souls
The cup of strength in some great agony,
Enkindle generous ardor, feed pure love,
Beget the smiles that have no cruelty—
Be the sweet presence of a good diffused,
And in diffusion ever more intense
So shall I join the choir invisible
Whose music is the gladness of the world.

IRONY.
(See Tone Drill No. 126.)

[Strictly speaking Irony has no tone, and yet it may belong to
all tones. Foreknowledge of the attitude of the speaker is, usually,
the key to Irony. Its intelligibility as a tone rests upon a slight
exaggeration of the genuine tone.]

Duluth.
J. PROCTOR KNOTT.

As I said, Sir, I was utterly at a loss to determine where
the terminus of this great and indispensable road should be,
until I accidentally overheard some gentleman the other day
mention the name of "Duluth." Duluth! The word fell
upon my ear with peculiar and indescribable charm, like the
gentle murmur of a low fountain stealing forth in the midst
of roses, or the soft, sweet accents of an angel's whisper, in
the bright joyous dream of sleeping innocence. Duluth.

'Twas the name for which my soul had panted for years, as the heart panteth for water-brooks. But where was Duluth? Never, in all my limited reading, had my vision been gladdened by seeing the celestial word in print.

Nevertheless, I was confident it existed somewhere, and that its discovery would constitute the crowning glory of the present century, if not of all modern times. I knew it was bound to exist in the very nature of things; that the symmetry and perfection of our planetary system would be incomplete without it, that the elements of material nature would long since have resolved themselves back into original chaos if there had been such a hiatus in creation as would have resulted from leaving out Duluth. In fact, Sir, I was overwhelmed with the conviction that Duluth not only existed somewhere, but that wherever it was, it was a great and glorious place.

I was convinced that the greatest calamity that ever befell the benighted nations of the ancient world was in their having passed away without a knowledge of the actual existence of Duluth; that their fabled Atlantis, never seen save by the hallowed vision of inspired poesy, was, in fact, but another name for Duluth; that the golden orchard of Hesperides was but a poetical synonym for the beer gardens in the vicinity of Duluth. I knew that if the immortal spirit of Homer could look down from another heaven than that created by his own celestial genius upon the long lines of pilgrims from every nation of the earth to the gushing fountain of poesy opened by the touch of his magic wand, if he could be permitted to behold the vast assemblage of grand and glorious productions of the lyric art called into being by his own inspired strains, he would weep tears of bitter anguish that instead of lavishing all the stores of his mighty genius upon the fall of Troy it had not been his more blessed lot to crystallize in deathless song the rising glories of Duluth.

TONE OF SOOTHING.

(See Tone Drill No. 53.)

[The tone of Soothing is akin to Assurance, and has in it, at times, Affection and Consolation. It calms and lulls.]

Sweet and Low, Sweet and Low.

ALFRED TENNYSON.

Sweet and low, sweet and low,
   Wind of the western sea,
Low, low, breathe and blow,
   Wind of the western sea!
Over the rolling waters go,
Come from the dying moon, and blow,
   Blow him again to me;
While my little one, while my pretty one, sleeps.

Sleep and rest, sleep and rest,
   Father will come to thee soon;
Rest, rest, on mother's breast,
   Father will come to thee soon;
Father will come to his babe in the nest,
Silver sails all out of the west
   Under the silver moon:
Sleep, my little one, sleep, my pretty one, sleep.

She Is Sleeping.

CHRISTINA G. ROSSETTI.

Some are laughing, some are weeping;
She is sleeping, only sleeping:
Round her rest wild flowers are creeping.
There the wind is heaping, heaping
Sweetest sweets of summer's keeping,
By the corn-fields, ripe for reaping.

There are lilies, and there blushes
The deep rose, and there the thrushes
Sing till latest sunlight flushes
In the west; a fresh wind brushes
Through the leaves while evening hushes.

There by day the lark is singing,
And the grass and weeds are springing;
There by night the bat is winging;
There for ever winds are bringing
Far-off chimes of church bells ringing.

Night and morning, noon and even,
Their sound fills her dreams with heaven;
The long strife at length is striven,
Till her grave-bands shall be riven.
Such is the good portion given
To her soul at rest and shriven.

TONE OF WARNING.

(See Tone Drill No. 210.)

[This tone implies caution or threatening; in its higher form it has a touch of prophecy.]

Our Duty.

DANIEL WEBSTER.

The world, at this moment, is regarding us with a willing, but something of a fearful admiration. Its deep and awful anxiety is to learn whether free states may be stable as well as free; whether popular power may be trusted as well as feared; in short, whether wise, regular, and virtuous self-government is a vision for the contemplation of theorists, or a truth established, illustrated, and brought into practice in the country of Washington. Sir, for the earth which we inhabit, and the whole circle of the sun, for all the unborn races of mankind, we seem to hold in our hands, for their weal or woe, the fate of this experiment.

If we fail, who shall venture the repetition? If our example shall prove to be one, not of encouragement but of terror, not to be imitated but fit only to be shunned, where else shall the world look for free models? If this great "Western Sun" be struck out of the firmament, at what other fountain shall the lamp of liberty hereafter be lighted? What other orb shall emit a ray to glimmer, even, on the darkness of the world?

Sir, there is no danger of our overrating or overstating the important part which we are now acting in human affairs. It should not flatter our personal self-respect, but it should reanimate our patriotic virtues, and inspire us with a deeper and more solemn sense both of our privileges and of our duties. We cannot wish better for our country, nor for the world, than that the same spirit which influenced Washington may influence all who succeed him; and that that same blessing from above which attended his efforts may also attend theirs.

A Warning to Young Men.

GEORGE W. CURTIS.

Show me a land in which the young men are cold and skeptical and prematurely wise; in which polite indifference is called political wisdom, contempt for ideas common sense, and honesty in politics Sunday-school statesmanship—show me a land in which the young men are more anxious about doing well than about doing right—and I will show you a country in which public corruption and ruin overtakes private infidelity and cowardice, and in which, if there were originally a hope for mankind, a faith in principle, and a conquering enthusiasm, that faith, hope, and enthusiasm are expiring like the deserted camp-fires of a retiring army. Woe to a man when his heart grows old! Woe to a nation when its young men shuffle in the gouty shoes and limp on the untimely crutches of age, instead of leaping along the course of life with the jubilant spring of their years and the sturdy play of their own muscles!

Henry V to Citizens of Harfleur.

WILLIAM SHAKESPEARE.

How yet resolves the governor of the town?
This is the latest parle we will admit:
Therefore, to our best mercy give yourselves,
Or, like the men proud of destruction,
Defy us to our worst; for, as I am a soldier,
A name that in my thoughts becomes me best,
If I begin the battery once again,
I will not leave the half-achieved Harfleur,
Till in her ashes she lie buried.
The gates of mercy shall be all shut up;
And the flesh'd soldier, rough and hard of heart,
In liberty of bloody hand shall range
With conscience wide as hell. . . .

Therefore, you men of Harfleur
Take pity of your town, and of your people,
Whiles yet my soldiers are in my command;
Whiles yet the cool and temperate wind of grace
O'erblows the filthy and contagious clouds
Of heady murder, spoil, and villainy.
If not, why, in a moment look to see
Your fathers taken by the silver beards,
And their most reverend heads dash'd to the walls;
Your naked infants spitted upon pikes,

Whiles the mad mothers with their howls confus'd
Do break the clouds, as did the wives of Jewry
At Herod's bloody-hunting slaughtermen.
What say you? will you yield, and this avoid,
Or, guilty, in defence, be thus destroyed?
—Henry V, iii., 3.

TONE OF SUBLIMITY.

(See Tone Drill No. 194.)

[The tone of Sublimity manifests an extreme admiration which almost overwhelms. The speaker seems uplifted by the majesty and the grandeur. While akin to Awe, Sublimity has in it less of Fear and more of Joy.]

The Avalanches of the Jungfrau.

G. B. CHEEVER.

Figure to yourself a cataract like that of Niagara, poured in foaming grandeur, not merely over one great precipice of two hundred feet, but over the successive ridgy precipices of two or three thousand, in the face of a mountain eleven thousand feet high, and tumbling, crashing, thundering down with a continuous din of far greater sublimity than the sound of the grandest cataract. The roar of the falling mass begins to be heard the moment it is loosened from the mountain; it pours on with the sound of a vast body of rushing water; then comes the first great concussion, a booming crash of thunders, breaking on the still air in mid-heaven; your breath is suspended, and you listen and look; the mighty glittering mass shoots headlong over the main precipice, and the fall is so great that it produces to the eye that impression of dread majestic slowness of which I have spoken, though it is doubtless more rapid than Niagara.

But if you should see the cataract of Niagara itself coming down five thousand feet above you in the air, there would be the same impression. The image remains in the mind, and can never fade from it; it is as if you had seen an alabaster cataract from heaven. The sound is far more sublime than that of Niagara, because of the preceding stillness in those Alpine solitudes. In the midst of such silence and solemnity, from out the bosom of those glorious, glittering forms of nature, comes that rushing, crashing thunderburst of sound! If it were not that your soul, through the eye, is as filled and fixed with the sublimity of the vision as, through the sense of hearing, with that of the audible report, methinks you would wish to bury your face in your hands, and fall prostrate, as at the voice of the Eternal.

TONE OF BITTERNESS.
(See Tone Drill No. 31.)

[The tone of Bitterness has in it the note of grievance, but manifests a deeper resentment.]

The American War.
CHARLES JAMES FOX.

Who is he who arraigns gentlemen on this side of the House with causing, by their inflammatory speeches, the misfortunes of their country? The accusation comes from one whose inflammatory harangues have led the Nation, step by step, from violence to violence, in that inhuman, unfeeling system of blood and massacre, which every honest man must detest, which every good man must abhor, and every wise man condemn! And this man imputes the guilt of such measures to those who had all along foretold the consequences; who had prayed, entreated and supplicated, not only for America, but for the credit of the Nation and its eventual welfare, to arrest the hand of Power, meditating slaughter, and directed by injustice!

What was the consequence of the sanguinary measures recommended in those bloody, inflammatory speeches? Though

Boston was to be starved, though Hancock and Adams were proscribed, yet at the feet of these very men the Parliament of Great Britain was obliged to kneel, flatter, and cringe; and, as it had the cruelty at one time to denounce vengeance against these men, so it had the meanness afterwards to implore their forgiveness. Shall he who called the American "Hancock and his crew,"—shall he presume to reprehend any set of men for inflammatory speeches?

It is this accursed American war that has led us, step by step, into all our present misfortunes and national disgraces. What was the cause of our wasting forty millions of money, and sixty thousand lives? The American war! What was it that produced the French rescript and a French war? The American war! What was it that produced the Spanish manifesto and Spanish war? The American war! What was it that armed forty-two thousand men in Ireland with the arguments carried on the points of forty thousand bayonets? The American war! For what are we about to incur an additional debt of twelve or fourteen millions? This accursed, cruel, diabolical American war!

The Patriot.

ROBERT BROWNING.

It was roses, roses, all the way,
    With myrtle mixed in my path like mad:
The house-roofs seemed to heave and sway,
    The church-spires flamed, such flags they had,
A year ago on this very day.

The air broke into a mist with bells,
    The old walls rocked with the crowd and cries.
Had I said, "Good folk, mere noise repels—
    But give me your sun from yonder skies!"
They had answered "And afterward, what else?"

Alack, it was I who leaped at the sun
  To give it my loving friends to keep!
Naught man could do, have I left undone:
  And you see my harvest, what I reap
This very day, now a year is run.

There's nobody on the house-tops now—
  Just a palsied few at the windows set;
For the best of the sight is, all allow,
  At the Shambles' Gate—or, better yet,
By the very scaffold's foot, I trow.

I go in the rain, and, more than needs,
  A rope cuts both my wrists behind;
And I think, by the feel, my forehead bleeds,
  For they fling, whoever has a mind,
Stones at me for my year's misdeeds.

Thus I entered, and thus I go!
  In triumphs, people have dropped down dead.
"Paid by the world, what dost thou owe
  Me?"—God might question; now instead,
'Tis God shall repay: I am safer so.

TONE OF SOLEMN CONDEMNATION.
(See Tone Drill No. 48.)

[The tone of Solemn Condemnation implies that the judgment
has weighed and considered before passing sentence.]

Impeachment of Warren Hastings.
EDMUND BURKE.

I impeach Warren Hastings, Esquire, of high crimes and
misdemeanors.

I impeach him in the name of the Commons of Great

Britain, in Parliament assembled, whose parliamentary trust he has betrayed.

I impeach him in the name of all the Commons of Great Britain, whose national character he has dishonored.

I impeach him in the name of the people of India, whose laws, rights, and liberties he has subverted, whose property he has destroyed, whose country he has laid waste and desolate.

I impeach him in the name, and by virtue, of those eternal laws of justice which he has violated.

I impeach him in the name of human nature itself, which he has cruelly outraged, injured, and oppressed, in both sexes, in every age, rank, situation, and condition of life.

Henry V's Sentence on the Conspirators.

WILLIAM SHAKESPEARE.

Hear your sentence.
You have conspired against our royal person,
Join'd with an enemy proclaim'd, and from his coffers
Received the golden earnest of our death;
Wherein you would have sold your king to slaughter,
His princes and his peers to servitude,
His subjects to oppression and contempt,
And his whole kingdom into desolation.
Touching our person seek we no revenge;
But we our kingdom's safety must so tender,
Whose ruin you have sought, that to her laws
We do deliver you. Get you therefore hence,
Poor miserable wretches, to your death:
The taste whereof, God of his mercy give
You patience to endure, and true repentance
Of all your dear offences! Bear them hence.
                              —Henry V, ii., 2.

TONE OF MEDITATION.

(See Tone Drill No. 135.)

[The tone of Meditation is always linked with some other (usually Argument) and indicates to the listener self-communion. The speaker is subjective. He is thinking aloud.]

Cato's Soliloquy.

JOSEPH ADDISON.

It must be so—Plato, thou reasonest well!
Else whence this pleasing hope, this fond desire,
This longing after immortality?
Or whence this secret dread, and inward horror
Of falling into naught? Why shrinks the soul
Back on herself, and startles at destruction?—
'Tis the Divinity that stirs within us;
'Tis Heaven itself that points out a *hereafter,*
And intimates Eternity to man.
Here will I hold. If there's a Power above us
(And that there is, all Nature cries aloud
Through all her works), He must delight in virtue:
And that which He delights in, must be happy.
Eternity!—thou pleasing, dreadful thought!
Through what variety of untried being,
Through what new scenes and changes must we pass?
The wide, the unbounded prospect lies before me;
But shadows, clouds, and darkness, rest upon it.

Hamlet's Soliloquy on Life and Death.

WILLIAM SHAKESPEARE.

To be, or not to be: that is the question:
Whether 'tis nobler in the mind to suffer
The slings and arrows of outrageous fortune,
Or to take arms against a sea of troubles,

And by opposing end them. To die: to sleep;
No more; and by a sleep to say we end
The heart-ache, and the thousand natural shocks
That flesh is heir to, 'tis a consummation
Devoutly to be wish'd. To die;—to sleep;—
To sleep! perchance to dream! ay, there's the rub;
For in that sleep of death what dreams may come,
When we have shuffled off this mortal coil,
Must give us pause: there's the respect
That makes calamity of so long life;
For who would bear the whips and scorns of time,
The oppressor's wrong, the proud man's contumely,
The pangs of despised love, the law's delay,
The insolence of office, and the spurns
That patient merit of the unworthy takes,
When he himself might his quietus make
With a bare bodkin? who would fardels bear,
To grunt and sweat under a weary life,
But that the dread of something after death,
The undiscover'd country from whose bourn
No traveller returns, puzzles the will,
And makes us rather bear those ills we have
Than fly to others that we know not of?
Thus conscience does make cowards of us all,
And thus the native hue of resolution
Is sicklied o'er with the pale cast of thought,
And enterprises of great pith and moment,
With this regard their currents turn awry
And lose the name of action.

—Hamlet iii., 1.

TONE OF CONVICTION.
(See Tone Drill No. 55.)

[The tone of Conviction aims not so much to prove as to proclaim what the speaker feels to be inevitable or absolute. In it, often, is the note of the seer. Assertion asserts aggressively, Conviction asserts calmly.]

The Human Race Progresses.

GEORGE BANCROFT.

The irresistible tendency of the human race is to advancement, for absolute power has never succeeded and can never succeed in suppressing a single truth. An idea once revealed may find its admission into every living breast and live there. Like God, it becomes immortal and omnipresent. The movement of the species is upward, irresistibly upward. The individual is often lost; Providence never disowns the race. No principle once promulgated has ever been forgotten. No "timely tramp" of a despot's foot ever trod out one idea. The world cannot retrograde; the dark ages cannot return. Dynasties perish, states are buried, nations have been victims of error, martyrs for right; humanity has always been on the advance, gaining maturity, universality and power.

Yes, Truth is immortal; it cannot be destroyed; it is invincible; it cannot long be resisted. Not every great principle has yet been generated, but when once proclaimed and diffused, it lives without end in the safe custody of the race. States may pass away, every just principle of legislation which has been once established will endure. Philosophy has sometimes forgotten God, a great people never did. The skepticism of the last century could not uproot Christianity because it lived in the hearts of the millions. Do you think that infidelity is spreading? Christianity never lived in the hearts of so many millions as at this moment. The forms under which it is professed may decay, for they, like all that is the work of man's hands, are subject to changes and chances of mortal being, but the spirit of truth is incorruptible; it may be developed, illustrated and applied; it never can die, never can decline.

No truth can perish, no truth can pass away; the flame is undying, though generations disappear. Wherever moral truth has struck into being, humanity claims and guards the greatest bequest. Each generation gathers together imperishable children of the past, and increases them by new sons of light alike radiant with immortality.

The Right.

VICTOR HUGO.

Ah! Whether you will or no the past is passed. Your law is null, void and dead, even before its birth; because it is not just; because it is not true; because, while it goes furtively to plunder the poor man and the weak of his right of suffrage, it encounters the withering glance of a Nation's probity and sense of right, before which your work of darkness shall vanish; because in the depths of the conscience of every citizen,—of the humblest as well as the highest—there is a sentiment sublime, sacred, indestructible, incorruptible, eternal,—the Right.

This sentiment, which is the very element of reason in man, the granite of the human conscience,—this Right, is the rock upon which shall split and go to pieces the iniquities, the hypocrisies, the bad laws and bad governments, of the world. There is the obstacle, concealed, invisible,—lost to view in the soul's profoundest deep, but eternally present and abiding,—against which you shall always strike, and which you shall never wear away, do what you will! I repeat it, your efforts are in vain. You cannot deracinate, you cannot shake it. You might sooner tear up the eternal Rock from the bottom of the sea, than the Right from the heart of the people.

Richard's Trust in Heaven.

WILLIAM SHAKESPEARE.

Discomfortable cousin! know'st thou not
That when the searching eye of heaven is hid
Behind the globe, that lights the lower world,
Then thieves and robbers range abroad unseen
In murders and in outrage, boldly here;
But when from under this terrestrial ball
He fires the proud tops of the eastern pines
And darts his light through every guilty hole,
Then murders, treasons and detested sins,
The cloak of night being pluck'd from off their backs,
Stand bare and naked, trembling at themselves?
So when this thief, this traitor, Bolingbroke,
Who all this while hath revell'd in the night,
Whilst we were wandering with the antipodes,
Shall see us rising in our throne, the east,
His treasons will sit blushing in his face,
Not able to endure the sight of day,
But self-affrighted tremble at his sin.
Not all the water in the rough rude sea
Can wash the balm off from an anointed king;
The breath of worldly men cannot depose
The deputy elected by the Lord:
For every man that Bolingbroke hath press'd
To lift shrewd steel against our golden crown,
God for his Richard hath in heavenly pay
A glorious angel; then, if angels fight,
Weak men must fall, for heaven still guards the right.
—Richard II, iii., 2.

TONE OF HATRED.
(See Tone Drill No. 134.)

[The tone of Hatred indicates dislike in the most intense degree. It says to the listener, "Every inch of me detests this person or thing."]

The Seminole's Defiance.
G. W. PATTEN.

Blaze, with your serried columns! I will not bend the knee:
The shackle ne'er again shall bind the arm which now is free!
I've mailed it with the thunder, when the tempest muttered
    low;
And where it falls, ye well may dread the lightning of its
    blow.
I've scared you in the city, I've scalped you on the plain;
Go, count your chosen where they fell beneath my leaden
    rain!
I scorn your proffered treaty; the pale-face I defy;
Revenge is stamped upon my spear, and "blood" my battle-
    cry!

Some strike for hope of booty; some to defend their all—
I battle for the joy I have to see the white man fall.
I love, among the wounded, to hear his dying moan,
And catch, while chanting at his side, the music of his groan.
You've trailed me through the forest; you've tracked me
    o'er the stream;
And struggling through the everglade your bristling bayonets
    gleam.
But I stand as should the warrior, with his rifle and his
    spear;
The scalp of vengeance still is red, and warns you—"Come
    not here!"

Think ye to find my homestead?—I gave it to the fire.
My tawny household do you seek?—I am a childless sir

But, should you crave life's nourishment, enough I have, and
    good;
I live on hate—'tis all my bread; yet light is not my food.
I loathe you with my bosom! I scorn you with mine eye!
And I'll taunt you with my latest breath, and fight you till
    I die!
I ne'er will ask for quarter, and I ne'er will be your slave;
But I'll swim the sea of slaughter till I sink beneath the
    wave!

Shylock's Hatred of Antonio.

WILLIAM SHAKESPEARE.

How like a fawning publican he looks!
I hate him for he is a Christian;
But more for that in low simplicity
He lends out money gratis and brings down
The rate of usance here with us in Venice.
If I can catch him once upon the hip,
I will feed fat the ancient grudge I bear him.
He hates our sacred nation; and he rails,
Even there where merchants most do congregate,
On me, my bargains, and my well-won thrift,
Which he calls interest. Cursed be my tribe,
If I forgive him!

—Merchant of Venice, i., 3.

TONE OF HORROR.

(See Tone Drill No. 113.)

[The tone of Horror manifests an extreme fear or detestation.]

The Death Penalty.

VICTOR HUGO.

A man, a convict, a sentenced wretch, is dragged, on a
certain morning, to one of our public squares. There he

finds the scaffold! He shudders, he struggles, he refuses to die. He is young yet—only twenty-nine. Ah! I know what you will say,—"He is a murderer!" But hear me. Two officers seize him. His hands, his feet, are tied. He throws off the two officers. A frightful struggle ensues. His feet, bound as they are, become entangled in the ladder. He uses the scaffold against the scaffold! The struggle is prolonged. Horror seizes on the crowd. The officers,—sweat and shame on their brows,—pale, panting, terrified, despairing,—despairing with I know not what horrible despair,—shrinking under that public reprobation which ought to have visited the penalty, and spared the passive instrument, the executioner,—the officers strive savagely.

The victim clings to the scaffold, and shrieks for pardon. His clothes are torn,—his shoulders bloody,—still he resists. At length, after three quarters of an hour of this monstrous effort, of this spectacle without a name, of this agony,— agony for all, be it understood,—agony for the assembled spectators as well as for the condemned man,—after this age of anguish, Gentlemen of the Jury, they take back the poor wretch to his prison. The People breathe again.

The People, naturally merciful, hope that the man will be spared. But no,—the guillotine, though vanquished, remains standing. There it frowns all day, in the midst of a sickened population. And at night, the officers, reinforced, drag forth the wretch again, so bound that he is but an inert weight,—they drag him forth, haggard, bloody, weeping, pleading, howling for life,—calling upon God, calling upon his father and mother,—for like a very child had this man become in the prospect of death,—they drag him forth to execution. He is hoisted on to the scaffold, and his head falls!—And then through every conscience runs a shudder. Never had legal murder appeared with an aspect so indecent, so abominable.

Clarence's Dream.

WILLIAM SHAKESPEARE.

O! I have pass'd a miserable night,
So full of fearful dreams, of ugly sights,
That, as I am a Christian faithful man,
I would not spend another such a night,
Though 't were to buy a world of happy days,
So full of dismal terror was the time.
Methought, that I had broken from the Tower,
And was embark'd to cross to Burgundy;
And, in my company, my brother Gloster,
Who from my cabin tempted me to walk
Upon the hatches: thence we look'd toward England,
And cited up a thousand heavy times,
During the wars of York and Lancaster,
That had befall'n us. As we pac'd along
Upon the giddy footing of the hatches,
Methought, that Gloster stumbled; and, in falling,
Struck me (that thought to stay him) over-board,
Into the tumbling billows of the main.
O Lord! methought what pain it was to drown!
What dreadful noise of water in mine ears!
What sights of ugly death within mine eyes!
Methought I saw a thousand fearful wrecks;
A thousand men that fishes gnaw'd upon;
Wedges of gold, great anchors, heaps of pearl,
Inestimable stones, unvalued jewels,
All scatter'd in the bottom of the sea:
Some lay in dead men's skulls; and in the holes
Where eyes did once inhabit, there were crept
(As 't were in scorn of eyes) reflecting gems,
That woo'd the slimy bottom of the deep,
And mock'd the dead bones that lay scatter'd by.
My dream was lengthen'd after life.

O! then began the tempest to my soul!
I pass'd, methought, the melancholy flood,
With that sour ferryman which poets write of,
Unto the kingdom of perpetual night.
The first that there did greet my stranger soul,
Was my great father-in-law, renowned Warwick,
Who cried aloud,—"What scourge for perjury
Can this dark monarchy afford false Clarence?"
And so he vanish'd. Then, came wandering by
A shadow like an angel, with bright hair
Dabbled in blood; and he shriek'd out aloud,—
"Clarence is come,—false, fleeting, perjur'd Clarence,—
That stabb'd me in the field by Tewksbury;—
Seize on him, furies! take him unto torment!"
With that, methought, a legion of foul fiends
Environ'd me, and howled in mine ears
Such hideous cries, that with the very noise,
I trembling wak'd, and, for a season after,
Could not believe but that I was in hell;
Such terrible impression made my dream.

—Richard III, i., 4.

TONE OF BELITTLING.

(See Tone Drill No. 29.)

[The tone of Belittling indicates a mild form of Contempt. It says to the listener, "I set little value on this."]

The Lake School of Poetry.

WILLIAM HAZLITT.

The Lake school of poetry had its origin in the French Revolution, or rather in those sentiments and opinions which produced that revolution. According to the prevailing notions, all was to be natural and new. Nothing that was established was to be tolerated. All the commonplace figures of poetry, tropes, allegories, personifications, with the whole heathen mythology, were instantly discarded; a classical allusion was considered as a piece of antiquated foppery; capital letters were no more allowed in print than letters-patent of nobility were permitted in real life; kings and queens were dethroned from their rank and station in legitimate tragedy or epic poetry, as they were decapitated elsewhere; rhyme was looked upon as a relic of the feudal system, and regular metre was abolished, along with regular government. Authority and fashion, elegance or arrangement, were hooted out of countenance as pedantry and prejudice. Everyone did that which was good in his own eyes. The object was to reduce all things to an absolute level; and a singularly affected and outrageous simplicity prevailed in dress and manners, in style and sentiment.

A thorough adept in this school of poetry and philanthropy is jealous of all excellence but his own. He sees nothing but himself and the universe. He hates all greatness and all pretentions to it, whether well or ill-founded. His egotism is in some respects a madness; for he scorns even the admiration of himself, thinking it a presumption in anyone to suppose that he has taste or sense enough to understand him. He hates all science and all art; he hates chemistry; he hates conchology; he hates Voltaire; he hates Sir Isaac Newton; he hates wisdom; he hates wit; he hates metaphysics, which he says are unintelligible, and yet he would be thought to understand them; he hates prose; he hates all poetry but his own; he hates the dialogues in Shakespeare; he hates music, dancing and painting; he hates Reubens; he hates Rembrandt; he hates Raphael; he hates Titian; he hates Vandyke; he hates the antique; he hates the Apollo Belvidere; he hates the Venus of Medicis. This is the reason that so few people take an interest in his writings, because he takes an interest in nothing that others do!

Richard on the Vanity of State.

WILLIAM SHAKESPEARE.

Of comfort no man speak:
Let 's talk of graves, of worms and epitaphs;
Make dust our paper and with rainy eyes
Write sorrow on the bosom of the earth.
Let 's choose executors and talk of wills:
And yet not so, for what can we bequeath
Save our deposed bodies to the ground?
Our lands, our lives and all are Bolingbroke's,
And nothing can we call our own but death,
And that small model of the barren earth
Which serves as paste and cover to our bones.
For God's sake, let us sit upon the ground
And tell sad stories of the death of kings:
How some have been deposed; some slain in war;
Some haunted by the ghosts they have deposed;
Some poison'd by their wives; some sleeping kill'd;
All murder'd: for within the hollow crown
That rounds the mortal temples of a king
Keeps Death his court, and there the antic sits,
Scoffing his state and grinning at his pomp,
Allowing him a breath, a little scene,
To monarchize, be fear'd and kill with looks,
Infusing him with self and vain conceit,
As if this flesh which walls about our life
Were brass impregnable, and humour'd thus
Comes at the last and with a little pin
Bores through his castle wall, and farewell king!
Cover your heads and mock not flesh and blood
With solemn reverence: throw away respect,
Tradition, form and ceremonious duty,
For you have but mistook me all this while:

I live with bread like you, feel want,
Taste grief, need friends: subjected thus,
How can you say to me, I am a king?
                                    —Richard II, iii., 2.

THE TONE OF ADORATION.
(See Tone Drill No. 3.)

[The tone of Adoration indicates a deep love, mingled with reverence. While human beings may inspire this feeling, it arises more often from the contemplation of Divinity.]

God.

DERZHAVIN.

O thou eternal One! whose presence bright
    All space doth occupy, all motion guide;
Unchanged through Time's all devastating flight!
    Thou only God—there is no God beside!
Being above all beings! Mighty One.
    Whom none can comprehend and none explore,
Who fill'st existence with thyself alone,
    Embracing all, supporting, ruling o'er;
    Being whom we call God, and know no more! .   .   .

Creator, yes. Thy wisdom and thy word
    Created me. Thou source of life and good.
Thou spirit of my spirit, and my Lord,
    Thy light, thy love, in their bright plenitude
Filled me with an immortal soul, to spring
    Over the abyss of death, and bade it wear
The garments of eternal day, and wing
    Its heavenly flight beyond this little sphere,
    Even to its source—to thee—its Author there.

O thoughts ineffable! O visions blest!
    Though worthless our conceptions all of thee,

Yet shall thy shadowed image fill our breast,
   And waft its homage to thy Deity.
God! thus alone my lowly thoughts can soar,
   Thus seek thy presence—Being wise and good!
'Midst thy vast works admire, obey, adore;
And when the tongue is eloquent no more
   The soul shall speak in tears of gratitude.

TONE OF REMORSE.
(See Tone Drill No. 166.)

[The tone of Remorse proclaims agony of mind. It indicates that something troubles the conscience.]

Dream of Richard III.
WILLIAM SHAKESPEARE.

Give me another horse!—bind up my wounds!—
Have mercy, Jesu!—Soft! I did but dream.—
O, coward conscience, how dost thou afflict me!—
The lights burn blue.—It is now dead midnight.
Cold fearful drops stand on my trembling flesh.
What do I fear? myself? there's none else by:
Richard loves Richard; that is, I am I.
Is there a murderer here? No;—yes; I am:
Then fly,—What, from myself? Great reason: why?
Lest I revenge. What! Myself upon myself?
Alack! I love myself. Wherefore? for any good,
That I myself have done unto myself?
O! no: alas! I rather hate myself.
For hateful deeds committed by myself.
I am a villain. Yet I lie; I am not.
Fool, of thyself speak well:—Fool, do not flatter.
My conscience hath a thousand several tongues,
And every tongue brings in a several tale,
And every tale condemns me for a villain.

Perjury, foul perjury, in the high'st degree;
Murder, stern murder, in the dir'st degree:
All several sins, all us'd in each degree,
Throng to the bar, crying all,—Guilty! guilty!
I shall despair.—There is no creature loves me;
And if I die, no soul shall pity me:—
Nay, wherefore should they? since that I myself
Find in myself no pity to myself.
Methought, the souls of all that I had murder'd
Came to my tent; and every one did threat
To-morrow's vengeance on the head of Richard.

—Richard III, i., 3

Wolsey on His Fall.

WILLIAM SHAKESPEARE.

Farewell, a long farewell, to all my greatness!
This is the state of man; to-day he puts forth
The tender leaves of hope, to-morrow blossoms,
And bears his blushing honors thick upon him;
The third day, comes a frost, a killing frost;
And,—when he thinks, good easy man, full surely
His greatness is a ripening,—nips his root,
And then he falls, as I do. I have ventured,
Like little wanton boys that swim on bladders,
This many summers in a sea of glory;
But far beyond my depth: My high-blown pride
At length broke under me; and now has left me,
Weary, and old with service, to the mercy
Of a rude stream, that must forever hide me.
Vain pomp and glory of this world, I hate ye;
I feel my heart new opened: O, how wretched
Is that poor man, that hangs on princes' favors!
There is, betwixt that smile we would aspire to,
That sweet aspect of princes, and their ruin,

More pangs and fears than wars or women have;
And when he falls, he falls like Lucifer,
Never to hope again.
                              —Henry VIII, iii., 2.

THE TONE OF EXULTATION.
(See Tone Drill No. 96.)

[The tone of Exultation indicates a personal joy bordering on gloating.]

Gloster on His Wooing of Lady Anne.
WILLIAM SHAKESPEARE.

Was ever woman in this humour woo'd?
Was ever woman in this humour won?
I'll have her; but I will not keep her long.
What! I, that kill'd her husband and his father,
To take her in her heart's extremest hate,
With curses in her mouth, tears in her eyes,
The bleeding witness of her hatred by;
Having God, her conscience, and these bars against me,
And I nothing to back my suit at all,
But the plain devil and dissembling looks,
And yet to win her, all the world to nothing!
Ha!
Hath she forgot already that brave prince,
Edward, her lord, whom I, some three months since,
Stabb'd in my angry mood at Tewksbury?
A sweeter and a lovelier gentleman,
Framed in the prodigality of nature,
Young, valiant, wise, and, no doubt, right royal,
The spacious world cannot again afford:
And will she yet debase her eyes on me,
That cropp'd the golden prime of this sweet prince,
And made her widow to a woful bed?
On me, whose all not equals Edward's moiety?

On me, that halt and am unshapen thus?
My dukedom to a beggarly denier,
I do mistake my person all this while:
Upon my life, she finds, although I cannot,
Myself to be a marvellous proper man.
I'll be at charges for a looking-glass,
And entertain some score or two of tailors,
To study fashions to adorn my body:
Since I am crept in favour with myself,
I will maintain it with some little cost.
But first I'll turn yon fellow in his grave;
And then return lamenting to my love.
Shine out, fair sun, till I have bought a glass,
That I may see my shadow as I pass.

—Richard III, i., 2.

TONE OF DESPAIR.
(See Tone Drill No. 66.)

[The tone of Despair manifests absolute helplessness.]

Lament for James, Earl of Glencairn.

ROBERT BURNS.

"Ye scattered birds that faintly sing,
    The reliques of the vernal quire!
Ye woods that shed on a' the winds
    The honors of the agèd year!
A few short months, and glad and gay,
    Again ye'll charm the ear and e'e;
But nocht in all revolving time
    Can gladness bring again to me.

"I am a bending, agèd tree,
    That long has stood the wind and rain;
But now has come a cruel blast,

And my last hald of earth is gane:
Nae leaf o' mine shall greet the spring,
Nae simmer sun exalt my bloom;
But I maun lie before the storm,
And ithers plant them in my room.

"I've seen sae mony changefu' years,
On earth I am a stranger grown;
I wander in the ways of men,
Alike unknowing and unknown:
Unheard, unpitied, unrelieved,
I bear alane my lade o' care,
For silent, low, on beds of dust
Lie a' that would my sorrows share.

"And last (the sum of a' my griefs!)
My noble master lies in clay;
The flower amang our barons bold,
His country's pride, his country's stay:
In weary being now I pine,
For a' the life of life is dead,
And hope has left my agèd ken,
On forward wing for ever fled. . . .

TONE OF MALEDICTION.
(See Tone Drill No 134.)

[The tone of Malediction denotes that the speaker wishes evil
to come to some person or thing. It is usually the accompaniment
of hatred.]

Curse on Rome.

CORNEILLE.

Rome, sole object of my resentment! Rome, to which thy
arm has just sacrificed my lover! Rome, which has seen thee
born, and which thy heart adores! Rome, in short, which I

hate because it adores thee! May all its neighbors, conspiring together, be able to sap its foundations! And if Italy be not sufficient, may the East ally itself with the West against her! May a hundred nations from all ends of the universe press on to level her hills and walls! let her hurl her walls on her own head, and tear out her entrails with her own hands; let the wrath of Heaven, called down by my prayers, rain upon her a deluge of fires! May I, with these eyes of mine, see this thunderbolt fall, see her houses in ashes, and laurels in the dust! see the last Roman heave his last sigh.

—Horace iv., 5.

Curse of Kehama.

ROBERT SOUTHEY.

I charm thy life
From the weapons of strife,
From stone and from wood,
From fire and from flood,
  From the serpent's tooth,
And the beasts of blood.
From sickness I charm thee,
And time shall not harm thee;
But earth, which is mine,
  Her fruits shall deny thee.
And the winds shall not touch thee
  When they pass by thee,
And the dews shall not wet thee
  When they fall nigh thee;
And thou shalt seek death
  To release thee in vain.
  Thou shalt live in thy pain
  While Kehama shall reign,
With a fire in thy heart
  And a fire in thy brain;

And sleep shall obey me,
    And visit thee never,
And the curse shall be on thee
    For ever and ever!

Duchess of York to Richard III.

WILLIAM SHAKESPEARE.

Either thou wilt die, by God's just ordinance,
Ere from this war thou turn a conqueror,
Or I with grief and extreme age shall perish
And never look upon thy face again.
Therefore take with thee my most heavy curse;
Which, in the day of battle, tire thee more
Than all the complete armour that thou wear'st!
My prayers on the adverse party fight;
And there the little souls of Edward's children
Whisper the spirits of thine enemies,
And promise them success and victory.
Bloody thou art, bloody will be thy end;
Shame serves thy life and doth thy death attend.
                —Richard III, iv., 4.

THE TONE OF CONFUSION.
(See Tone Drill No. 52.)

[The tone of Confusion implies a checking or stoppage of the flow of utterance. Either the mind has ceased to think continuously or the speaker is trying to repress his real thoughts.]

An Orator's First Speech in Parliament.

ALEXANDER BELL.

The pillar of "ten-pounders" rises now, and towards the Speaker makes profoundest bow. Unused to so much honour, his weak knees bend with the weight of senate-dignities. He staggers—almost falls—stares—strokes his chin—clears out

his throat, and ventures to begin. "Sir, I am sensible"—
(some titter near him)—"I am, Sir, sensible"—"Hear!
hear!" (they cheer him.) Now bolder grown, for praise mis-
taking pother, teapots one arm, and spouts out with the other.
"I am, Sir, sensible—I am, indeed—that, though—I should—
want—words—I must proceed; and, for the first time in my
life I think—I think—that—no great orator—should shrink:
—and, therefore,—Mr. Speaker—I for one—will speak out
freely. Sir—*I've not yet done.* Sir, in the name of those
enlightened men who sent me here to—*speak* for them—
why, then, to do my duty—as I said before—to my con-
stituency—I'LL SAY NO MORE."

GASPING.
(See Tone Drill No. 105.)

[Gasping indicates a struggle for breath. This spasmodic tone
may be caused by overexertion or by a great mental shock or by a
physical injury.]

Wounded.

WILLIAM E. MILLER.

Let me lie down
Just here, in the shade of this cannon-torn tree,
Here, low on the trampled grass, where I may see
The surge of the combat, and where I may hear
The glad cry of victory, cheer upon cheer:
Let me lie down. . . .

Dying at last!
My mother, dear mother! with meek tearful eye,
Farewell! and God bless you, for ever and aye!
O that I now lay on your pillowing breast,
To breathe my last sigh on the bosom first prest!
Dying at last!

Great Heaven! this bullet-hole gapes like a grave;
A curse on the aim of the traitorous knave!
Is there never a one of you knows how to pray,
Or speak for a man as his life ebbs away?
Pray! Pray!

Our Father! our Father! why don't you proceed?
Can't you see I am dying? Great God, how I bleed!
Ebbing away!
Ebbing away! The light of the day is turning to gray. . . .

I am dying; bend down, till I touch you once more;
Don't forget me, old fellow: God prosper this war!

MOANING.
(See Tone Drill No. 140.)

[Moaning manifests mental or physical pain, with exhaustion.
It is agony in its weaker states. Sometimes there is unconsciousness.]

Lady Macbeth in Her Sleep.
WILLIAM SHAKESPEARE.

Yet here's a spot. . . . Out, damned spot! out, I say!
One: two: why, then 'tis time do do 't. Hell is murky. Fie,
my lord, fie! a soldier, and afeard? What need we fear who
knows it, when none can call our power to account? Yet who
would have thought the old man to have had so much blood
in him? . . . The thane of Fife had a wife; where is
she now? What, will these hands ne'er be clean? No more
o' that, my lord, no more o' that: you mar all with this
starting. . . . Here's the smell of the blood still: all
the perfumes of Arabia will not sweeten this little hand.
Oh, oh, oh! . . . Wash your hands; put on your nightgown; look not so pale: I tell you yet again, Banquo's
buried; he cannot come out on 's grave. To bed, to bed;

there's knocking at the gate: come, come, come, come, give me your hand: what's done cannot be undone: to bed, to bed, to bed.—Macbeth, v., 1.

TONE OF UPROAR.
(See Tone Drill No. 207.)

[The tone of Uproar manifests great perturbation, commotion or turmoil. It is akin to Excitement.]

The War in Heaven.

JOHN MILTON.

Immediate in a flame
But soon obscured with smoke, all Heaven appeared,
From those deep-throated engines belched, whose roar
Embowelled with outrageous noise the air,
And all their entrails tore, disgorging foul
Their devilish glut, chained thunderbolts and hail
Of iron globes; which, on the victor host
Levelled, with such impetuous fury smote
That whom they hit none on their feet might stand,
Though standing else as rocks, but down they fell
By thousands, Angel on Archangel rolled. . . .
But they stood not long;
Rage prompted them at length, and found them arms
Against such hellish mischief fit to oppose.
Forthwith—behold the excellence, the power,
Which God hath in his mighty Angels placed!—
Their arms away they threw, and to the hills
—For Earth hath this variety from Heaven
Of pleasure situate in hill and dale—
Light as the lightning-glimpse, they ran, they flew;
From their foundations loosening to and fro
They plucked the seated hills, with all their load,
Rocks, waters, woods, and by their shaggy tops

Uplifting bore them in their hands.   Amaze,
Be sure, and terror seized the rebel host,
When coming toward them so dread they saw
The bottom of the mountains upward turned;
Till on those cursed engines' triple row
They saw them whelmed, and all their confidence
Under the weight of mountains buried deep;
Themselves invaded next, and on their heads
Main promontories flung, which in the air
Came shadowing, and oppressed whole legions armed.
Their armour helped their harm, crushed-in and bruised
Into their substance pent, which wrought them pain
Implacable, and many a dolorous groan,
Long struggling underneath, ere they could wind
Out of such prison; though Spirits of purest light,
Purest at first, now gross by sinning grown.
The rest, in imitation, to like arms
Betook them, and the neighbouring hills up-tore;
So hills amid the air encountered hills,
Hurled to and fro, with jaculation dire,
That underground they fought in dismal shade;
Infernal noise; war seemed a civil game
To this uproar; horrid confusion heaped
Upon confusion rose.

—Paradise Lost, Book VI.

TONE OF CUNNING.
(See Tone Drills Nos. 96a, 37a, 204b.)

[The tone of Cunning has in it Triumph, Exultation, and Carefulness; it manifests a subtle pride, bordering at times on fiendishness.]

The Telltale Heart.
EDGAR ALLAN POE.

True!—nervous—very dreadfully nervous I had been and am; but why will you say that I am mad? Hearken! and observe how healthily—how calmly I can tell you the whole story.

It is impossible to say how first the idea entered my brain; but once conceived, it haunted me day and night. Object, there was none. Passion, there was none. I loved the old man. He had never wronged me. He had never given me insult. For his gold I had no desire. I think it was his eye! yes, it was this! One of his eyes resembled that of a vulture—a pale-blue eye with a film over it. Whenever it fell upon me, my blood ran cold; and so by degrees—very gradually I made up my mind to take the life of the old man, and thus rid myself of the eye forever.

You fancy me mad. Madmen know nothing. But you should have seen me. You should have seen how wisely I proceeded—with what caution—with what foresight—with what dissimulation I went to work! I was never kinder to the old man than during the whole week before I killed him. Every night, about midnight, I turned the latch of his door and opened it—oh, so gently! and then, when I had made an opening sufficient for my head, I put in a dark lantern, all closed, closed so that no light shone out, and then I thrust in my head. Oh, you would have laughed to see how cunningly I thrust it in! I moved it slowly—very, very slowly, so that I might not disturb the old man's sleep. Would a madman have been so wise as this? And then, when my head was well in the room, I undid the lantern cautiously—oh, so cautiously (for the hinges creaked). I undid it just so much that a single thin ray fell upon the vulture eye. And this I did for seven long nights—every night just at midnight—but I found the eye always closed; and so it was impossible to do the work; for it was not the old man who vexed me, but his evil eye.

Upon the eighth night I was more than usually cautious in opening the door. To think that there I was, opening the door, little by little, and he not even to dream of my secret deeds or thoughts. I fairly chuckled at the idea; and perhaps he heard me; for he moved on the bed suddenly, as if startled. Now, you may think that I drew back—but no. I kept pushing the door open steadily, steadily.

I had my head in, and was about to open the lantern, when my thumb slipped upon the tin fastening, and the old man sprang up in the bed, crying out, "Who's there?"

I kept quite still and said nothing. For a whole hour I did not move a muscle, and meantime I did not hear him lie down.

When I had waited a long time, very patiently, without hearing him lie down, I resolved to open a little—a very, very little crevice in the lantern. So I opened it—you cannot imagine how stealthily, stealthily—until at length a single dim ray, like the thread of the spider, shot from out the crevice and fell upon the vulture eye.

It was open—wide, wide open—and I grew furious as I gazed upon it. I saw it with perfect distinctness—all a dull blue, with a hideous veil over it that chilled the very marrow in my bones; but I could see nothing else of the old man's face or person; for I had directed the ray, as if by instinct, precisely upon the eye.

Now, there came to my ears a low, dull, quick sound, such as a watch makes when enveloped in cotton. I knew that sound well, too. It was the beating of the old man's heart. I scarcely breathed; I held the lantern motionless. I tried how steadily I could maintain the ray upon the eye. Meantime the hellish tattoo of the heart increased. It grew quicker and quicker, and louder and louder every instant. I thought the heart must burst.

And now a new anxiety seized me—the sound could be heard by a neighbor! The old man's hour had come! With a loud yell I threw open the lantern and leaped into the room. He shrieked once—once only. In an instant I dragged him to the floor, and pulled the heavy bed over him. I then smiled gayly to find the deed so far done. But for many minutes the heart beat on with a muffled sound. This, however, did not vex me; it would not be heard through the wall. At length it ceased. The old man was dead.

If still you think me mad, you will think so no longer when I describe the wise precautions I took for the concealment of the body. The night waned, and I worked hastily, but in silence.

I took up three planks from the flooring of the chamber and deposited all between the scantlings. I then replaced the boards so cleverly, so cunningly, that no human eye—not even his—could have detected anything wrong.

When I had made an end of these labors it was four o'clock—still dark as midnight. As the bell sounded the hour, there came a knocking at the street door I went down to open it with a light heart—for what had I now to fear? Then entered three men, who introduced themselves, with perfect suavity, as officers of the police A shriek had been heard by a neighbor during the night; suspicion of foul play had been aroused; information had been lodged at the police office, and they (the officers) had been deputed to search the premises.

I smiled—for what had I to fear? I bade the gentlemen welcome. The shriek, I said, was my own in a dream. The old man, I mentioned, was absent in the country. I took my visitors all over the house. I bade them search—search well. I led them at length to his chamber. I showed them his treasures, secure, undisturbed. In the enthusiasm of my confidence I brought chairs into the room, and desired them here to rest from their fatigues, while I myself, in the wild audacity of my perfect triumph, placed my own seat upon the very spot beneath which reposed the corpse of the victim.

The officers were satisfied. My manner had convinced them. I was singularly at ease. But erelong I felt myself getting pale, and wished them gone. My head ached, and I fancied a ringing in my ears; but still they sat and still chatted. The ringing became more distinct; it continued and gained definiteness—until at length I found that the noise was not within my ears.

No doubt I now grew very pale; but I talked more fluently, and with a heightened voice. Yet the sound increased—and what could I do? It was a low, dull, quick sound—much such a sound as a watch makes when enveloped in cotton. I gasped for breath—and yet the officers heard it not. I talked more quickly—more vehemently; but the noise steadily increased. I arose and argued about trifles, in a high key, and with violent gesticulations; but the noise steadily increased. Why would they not be gone? I paced the floor to and fro, with heavy strides, as if excited to fury by the observations of the men—but the noise steadily increased. O God! what could I do? I foamed—I raved—I swore! I swung the chair upon which I had been sitting, and grated it upon the boards, but the noise arose over all and continually increased. It grew louder—louder—louder. And still the men chatted pleasantly and smiled. Was it possible they heard not?

They heard!—they suspected!—they knew!—they were making a mockery of my horror! I felt that I must scream or die!—and now—again!—hark!—louder!—louder! louder!

"Villains!" I shrieked, "dissemble no more! I admit the deed—tear up the planks! here! here! it is the beating of his hideous heart!"

ATMOSPHERE.

[Atmosphere is the feeling or spirit which pervades the thing seen or done. It is that something which seems to the speaker to envelop all, as the mist envelops a house or the sunshine a landscape. Atmosphere has no distinctive tone. It frequently demands the tone of Awe, or of Uproar.]

The Field of Waterloo Today.

VICTOR HUGO.

The field of Waterloo to-day has that calm which belongs to the earth, impassive support of man; it resembles any other plain.

At night, however, a sort of visionary mist arises from it, and if some traveller be walking there, if he looks, if he listens, if he dreams like Virgil in the fatal plain of Philippi, he becomes possessed by the hallucination of the disaster. The terrible 18th of June is again before him; the artificial hill of the monument fades away, this lion, whatever it be, is dispelled; the field of battle resumes its reality; the lines of infantry undulate in the plain, furious gallops traverse the horizon; the bewildered dreamer sees the flash of sabres, the glistening of bayonets, the bursting of shells, the awful intermingling of the thunders; he hears, like a death-rattle from the depths of a tomb, the vague clamor of the phantom battle; these shadows are grenadiers; these gleams are cuirassiers; this skeleton is Napoleon; that skeleton is Wellington; all this is unreal, and yet it clashes and combats; and the ravines run red, and the trees shiver, and there is fury even in the clouds, and, in the darkness, all those savage heights, Mont Saint Jean, Hougomont, Frischemont, Papelotte, Planchenoit, appear confusedly crowned with whirlwinds of spectres exterminating each other.

Atmosphere of Macbeth.

ARTHUR E. PHILLIPS.

Thus understood, the atmosphere of this play of Macbeth is the most awful, and, withal, majestic, in literature. With a sweep of his titanic genius Shakespeare snatches from the universe a segment of Chaos, and charms it into a wild symphony for human ears—a symphony terrible and bloody—but yet a symphony. Listen to its awful music. The roaring and flashing of nature's artillery: in its midst strange, weird creatures, foul and filthy. Hell's unkenneled whelps, moaning and crooning. Blood on every side from war's awful conflict. Blasted and blackened meeting grounds; caverns hollow and hideous; cauldrons reeking with foul vapors of paddock and bat and toad; smoke tainted with the breath of hell; blood lettings of every kind,—executions, murders, carousals; things shrieking in their drunken dreams, animals gnawing at each other's entrails; the moon spirited away, the sun stopped in its course, darkness on the face of all! Owls shrieking, crickets crying, lamentations and screams of death—accents terrible—a universal roaring and shouting—chaos physical!

Aye, and chaos intellectual! The brain, peopled with strange and direful creatures and hideous, all in one horrid foment of insurrection. The good warring with the bad, hell struggling with heaven in the mind. The terrific clamor of Sin knocking at the door of Conscience, and laughing and shrieking in his triumph as he tortures his victim with visions of murderous daggers, gouts of blood, gory locks, sightless eyes, marrowless bones, graves and charnel houses! Matter physical and matter intellectual in one terrific upheaval—in a word, Chaos itself, mastered by our immortal Shakespeare and set to a mighty and majestic and awful dramatic symphony. Such is Macbeth.

PROPHECY.

(See Tone Drills Nos. 55, 144, 210.)

[Prophecy cannot be said to have a distinct tone. It is usually composed of Conviction, tinged with Omination or Awe. Sometimes there is mingled with it Joy, Anger or Hatred.]

The Utter Destruction.

ISAIAH XXXIV.

Come near, ye nations, to hear; and hearken, ye peoples: let the earth hear, and the fulness thereof; the world, and all things that come forth of it. For the Lord hath indignation against all nations, and fury against all their host: he hath utterly destroyed them, he hath delivered them to the slaughter. Their slain also shall be cast out, and the stink of their carcases shall come up, and the mountains shall be melted with their blood. And all the host of heaven shall be dissolved, and the heavens shall be rolled together as a scroll: and all their host shall fade away, as the leaf fadeth from off the vine, and as a fading leaf from the fig tree. For my sword hath drunk its fill in heaven: behold, it shall come down from Edom, and upon the people of my curse, to judgment. The sword of the Lord is filled with blood, it is made fat with fatness, with the blood of the lambs and goats, with the fat of the kidneys of rams: for the Lord hath a sacrifice in Bozrah, and a great slaughter in the land of Edom.

And the wild-oxen shall come down with them, and the bullocks with the bulls; and their land shall be drunken with blood, and their dust made fat with fatness. For it is the day of the Lord's vengeance, the year of recompense in the controversy of Zion And the streams thereof shall be turned into pitch, and the dust thereof into brimstone, and the land thereof shall become burning pitch. It shall not be quenched night nor day; the smoke thereof shall go up forever; from generation to generation it shall lie waste; none shall pass through it for ever and ever. But the pelican and the porcupine shall possess it; and the owl and the raven shall dwell therein: and he shall stretch over it the line of confusion, and the plummet of emptiness.

They shall call the nobles thereof to the kingdom, but none shall be there, and all her princes shall be nothing. And thorns shall come up in her palaces, nettles and thistles in the fortresses thereof: and it shall be an habitation of jackals, a court for ostriches. And the wild beasts of the desert shall meet with the wolves, and the satyr shall cry to his fellow; yea, the night-monster shall settle there, and shall find her a place of rest. There shall the arrowsnake make her nest, and lay, and hatch, and gather under shadow: yea, there shall the kites be gathered, every one with her mate.

The Great Restoration.

ISAIAH XXXV.

The wilderness and the solitary place shall be glad; and the desert shall rejoice, and blossom as the rose. It shall blossom abundantly, and rejoice even with joy and singing; the glory of Lebanon shall be given unto it, the excellency of Carmel and Sharon: they shall see the glory of the Lord, the excellency of our God.

Strengthen ye the weak hands, and confirm the feeble knees; say to them that are of a fearful heart, Be strong, fear not: behold, your God will come with vengeance, with the recompence of God he will come and save you.

Then the eyes of the blind shall be opened, and the ears of the deaf shall be unstopped. Then shall the lame man leap as an hart, and the tongue of the dumb shall sing; for in the wilderness shall waters break out, and the streams on the desert. And the glowing sand shall become a pool, and the thirsty ground springs of water: in the habitation of jackals, where they lay, shall be grass with reeds and rushes.

And an highway shall be there, and a way, and it shall be

called the way of holiness; the unclean shall not pass over it; but it shall be for those; the wayfaring men, yea fools, shall not err therein.   No lion shall be there, nor shall any raven- ous beast go up thereon, they shall not be found there; but the redeemed shall walk there; and the ransomed of the Lord shall return, and come with singing unto Zion; and everlasting joy shall be upon their heads: they shall obtain gladness and joy, and sorrow and sighing shall flee away.

PARENTHESIS.

Truth in Parenthesis.

THOMAS HOOD.

I really take it very kind—
  This visit, Mrs. Skinner—
I have not seen you such an age—
  (The wretch has come to dinner!)
Your daughters, too—what loves of girls!
  What heads for painters' easels!
Come here, and kiss the infant, dears—
  (And give it, p'rhaps, the measles!)

Your charming boys I see are home
  From Reverend Mr. Russell's—
'Twas very kind to bring them both—
  (What boots for my new Brussels!)
What! little Clara left at home?
  Well, now, I call that shabby!
I should have loved to kiss her so—
  (A flabby, dabby babby!)

And Mr. S., I hope he's well?
  But, though he lives so handy,
He never once drops in to sup—
  (The better for our brandy!)
Come, take a seat—I long to hear
  About Matilda's marriage;

You've come, of course, to spend the day
   (Thank Heaven! I hear the carriage!)

What! must you go?—next time I hope
   You'll give me longer measure.
Nay, I shall see you down the stairs—
   (With most uncommon pleasure!)
Good bye! good bye! Remember, all,
   Next time you'll take your dinners—
(Now, David—mind, I'm not home,
   In future, to the Skinners.)

TRANSITION.

Ode to My Infant Son.

THOMAS HOOD.

Thou happy, happy elf!
   (But stop—first let me kiss away that tear,)
Thou tiny image of myself!
   (My love, he's poking peas into his ear!)
   Thou merry, laughing sprite!
   With spirits feather light,
Untouched by sorrow, and unsoiled by sin
(Dear me! the child is swallowing a pin!)

   Thou little, tricksy duck!
With antic toys so funnily bestuck,
Light as the singing bird that wings the air,
(The door! the door! he'll tumble down the stair!)
   Thou darling of thy sire!
(Why, Jane, he'll set his pinafore afire!)
   Thou imp of mirth and joy!
In love's dear chain so strong and bright a link,
Thou idol of thy parents!—(Drat the boy!
   There goes my ink!)

   Thou cherub—but of earth;
Fit playfellow for fays by moonlight pale.

In harmless sport and mirth,
(That dog will bite him if he pulls his tail!)
Thou human humming-bee, extracting honey
From every blossom in the world that blows,
Singing in youth's Elysium ever sunny,
(Another tumble—that's his precious nose!)
          Thy father's pride and hope!
(He'll break the mirror with that skipping-rope!)
With pure heart newly stamped from nature's mint—
          (Where *did* he learn that squint?)

          Thou young domestic dove!
(He'll have that jug off, with another shove!)
          Dear nursling of the hymeneal nest!
(Are those torn clothes his best?)
          Little epitome of man!
(He'll climb upon the table—that's his plan!)
Touched with the beauteous tints of dawning life,
          (He's got a knife!)
          Thou enviable being!
No storms, no clouds, in thy blue sky foreseeing,
          Play on, play on,
          My elfin John!
Toss the light ball—bestride the stick,
(I knew so many cakes would make him sick!)
With fancies buoyant as the thistle-down,
Prompting the face grotesque, and antic brisk,
          With many a lamb-like frisk,
(He's got the scissors, snipping at your gown!)
          Thou pretty opening rose!
(Go to your mother, child, and wipe your nose!)
Balmy and breathing music like the south,
(He really brings my heart into my mouth!)
Fresh as the morn, and brilliant as its star,

(I wish that window had an iron bar!)
Bold as the hawk, yet gentle as the dove,
(I'll tell you what, my love,
I cannot write, unless he's sent above!)

SELECTIONS

CHOSEN FOR THEIR VALUE AS

STUDIES IN VARIETY OF TONE

AND AFFORDING

EXERCISES IN TONING

Bernardo del Carpio.

FELICIA HEMANS.

The warrior bowed his crested head, and tamed his heart of
    fire,
And sued the haughty king to free his long-imprisoned sire;
"I bring thee here my fortress-keys, I bring my captive train,
I pledge thee faith, my liege, my lord!—Oh! break my father's
    chain!"

"Rise, rise! even now thy father comes, a ransomed man this
    day:
Mount thy good horse; and thou and I will meet him on his
    way."
Then lightly rose that loyal son, and bounded on his steed,
And urged, as if with lance in rest, the charger's foamy speed.

And lo! from far, as on they pressed, there came a glittering
    band,
With one that 'midst them stately rode, as a leader in the
    land:

"Now haste, Bernardo, haste! for there, in very truth, is he,
The father whom thy faithful heart hath yearned so long
to see"

His dark eye flashed, his proud breast heaved, his cheek's hue
came and went:
He reached that gray-haired chieftain's side, and there,
dismounting, bent;
A lowly knee to earth he bent, his father's hand he took—
What was there in its touch that all his fiery spirit shook?

That hand was cold, a frozen thing,—it dropped from his like
lead!
He looked up to the face above,—the face was of the dead!
A plume waved o'er the noble brow,—the brow was fixed and
white:
He met at last, his father's eyes,—but in them was no sight!

Up from the ground he sprang and gazed;—but who could
paint that gaze?
They hushed their very hearts, that saw its horror and amaze:
They might have chained him, as before that stony form he
stood;
For the power was stricken from his arm, and from his lips
the blood.
"Father!" at length he murmured low, and wept like child-
hood then:
Talk not of grief till thou hast seen the tears of warlike men!
He thought on all his glorious hopes, and all his young
renown,—
He flung his falchion from his side, and in the dust sat down.

Then covering with his steel-gloved hands his darkly mourn-
ful brow,

"No more, there is no more," he said, "to lift the sword for,
    now;
My king is false—my hope betrayed! My father—oh! the
    worth,
The glory, and the loveliness, are passed away from earth!

"I thought to stand where banners waved, my sire, beside
    thee, yet!
I would that there our kindred blood on Spain's free soil had
    met!
Thou wouldst have known my spirit then;—for thee my fields
    were won;
And thou hast perished in thy chains, as though thou hadst
    no son!"

Then starting from the ground once more, he seized the
    monarch's rein,
Amidst the pale and 'wildered looks of all the courtier train;
And, with a fierce, o'ermastering grasp, the rearing war-horse
    led,
And sternly set them face to face—the king before the dead:

"Came I not forth, upon thy pledge, my father's hand to
    kiss?
Be still, and gaze thou on, false king! and tell me, what is
    this?
The voice, the glance, the heart I sought,—give answer, where
    are they?
If thou wouldst clear thy perjured soul, send life through this
    cold clay!

"Into these glassy eyes put light;—be still! keep down thine
    ire!—

Bid these white lips a blessing speak,—this earth is not my
    sire:
Give me back him for whom I strove, for whom my blood
    was shed!—
Thou canst not? and a king!—his dust be mountains on thy
    head!"

He loosed the steed,—his slack hand fell;—upon the silent
    face
He cast one long, deep, troubled look, then turned from that
    sad place:
His hope was crushed, his after fate untold in martial
    strain:—
His banner led the spears no more, amidst the hills of Spain.

Lady Clare.

ALFRED TENNYSON.

It was the time when lilies blow,
    And clouds are highest up in air,
Lord Ronald brought a lily-white doe
    To give his cousin Lady Clare.

I trow they did not part in scorn:
    Lovers long-betrothed were they:
They two shall wed the morrow morn;
    God's blessing on the day.

"He does not love me for my birth,
    Nor for my lands, so broad and fair;
He loves me for my own true worth,
    And that is well," said Lady Clare;

In there came old Alice, the nurse,
    Said, "Who was this that went from thee?"

"It was my cousin," said Lady Clare;
　"To-morrow he weds with me."

"Oh God be thanked!" said Alice, the nurse,
　"That all comes round so just and fair:
Lord Ronald is heir of all your lands,
　And you are not the Lady Clare."

"Are ye out of your mind, my nurse, my nurse?"
　Said Lady Clare, "that ye speak so wild?"
"As God's above," said Alice, the nurse,
　"I speak the truth; you are my child.

"The old earl's daughter died at my breast:
　I speak the truth as I live by bread!
I buried her like my own sweet child,
　And put my child in her stead."

"Falsely, falsely have ye done,
　O mother," she said, "if this be true,
To keep the best man under the sun
　So many years from his due."

"Nay now, my child," said Alice the nurse,
　"But keep the secret for your life,
And all you have will be Lord Ronald's
　When you are man and wife."

"If I'm a beggar born," she said,
　"I will speak out, for I dare not lie:
Pull off, pull off the brooch of gold,
　And fling the diamond necklace by."

"Nay now, my child," said Alice the nurse,
　"But keep the secret all ye can."

She said, "Not so: but I will know,
    If there be any faith in man."

"Nay now, what faith?" said Alice the nurse:
    "The man will cleave unto his right."
"And he shall have it," the lady replied,
    "Though I should die to-night."

"Yet give one kiss to your mother dear!
    Alas, my child, I sinned for thee."
"O mother, mother, mother!" she said,
    "So strange it seems to me.

"Yet here's a kiss for my mother dear,
    My mother dear, if this be so;
And lay your hand upon my head,
    And bless me, mother, ere I go."

She clad herself in a russet gown—
    She was no longer Lady Clare:
She went by dale, and she went by down,
    With a single rose in her hair.

The lily-white doe Lord Ronald had brought
    Leapt up from where she lay,
Dropt her head in the maiden's hand,
    And followed her all the way.

Down stept Lord Ronald from his tower:
    "O Lady Clare, you shame your worth!
Why come you drest like a village maid,
    That are the flower of the earth?"

"If I come drest like a village maid,
    I am but as my fortunes are:

I am a beggar born," she said,
   "And not the Lady Clare."

"Play me no tricks," said Lord Ronald,
   "For I am yours in word and deed.
Play me no tricks," said Lord Ronald,
   "Your riddle is hard to read."

Oh, and proudly stood she up!
   Her heart within her did not fail:
She looked into Lord Ronald's eyes,
   And told him all her nurse's tale.

He laughed a laugh of merry scorn:
   He turned and kissed her where she stood:
"If you are not the heiress born,
   And I," said he, "the next of blood—

"If you are not the heiress born,
   And I," said he, "the lawful heir,
We two will wed to-morrow morn,
   And you shall still be Lady Clare."

The Battle of Waterloo.

LORD BYRON.

There was a sound of revelry by night,
And Belgium's capital had gathered then
Her beauty and her chivalry; and bright
The lamps shone o'er fair women and brave men;
A thousand hearts beat happily; and when
Music arose with its voluptuous swell,
Soft eyes looked love to eyes which spake again,
And all went merry as a marriage-bell:
But hush! hark! a deep sound strikes like a rising knell!

Did ye not hear it?—No; 'twas but the wind,
Or the car rattling o'er the stony street;
On with the dance! Let joy be unconfined;
No sleep till morn, when Youth and Pleasure meet;
To chase the glowing hours with flying feet—
But, hark!—that heavy sound breaks in once more,
As if the clouds its echo would repeat;
And nearer, clearer, deadlier than before!
Arm! arm! it is—it is the cannon's opening roar! . . .

Ah! then and there was hurrying to and fro,
And gathering tears and tremblings of distress,
And cheeks all pale, which but an hour ago
Blushed at the praise of their own loveliness;
And there were sudden partings, such as press
The life from out young hearts, and choking sighs
Which ne'er might be repeated: who could guess
If ever more should meet those mutual eyes,
Since upon night so sweet such awful morn could rise?

And there was mounting in hot haste: the steed,
The mustering squadron, and the clattering car,
Went pouring forward with impetuous speed,
And swiftly forming in the ranks of war;
And the deep thunder peal on peal afar;
And near, the beat of the alarming drum
Roused up the soldier ere the morning star;
While thronged the citizens with terror dumb,
Or whispering, with white lips, "The foe! They come! they
   come!"

And wild and high the "Camerons' gathering" rose!
The war-note of Lochiel, which Albyn's hills
Have heard,—and heard, too, have her Saxon foes:

How in the noon of night that pibroch thrills,
  Savage and shrill! But with the breath which fills
Their mountain-pipe, so fill the mountaineers
  With the fierce native daring which instils
The stirring memory of a thousand years,
And Evan's, Donald's fame rings in each clansman's ears!

And Ardennes waves above them her green leaves,
  Dewy with Nature's tear-drops, as they pass,
Grieving, if aught inanimate e'er grieves,
  Over the unreturning brave,—alas!
Ere evening to be trodden like the grass
  Which now beneath them, but above shall grow
In its next verdure, when this fiery mass
  Of living valor, rolling on the foe,
And burning with high hope, shall moulder cold and low.

Last noon beheld them full of lusty life,
  Last eve in Beauty's circle proudly gay,
The midnight brought the signal-sound of strife,
  The morn the marshalling in arms,—the day,
Battle's magnificently stern array!
  The thunder-clouds close o'er it, which when rent,
The earth is covered thick with other clay,
  Which her own clay shall cover, heaped and pent,
Rider and horse,—friend, foe,—in one red burial blent!

The Defense of Hofer, the Tyrolese Patriot.

You ask what I have to say in my defense, you, who
glory in the name of France, who wander through the world
to enrich and exalt the land of your birth; you demand how
I could dare arm myself against the invaders of my native
rocks. Do you confine the love of home to yourselves? Do

you punish in others the actions which you dignify among yourselves? Those stars which glitter on your breasts, do they hang there as a recompense for patient servitude?

I see the smile of contempt which curls your lips. You say, "This brute! he is a ruffian! a beggar! That patched jacket, that ragged cap, that rusty belt! Shall barbarians such as he close the pass against us, shower rocks on our heads, and single out our leaders with unfailing aim; these groveling mountaineers, who know not the joys and brilliance of life, creeping amid eternal snows, and snatching with greedy hand their stinted ear of corn!"

Yet, poor as we are, we never envied our neighbors their smiling sun, their gilded palaces. We never strayed from our peaceful huts to blast the happiness of those who have injured us. The traveler who visited our valleys met every hand outstretched to welcome him; for him every hearth blazed as we listened to his tale of distant lands. Too happy for ambition, we were not jealous of wealth; we have even refused to partake of it.

Frenchmen! you have wives and children. When you return to your beautiful cities, amid the roar of trumpets, the smiles of the lovely, and the multitude shouting their triumphs, they will ask, "Where have you roamed? What have you achieved? What have you brought back to us?" Those laughing babes who climb to your knees, will you have the heart to tell them, "We have pierced the barren crags, we have entered the naked cottage to level it to the ground; we found no treasures but honest hearts, and those we have broken because they throbbed with love for the wilderness around them. Clasp this old firelock in your little hands, it was snatched from a peasant of Tyrol, who died in the vain effort to stem the torrent?" Seated by your firesides, will you boast to your generous and blooming wives that you have extinguished the last ember that lighted our gloom?

Happy scenes! I shall never see you more! In those cold, stern eyes I read my fate. Think not that your sentence can be terrible to me, but I have sons, daughters, and a wife who has shared all my labors; she has shared, too, my little pleasures, such pleasures as that humble roof can yield, pleasures that you cannot understand. My little ones! should you live to bask in the sunshine of manhood, dream not of your father's doom! Should you live to know it, know, too, that the man who has served his God and his country with all his heart can smile at the musket leveled to pierce it!

What is death to me? I have not revelled in pleasures wrung from innocence and want; rough and discolored as these hands are, they are pure. My death is nothing. Oh, that my country could live! Oh, that ten thousand such deaths could make her immortal! Do I despair then? No. We have rushed to the sacrifice, and the offering has been in vain for us; but our children shall burst these fetters; the blood of virtue was never shed in vain; Freedom can never die. I have heard that you killed your king once because he enslaved you, yet, now, again you crouch before a single man who bids you trample on all who abjure his yoke, and shoots you if you have courage to disobey.

Do you think that, when I am buried, there shall breathe no other Hofers? Dream you that, if today you prostrate Hofer in the dust, tomorrow Hofer is no more? In the distance I see liberty which I shall not taste; behind I look on my slaughtered countrymen, on my orphans, on my desolate fields; but a star rises before my aching sight which points to justice,—and it shall come!

SELECTIONS

CHOSEN FOR THEIR VALUE AS

STUDIES IN PAUSE

Pause is concerned with the silences in speech. All those cessations of sound that occur in the course of utterance, whether between words, sentences, or paragraphs, come under Pause.

Pause has relation to both thought and feeling. If we listen attentively to animated conversation we shall observe that the silences of the speaker have a bearing upon the idea itself, and also upon the emotional attitude toward the thought.

Pause as concerned with thought manifests the relationship of words. In the phrase, "deep and dark blue ocean," if a longer pause is made after "deep" than after the other words, we understand that the ocean is deep and the color a dark blue. If this longer pause is after "dark" it indicates to us that the ocean is not of dark blue color but of blue, and that it (the ocean) is not only deep but dark. If the longer pause is after "blue" we understand that the ocean is of a blue color that is deep and dark. *In each case a change in the relative length of the pause after a given word indicated a new relationship of words*. Applied to thought, therefore, the listener understands pause as follows: the longer the pause the less close the verbal relationship, and, obversely, the shorter the pause the closer the relationship. The law, then,

281

for the speaker, if he would be clearly understood by the listener, is:—*increase the length of the pause in proportion to the irrelation of the words,* and, obversely, *decrease the length of the pause in proportion to their relation.*

This variation in the length of pauses, it is apparent, marks off words into groups, and the task of determining this relation of words is usually called "grouping." This grouping has been discussed and illustrated in a preceding section.

Besides manifesting the relationship of words, pause is one of the means by which the listener is enabled to grasp the full significance of each group in itself, and of the whole, both with regard to the thought and to the feeling. The speaker, appreciating this, will adjust his delivery accordingly. In respect to the thought, the speaker will increase the pause in proportion to the importance of the idea, the difficulty of apprehension or the difficulty of belief. In respect to the feeling the pause will be increased in proportion to the height or intensity of the emotion. The various aspects of these pauses are illustrated in this section of selections.

PAUSE AND THE INFREQUENT.

[A word or group of words, while known to the listener, may be so rarely heard or used by him that additional time must be allowed in which to be fully comprehended. Ex. (Lord Beaconsfield's humorous description of W. E. Gladstone): "A sophisticated rhetorician inebriated with the exuberance of his own verbosity."]

Universal Adaptation.

JAMES McCOSH.

The mind is suited to the position in which it is placed in the world, and the world is adapted to the minds which are to observe and use it. There is order in the world, and man is so constituted as to discover and to admire it. There is reason in the works of God, and reason in man's mind to appreciate it. "If the laws of our reason," says Oersted, "did not exist in nature, we would vainly attempt to force them upon her; if the laws of nature did not exist in our reason, we should not be able to comprehend them." The forms which minerals assume when they crystallize; the elliptic orbits of the planets; the hyperbolic curves of the comets; the spiral conformations of the nebular groups of the heavens, of the appendages of plants around their axes, and of the whorls of the shells of molluscs; the conical shape of the fruit of pines and firs with the rhomboids on their surface, are all constructed according to mathematical laws which have their seat in the intelligence and can be evolved by pure thought. When we ascend to the higher manifestations of life, in particular, when we rise to the human form, we do not find the same rigid lines as in crystals, nor are the invariable curves of the nebulæ and plants so observable; but I believe they are still there blended in innumerable ways, so as to give an infinite sweep and variety to the graceful forms on which the eye ever delights to rest, and which the mind never wearies to contemplate, and unconsciously follows now the one and now the other till it is lost in a perfect wilderness of beauty.

PAUSE AND INVOLVED CONSTRUCTION.

[Some sentences are so unusual or involved in their construction that increased pause must be made to enable the listener to grasp the proper relation of each to the whole, as, "Deep in human nature, he thus demonstrates, and obligatory upon individuals, has been planted one great law."]

Introduction, Paradise Lost.

JOHN MILTON.

Of man's first disobedience, and the fruit
Of that forbidden tree, whose mortal taste

Brought death into the world, and all our woe,
With loss of Eden, till one greater Man
Restore us, and regain the blissful seat,
Sing, heavenly Muse, that on the secret top
Of Oreb, or of Sinai, didst inspire
That shepherd, who first taught the chosen seed,
In the beginning, how the Heavens and Earth
Rose out of Chaos: or, if Sion hill
Delight thee more, and Siloa's brook that flow'd
Fast by the oracle of God; I thence
Invoke thy aid to my adventurous song,
That with no middle flight intends to soar
Above the Aonian mount, while it pursues
Things unattempted yet in prose or rhyme.
And chiefly thou, O Spirit, that dost prefer
Before all temples the upright heart and pure,
Instruct me, for thou know'st; thou from the first
Wast present, and, with mighty wings out-spread,
Dove-like sat'st brooding on the vast abyss
And mad'st it pregnant: what in me is dark
Illumine; what is low raise and support;
That to the height of this great argument
I may assert eternal Providence,
And justify the ways of God to man.

PAUSE AND LONG SENTENCE.

[Frequently a sentence may be of such length that the pauses must be longer than the normal in order to give the listener time to adequately comprehend the complete thought. Ex. (Lord Erskine): "If indeed he writes what he does not think; if, contemplating the misery of others, he wickedly condemns what his own understanding approves; or even, admitting his real disgust against the government or the corruptions, if he calumniates living magistrates or holds out to individuals that they have a right to run before the public mind in their conduct; that they may oppose by contumacy or force what private reason only disapproves; that they may disobey the law, because their judgment condemns it, or resist the public will, because they honestly wish to change it—he is then a criminal upon every principle of rational policy, as well as upon the immemorial precedents of English justice; because such a person seeks to disunite individuals from their duty to the whole, and excites to overt acts of misconduct in a part of the community, instead of endeavoring to change, by the impulse of reason, that universal assent, which, in this and in every country, constitutes the law for all.."]

The Field of Religion.

ALEXANDER DUFF.

The field of divine appointment is not Scotland or England, but "the world"—the world of "all nations." The prayer of divine inspiration is, "God bless and pity us," not that thy way may be known in all Britain, and thy saving health among all its destitute families, but "that thy way may be known on all the earth, and thy saving health among all nations." The command of divine obligation is not, "Go to the people of Scotland or of England," but, "Go unto all the world and preach the gospel to every creature." And if we take our counsel from those blind and deluded guides that would, in spite of the Almighty's appointment, and in derision of our own prayers, persuade us, altogether, or for an indefinite period onward, to abandon the real proper Bible field, and direct the whole of our time, and strength and resources to home; if, at their antiscriptural suggestions, we do thus dislocate the divine order of proportion; if we do thus invert the divine order of magnitude, if we daringly presume to put that last which God hath put first; to reckon that least which God hath pronounced greatest, what can we expect but that he shall be provoked, in some displeasure, to deprive us of the precious deposit of misappropriated grace, and inscribe "Ichabod" on all our towers, bulwarks and palaces.

And if he do, then, like beings smitten with judicial blindness, we may hold hundreds of meetings, deliver thousands of speeches, and publish tens of thousands of tracts and pamphlets and volumes in defense of our chartered rights and birthright liberties; and all this we may hail as religious zeal, and applaud as patriotic spirit; but if such prodigious activities be designed solely, or even chiefly, to concentrate all hearts, affections, and energies on the limited interests of our own land; if such prodigious activities recognize and aim at no higher terminating object than the simple maintenance and extension of our home institutions, and that, too, for the exclusive benefit of our own people, while, in contempt of the counsels of the Eternal, the hundreds of millions of a guilty world are cruelly abandoned to perish, oh! how can all this appear in the sight of heaven as anything better than a national outburst of monopolizing selfishness?

PAUSE AND THE PICTURE.

[Some descriptions are essentially suggestive, and their charm lies in the listener filling in the details from his own imagination. In other cases, the details, while concrete and arbitrary (as shape or dimension), may require time to enable the listener to put them together. Both processes take time, and an increase of the normal pause should be made just in the degree that the picture is hard to reconstruct or vast in its sweep.]

Prologue of Act III, Henry V.

WILLIAM SHAKESPEARE.

Suppose that you have seen
The well-appointed king at Hampton pier
Embark his royalty; and his brave fleet
With silken streamers the young Phœbus fanning:
Play with your fancies, and in them behold
Upon the hempen tackle ship-boys climbing;

Hear the shrill whistle which doth order give
To sounds confused; behold the threaden sails,
Borne with the invisible and creeping wind,
Draw the huge bottoms through the furrow'd sea,
Breasting the lofty surge: O, do but think
You stand upon the rivage and behold
A city on the inconstant billows dancing;
For so appears this fleet majestical,
Holding due course to Harfleur. Follow, follow:
Grapple your minds to sternage of this navy,
And leave your England, as dead midnight still,
Guarded with grandsires, babies and old women,
Either past or not arrived to pith and puissance;
For who is he, whose chin is but enrich'd
With one appearing hair, that will not follow
These cull'd and choice-drawn cavaliers to France?
Work, work your thoughts, and therein see a siege;
Behold the ordnance on their carriages,
With fatal mouths gaping on girded Harfleur.
Suppose the ambassador from the French comes back;
Tells Harry that the king doth offer him
Katharine his daughter, and with her, to dowry,
Some petty and unprofitable dukedoms.
The offer likes not: and the nimble gunner
With linstock now the devilish cannon touches,
And down goes all before them. Still be kind,
And eke out our performance with your mind.

Niagara Falls.

EDWIN ARNOLD.

Before my balcony the great cataract is thundering, smoking, glittering with green and white rollers and rapids, hurling the waters of a whole continent in splendor and speed

over the sharp ledges of the long, brown rock by which Erie, "the Broad," steps proudly down to Ontario, "the Beautiful." The smaller but very imposing American Falls speaks with the louder voice of the two, because its coiling spirals of twisted and furious flood crash in full impulse of descent upon the talus of massive boulders heaped up at its foot. The resounding impact of water on rocks, the clouds of water-smoke which rise high in air, and the river below churned into a whirling cream of eddy and surge and backwater, unite in a composite effect, at once magnificent and bewildering.

Far away, Niagara river is seen winding eagerly to its prodigious leap. You can discern the line of the first breakers, where the river feels the fatal draw of the cataracts, its current seeming suddenly to leap forward, stimulated by mad desire, a hidden spell, a dreadful and irresistible doom.

Far back along the gilded surface of the upper stream, these lines of dancing, tossing, eager, anxious and fate-impelled breakers and billows multiply their white ranks and spread and close together their leaping ridges into a wild chaos of racing waves as the brink is approached. And then, at the brink, there is a curious pause—the momentary peace of the irrevocable. Those mad upper waters—reaching the great leap—are suddenly all quiet and glassy, and rounded and green as the border of a field of rye, while they turn the angle of the dreadful ledge and hurl themselves into the snow-white gulf of noise and mist and mystery underneath.

There is nothing more translucently green, nor more perennially still and lovely, than Niagara the greater. At this, her awful brink, the whole architrave of the main abyss gleams like a fixed and glorious work wrought in polished aquamarine or emerald. This exquisitely-colored cornice of the enormous waterfall—this brim of bright tranquillity between fervor of rush and fury of plunge—is its principal feature, and stamps it as far more beautiful than terrible. Even the central solemnity and shudder-fraught miracle of the monstrous uproar and glory is rendered exquisite, reposeful and soothing by the lovely rainbows hanging over the turmoil and clamor.

From its crest of chrysoprase and silver, indeed, to its broad foot of milky foam and of its white-stunned waves, too broken and too dazed to begin at first to float away, Niagara appears not terrible, but divinely and deliciously graceful, glad and lovely—a specimen of the splendor of water at its finest—a sight to dwell and linger in the mind with ineffaceable images of happy and grateful thought, by no means to affect it in seeing or to haunt it in future days of memory with any wild reminiscences of terror or of gloom.

Shakespeare's Imagination.

ROBERT G. INGERSOLL.

Shakespeare exceeded all the sons of men in the splendor of his imagination. To him the whole world paid tribute, and Nature poured her treasures at his feet. In him all races lived again, and even those to be were pictured in his brain.

He was a man of imagination—that is to say, of genius, and having seen a leaf, and a drop of water, he could construct the forests, the rivers and the seas. In his presence all the cataracts would fall and foam, the mists rise, the clouds form and float.

If Shakespeare knew one fact, he knew its kindred and its neighbors. Looking at a coat of mail, he instantly imagined the society, the conditions, that produced it and what it, in turn, produced. He saw the castle, the moat, the drawbridge, the lady in the tower, and the knightly lover spurring across the plain. He saw the bold baron and the rude retainer, the trampled serf, and all the glory and the grief of feudal life.

He lived the life of all. He was a citizen of Athens in the days of Pericles. He listened to the eager eloquence of the great orators, and sat upon the cliffs, and with the tragic poet heard "the multitudinous laughter of the sea." He saw Socrates thrust the spear of question through the shield and heart of falsehood. He was present when the great man drank hemlock, and met the night of death, tranquil as a star meets morning. He listened to the peripatetic philosophers, and was unpuzzled by the sophists. He watched Phidias as he chiseled shapeless stone to forms of love and awe.

He walked the ways of mighty Rome, and saw great Cæsar with his legions in the field. He stood with vast and motley throngs, and watched the triumphs given to victorious men, followed by uncrowned kings, the captured hosts, and all the spoils of ruthless war. He heard the shout that shook the Coliseum's roofless walls, when from the reeling gladiator's hand the short sword fell, while from his bosom gushed the stream of wasted life.

The Imagination had a stage in Shakespeare's brain, whereon were set all scenes that lie between the morn of laughter and the night of tears, and where his players bodied forth the false and true, the joys and griefs, the careless shallows and the tragic deeps of universal life.

Shakespeare was an intellectual ocean, whose waves touched all the shores of thought; within which were all the tides and waves of destiny and will; over which swept all the storms of fate, ambition, and revenge; upon which fell the gloom and darkness of despair and death and all the sunlight of content and love, and within which was the inverted sky, lit with the eternal stars—an intellectual ocean—towards which all rivers ran, and from which now the isles and continents of thought receive their dew and rain.

A Cottage.

EDGAR ALLEN POE.

The point of view from which I first saw the valley was
not altogether, although it was nearly, the best point from
which to survey the house. I will therefore describe it as I
afterwards saw it—from a position on the stone wall at the
southern extreme of the amphitheater.

The main building was about twenty-four feet long and
sixteen broad—certainly not more. Its total height, from
the ground to the apex of the roof, could not have exceeded
eighteen feet. To the west end of this structure was attached
one about a third smaller in all its proportions—the line of
its front standing back about two yards from that of the
larger house; and the line of its roof, of course, being con-
siderably depressed below that of the roof adjoining. At
right angles to these buildings, and from the rear of the
main one—not exactly in the middle—extended a third com-
partment, very small—being, in general, one-third less than
the western wing. The roofs of the two larger were very
steep—sweeping down from the ridge-beam with a long concave curve, and extending at least four feet beyond the walls
in front, so as to form the roofs of two piazzas. These latter
roofs, of course, needed no support; but as they had the air
of needing it, slight and perfectly plain pillars were inserted
at the corners alone. The roof of the northern wing was
merely an extension of a portion of the main roof. Between
the chief building and western wing arose a very tall and
rather slender square chimney of hard Dutch bricks, alternately black and red—a slight cornice of projecting bricks at
the top. Over the gables the roofs also projected very much
—in the main building about four feet to the east and two
to the west.

The piazzas of the main building and western wing had

no floors, as is usual; but at the doors and at each window, large, flat, irregular slabs of granite lay imbedded in the delicious turf, affording comfortable footing in all weather. Excellent paths of the same material—not nicely adapted, but with the velvety sod filling frequent intervals between the stones, led hither and thither from the house, to a crystal spring about five paces off, to the road, or to one or two out-houses that lay to the north, beyond the brook, and were thoroughly concealed by a few locusts and catalpas.

PAUSE AND THE UNUSUAL.

[As a rule, an unusual statement, to be adequately comprehended, demands increased pause to give the listener sufficient time to refer the idea to his experience. Ex. (Alexander McLaren): "The dead are the living;" (Milton): "stupidly good."]

Aphorisms.

JOHN MORLEY.

Lichtenberg, a professor of physics, who was also a considerable hand at satire a hundred years ago, composed a collection of sayings, with a little wheat amid much chaff, among which were, "People who never have any time are the people who do least," and "He who has less than he desires should know that he has more than he deserves," and "Enthusiasts without capacity are the really dangerous people." This last, by the way, recalls a saying of the great French reactionary, De Bonald, and which is never quite out of date: "Follies committed by the sensible, extravagances uttered by the clever, crimes committed by the good—that is what makes revolutions."

Some have found light in the sayings of Balthasar Gracian, a Spaniard, who flourished at the end of the Seventeenth century. I do not myself find Gracian much of a companion, though some of his aphorisms give a neat turn to commonplace. Thus: "To equal a predecessor one must have twice his worth." And "What is easy ought to be entered upon as though it were difficult, and what is difficult as though it were easy"

One of the most commonly known of all books of maxims, after the Proverbs of Solomon, is the Moral Reflections of La Rochefoucauld. "Interest," he says, "speaks all sorts of tongues and plays all sorts of parts, even the part of the disinterested." And again, "Gratitude is with most people only a strong desire for greater benefits to come." And this—"Love of justice is with most of us nothing but the fear of suffering injustice."

No more important name is associated with the literature of aphorisms than that of Pascal. On man, as he exists in society, he said little; and what he said does not make us hopeful. He saw the darker side. "If everybody knew what one says of them, there would not be four friends left in the world." "Would you have men think well of you, then do not speak well of yourself." "What a chimera is Man!" said Pascal. "What a confused chaos! What a subject of contradiction! A professed judge of all things, and yet a feeble worm of the earth; the great depository and guardian of truth, and yet a mere huddle of uncertainty; the glory and the scandal of the universe!"

There is a smart spurious wisdom of the world which has the bitterness not of the salutary tonic, but of the mortal poison; and of this kind the master is Chamfort "If you live among men," he said, "the heart must either break or turn to brass." "The public! the public!" he cried, "how many fools does it take to make a public!" "What is celebrity? The advantage of being known to people who don't know you" We cannot be surprised to hear of the lady who said that a conversation with Chamfort in the morning made her melancholy until bedtime. Yet Chamfort is the author of the not unwholesome saying that "the most wasted of all days is that on which one has not laughed." One of his maxims lets us into the secret of his misanthropy. "Whoever," he said, "is not a misanthropist at forty can never have loved mankind."

Chamfort I will leave, with his sensible distinction between pride and vanity. "A man," he says, "has advanced far in the study of morals who has mastered the difference between pride and vanity. The first is lofty, calm, immovable; the second is uncertain, capricious, unquiet. The one adds to a man's stature; the other puffs him out. The one is the source of a thousand virtues; the other is that of nearly all vices and all perversities. There is a kind of pride in which are included all the commandments of God; and a kind of vanity which contains the seven mortal sins."

PAUSE AND LEADING STATEMENT.

[Where a statement is followed by one or more clauses or sentences that directly bear on it, the pause after the statement should be increased sufficiently to enable the listener to so fix the thought in his mind that the support can be seen in its proper relation to it. If the parent statement is lost to the listener or is not sufficiently grasped, the supporting matter may lose its full significance. Ex. (G. F. Pierce): "The spirit of Christianity is essentially a public spirit. It ignores all selfishness. It is benevolence embodied and alive, full of plans for the benefit of the world."]

Freedom—What Is It?

WILLIAM ELLERY CHANNING.

I call that mind free, which masters the senses, which protects itself against animal appetites, which contemns pleasure and pain in comparison with its own energy, which penetrates beneath the body and recognizes its own reality and greatness, which passes life, not in asking what it shall eat or drink, but in hungering, thirsting, and seeking after righteousness.

I call that mind free, which escapes the bondage of matter, which, instead of stopping at the material universe and making it a prison-wall, passes beyond it to its Author, and finds, in the radiant signatures which it everywhere bears of the Infinite Spirit, helps to its own spiritual enlargement.

I call that mind free, which jealously guards its intellectual rights and powers, which calls no man master, which does not content itself with a passive or hereditary faith, which opens itself to light whencesoever it may come, which receives new truth as an angel from heaven, which, while consulting others, inquires still more of the oracle within itself, and uses instruction from abroad, not to supersede, but to quicken and exalt its own energies.

I call that mind free, which sets no bounds to its love, which is not imprisoned in itself or in a sect, which recognizes in all human beings the image of God and the rights of his children, which delights in virtue and sympathizes with suffering, wherever they are seen, which conquers pride, anger, and sloth, and offers itself up a willing victim to the cause of mankind.

I call that mind free, which is not passively framed by outward circumstances, which is not swept away by the torrents of events, which is not the creature of accidental impulse, but which bends events to its own improvement, and acts from an inward spring, from immutable principles which it has deliberately espoused.

I call that mind free, which protects itself against the usurpations of society, which does not cower to human opinion, which feels itself accountable to a higher tribunal than man's, which respects a higher law than fashion, which respects itself too much to be the slave or tool of the many or the few.

I call that mind free, which, through confidence in God, and, in the power of virtue, has cast off all fear but that of wrong doing, which no menace or peril can enthrall, which is calm in the midst of tumults, and possesses itself, though all else be lost.

I call that mind free, which resists the bondage of habit, which does not mechanically repeat itself and copy the past, which does not live on its old virtues, which does not enslave itself to precise rules, but which forgets what is behind, listens for new and higher monitions of conscience, and rejoices to pour itself forth in fresh and higher exertions.

I call that mind free, which is jealous of its own freedom, which guards itself from being merged in others, which guards its empire over itself as nobler than the empire of the world.

PAUSE AND LARGE CONTENT.

[Some ideas, while easy to understand in themselves, have so large a content that time must be given for the vivid recalling of the associated ideas. Ex.: "What a piece of work is man! How noble in reason! How infinite in faculty!"]

Speech at Gettysburg.

ABRAHAM LINCOLN.

Fourscore and seven years ago our fathers brought forth upon this continent a new nation, conceived in liberty, and dedicated to the proposition that all men are created equal. Now we are engaged in a great civil war, testing whether that nation, or any nation so conceived and so dedicated, can long endure. We are met on a great battle-field of that war. We have come to dedicate a portion of that field as a final resting-place for those who here gave their lives that that nation might live. It is altogether fitting and proper that we should do this. But in a larger sense we cannot dedicate, we cannot consecrate, we cannot hallow this ground. The brave men, living and dead, who struggled here, have consecrated it far above our power to add or detract. The world will little note, nor long remember, what we say here; but it can never forget what they did here. It is for us, the living, rather to be dedicated here to the unfinished work which they who fought here have thus far so nobly advanced. It is rather for us to be here dedicated to the great task remaining before us, that from these honored dead we take increased devotion to that cause for which they gave the last full measure of devotion; that we here highly resolve that these dead shall not have died in vain; that this nation, under God, shall have a new birth of freedom, and that government of the people, by the people, and for the people, shall not perish from the earth.

Life.

ROBERT G. INGERSOLL.

Born of love and hope, of ecstasy and pain, of agony and fear, of tears and joy—dowered with the wealth of two united hearts—held in happy arms, with lips upon life's drifted front, blue-veined and fair, where perfect peace finds perfect form—rocked by willing feet and wooed to shadowy shores of sleep by siren mother singing soft and low—looking with wonder's wide and startled eyes at common things of life and day—taught by want and wish and contact with the things that touch the dimpled flesh of babes—lured by light and flame and charmed by color's wondrous robes, learning the use of hands and feet and by the love of mimicry beguiled to utter speech—releasing prisoned thoughts from crabbed and curious marks on soiled and tattered leaves—puzzling the brain with crooked numbers and their changing, tangled worth—and so through years of alternating day and night, until the captive grows familiar with the chains and walls and limitations of a life.

And time runs on in sun and shade, until the one of all this world is wooed and won, and all the lore of love is taught and learned again. Again a home is built, with the fair chamber where faint dreams, like cool and shadowy vales, divide the billowed hours of love. Again the miracle of birth —the pain and joy, the kiss of welcome and the cradle song, drowning the drowsy prattle of a babe.

And then sense of obligation and of wrong—pity for those who toil and weep—tears for the imprisoned and despised— love for the generous dead, and in the heart the rapture of a high resolve.

And then ambition, with its lust of pelf and place and power, longing to put upon its breast distinction's worthless badge. Then keener thoughts of men and eyes that see behind the smiling mask of craft—flattered no more by the obstreperous cringe of gain and greed—knowing the uselessness of hoarded gold and honor bought from those who charge the usury of self-respect—of power that only bends a coward's knees and forces from the lips of fear the lies of praise. Knowing at last the unstudied gesture of esteem, the reverend eyes made rich with honest thoughts and holding high above all other things—high as hope's great throbbing star about the darkness of the dead—the love of wife and child and friend.

Then locks of gray and growing love of other days and half-remembered things—then holding withered hands of those who first held his, while over dim and loving eyes death softly presses down the lids of rest.

And so, locking in marriage vows his children's hands, and crossing others on the breasts of peace, with daughters' babes upon his knees, the white hair mingling with the gold, he journeys on from day to day to the horizon where the dusk is waiting for that night—sitting by the holy hearth of home, as the last embers change from red to gray, he falls asleep within the arms of her he worshiped and adored, feeling upon his pallid lips love's last and holiest kiss.

PAUSE AND THOUGHT EMPHASIS.

[Frequently there is desired for a thought an importance more than the normal pause gives to it. This increase of emphasis can be obtained by an increase of pause. By this pause the speaker in spirit says: "Let this sink into your minds." In the following an increase of pause deepens the impression of absurdity: "It is hard to cure a hurt in a Frenchman's head, but easy in his leg; it is hard to cure a hurt in an Englishman's leg, but easy in his head."]

Bacon's Philosophy.

ROBERT G. INGERSOLL.

It seems to have been taken for granted that if Shakespeare was not the author of the great dramas, Lord Bacon must have been. It has been claimed that Bacon was the greatest philosopher of his time. And yet in reading his works we find that there was in his mind a strange mingling of foolishness and philosophy. He takes pains to tell us, and to write it down for the benefit of posterity that "snow is colder than water, because it hath more spirit in it, and that quicksilver is the coldest of all metals, because it is the fullest of spirit."

He stated that he hardly believed that you could contract air by putting opium on top of the weather-glass, and gave the following reason: "I conceive that opium and the like make spirits fly rather by malignity than by cold." The great philosopher gave the following recipe for staunching blood: "Thrust the part that bleedeth into the body of a capon, new ripped and bleeding. This will staunch the blood. The blood, as it seemeth, sucking and drawing up by similitude of substance the blood it meeteth with, and so itself going back." The philosopher also records this important fact: "Divers witches among heathen and Christians have fed upon man's flesh to aid, as it seemeth, their imagination with high and foul vapors."

Lord Bacon was not only a philosopher, but he was a biologist, as appears from the following: "As for living creatures, it is certain that their vital spirits are a substance compounded of an airy and flamy matter, and although air and flame being free will not mingle, yet bound in by a body that hath some fixing, will." Now and then the inventor of induction reasons by analogy. He says: "As snow and ice holpen, and their cold activated by nitre or salt, will turn water into ice, so it may be it will turn wood or stiff clay into stone." Bacon seems to have been a believer in the transmutation of metals, and solemnly gives a formula for turning silver or copper into gold. He also believed in the transmutation of plants, and had arrived at such a height in entomology that he informed the world that "insects have no blood."

It is claimed that he was a great observer, and as evidence of this he recorded the wonderful fact that "tobacco cut and dried by the fire loses weight"; that "bears in the winter wax fat in sleep, though they eat nothing"; that "tortoises have no bones"; that "there is a kind of stone, if ground and put in the water where cattle drink, the cows will give more milk"; that "it is hard to cure a hurt in a Frenchman's head, but easy in his leg; that it is hard to cure a hurt in an Englishman's leg, but easy in his head"; that "wounds made with brass weapons are easier to cure than those made with iron"; that "lead will multiply and increase, as in statues buried in the ground"; and that "the rainbow touching anything causeth a sweet smell."

PAUSE AND SILENT REPLY.

[While not wishing that the reply be oral, a speaker frequently asks his audience a question which he expects them to think over and silently answer. Where this is desired there must be increase of the normal pause. Ex. (Sydney Smith): ''Has your system of exclusion made Ireland rich? Has it made Ireland loyal? Has it made Ireland free?'']

Secession.

DANIEL WEBSTER.

SECESSION! Peaceable Secession! Sir, your eyes and mine are never destined to see that miracle. The dismemberment of this vast country without convulsion! The breaking up of the fountains of the great deep without ruffling the surface! Who is so foolish—I beg everybody's pardon—as to expect to see any such thing? Sir, he who sees these states, now revolving in harmony around a common centre, and expects to see them quit their places and fly off without convulsion, may look the next hour to see the heavenly bodies rush from their spheres and jostle against each other in the realms of space, without producing the crush of the universe. There can be no such thing as a peaceable secession. Peaceable secession is an utter impossibility. Is the great Constitution under which we live here—covering this whole country—is it to be thawed and melted away by secession, as the snows on the mountain melt under the influence of a vernal sun—disappear almost unobserved, and die off? No, sir! no, sir! I will not state what might produce the disruption of the states; but, sir, I see it as plainly as I see the sun in heaven—I see that disruption must produce such a war as I will not describe in its twofold characters.

Peaceable secession! peaceable secession! The concurrent agreement of all the members of this great Republic to separate! A voluntary separation with alimony on the one side and on the other. Why, what would be the result? Where is

the line to be drawn? What states are to secede? What is
to remain American? What am I to be?—an American no
longer? Where is the flag of the Republic to remain? Where
is the eagle still to tower? or is he to cower, and shrink, and
fall to the ground? Why, sir, our ancestors—our fathers,
and our grandfathers, those of them that are yet living among
us with prolonged lives—would rebuke and reproach us; and
our children, and our grandchildren, would cry out, shame
upon us! if we, of this generation, should dishonor these
ensigns of the power of the government, and the harmony of
the Union, which is every day felt among us with so much
joy and gratitude. What is to become of the army? What
is to become of the navy? What is to become of the public
lands? How is each of the thirty states to defend itself?

Sir, I am ashamed to pursue this line of remark. I dislike
it—I have an utter disgust for it. I would rather hear of
natural blasts and mildews, war, pestilence, and famine, than
to hear gentlemen talk of secession. To break up! to break
up this great government! to dismember this great country!
to astonish Europe with an act of folly, such as Europe for
two centuries has never beheld in any government! No, sir!
no, sir! There will be no secession.

PAUSE AND LAPSE OF TIME.

[Often in literature and speech, for various reasons, there is
implied a lapse of time. To effectively convey this the speaker must
increase the length of pause beyond the normal. Ex. (Bible): ''And
he cried, 'Cause every man to go out from me.' And there stood
no man with him.'']

The Prodigal Son.

BIBLE.

And he said, A certain man had two sons; and the younger
of them said to his father, Father, give me the portion of

goods that falleth to me. And he divided unto them his living. And not many days after, the younger son gathered all together, and took his journey into a far country, and there wasted his substance with riotous living. And when he had spent all, there arose a mighty famine in that land; and he began to be in want.

And he went and joined himself to a citizen of that country; and he sent him into his fields to feed swine. And he would fain have filled his belly with the husks that the swine did eat; and no man gave unto him. And when he came to himself, he said, How many hired servants of my father's have bread enough and to spare, and I perish with hunger! I will arise and go to my father, and will say unto him, Father, I have sinned against heaven, and before thee, and am no more worthy to be called thy son: make me as one of thy hired servants.

And he arose, and came to his father. But when he was yet a great way off, his father saw him and had compassion, and ran, and fell on his neck and kissed him. And the son said unto him, Father, I have sinned against heaven, and in thy sight, and am no more worthy to be called thy son. But the father said to his servants, Bring forth the best robe, and put it on him; and put a ring on his hand, and shoes on his feet: and bring hither the fatted calf and kill it; and let us eat and be merry: for this my son was dead, and is alive again; he was lost, and is found. And they began to be merry.

Now his elder son was in the field: and as he came and drew nigh to the house, he heard music and dancing. And he called one of the servants, and asked what these things meant. And he said unto him, Thy brother is come; and thy father hath killed the fatted calf because he hath received him safe and sound. And he was angry, and would not go in: therefore came his father out, and entreated him.

And he answering, said to his father, Lo, these many years do I serve thee, neither transgressed I at any time thy commandment; and yet thou never gavest me a kid, that I might make merry with my friends; but as soon as this thy son was come which hath devoured thy living with harlots, thou hast killed for him the fatted calf. And he said unto him, Son, thou art ever with me; and all that I have is thine. It was meet that we should make merry, and be glad: for this thy brother was dead, and is alive again; and was lost and is found.

PAUSE AND UNSUPPORTED STATEMENT.

[Where a statement (unless self-evident) is unsupported, there should be an increase in pause to give time for the listener to verify the assertion by reference to his experience. As no proof is offered of the following, time must be given to recall some concrete instance or instances, corroborative. Ex.: "The greatest men have been martyrs who, in order to pull down the evil, have had themselves to perish."]

The Poetic Principle.

EDGAR ALLEN POE.

An immortal instinct deep within the spirit of man is a sense of the Beautiful. This it is which administers to his delight in the manifold forms, and sounds, and odors, and sentiments, amid which he exists. And just as the lily is repeated in the lake, or the eyes of Amaryllis in the mirror, so is the mere oral or written repetition of these forms, and sounds, and colors, and odors, and sentiments, a duplicate source of delight. But this mere repetition is not poetry. He who shall simply sing with however glowing enthusiasm, or with however vivid a truth of description of the sights, and sounds, and odors, and colors, and sentiments, which greet him in common with all mankind—he, I say, has yet failed to prove his divine title. There is still a something in the distance which he has been unable to attain. We have still a thirst unquenchable, to allay which he has not shown us the crystal springs. This thirst belongs to the immortality of man. It is at once a consequence and an indication of his perennial existence. It is the desire of the moth for the star. It is no mere appreciation of the Beauty before us, but a wild effort to reach the Beauty above. Inspired by an ecstatic prescience of the glories beyond the grave, we struggle by multiform combinations among the things and thoughts of Time to attain a portion of that Loveliness whose very elements perhaps appertain to eternity alone. And thus when by Poetry, or when by Music, the most entrancing of the Poetic moods, we find ourselves melted into tears, we weep then, not as the Abbate Gravina supposes, through excess of pleasure, but through a certain petulant, impatient sorrow at our inability to grasp now, wholly, here on earth, at once and forever, those divine and rapturous joys of which through the poem, or through the music, we attain to but brief and indeterminate glimpses. The struggle to apprehend the supernal Loveliness—this struggle, on the part of souls fittingly constituted—has given to the world all that which it has ever been enabled at once to understand and to feel as poetic.

PAUSE AND IMPRESSIVENESS.

[Frequently a speaker wishes an idea not only to be understood but to be deeply felt. In such cases the pause must be long enough to permit of the necessary emotional association. Ex. (Henry Ward Beecher): "His (Lincoln's) life now is grafted upon the infinite, and will be fruitful as no earthly life can be."]

Death of Garfield.

JAMES G. BLAINE.

Surely, if happiness can ever come from the honors or triumphs of this world, that quiet July morning James A.

Garfield may well have been a happy man. No foreboding of evil haunted him; no slightest premonition of danger clouded his sky. His terrible fate was upon him in an instant. One moment he stood erect, strong, confident in the years stretching peacefully before him; the next he lay wounded, bleeding, helpless, doomed to weary weeks of torture, to silence and the grave.

Great in life, he was surpassingly great in death. For no cause, in the very frenzy of wantonness and wickedness by the red hand of murder, he was thrust from the full tide of this world's interests, from its hopes, its aspirations, its victories, into the visible presence of death, and he did not quail. Not alone for the one short moment in which stunned and dazed he could give up life, hardly aware of its relinquishment, but through days of deadly languor, through weeks of agony that was not less agony because silently borne, with clear sight and calm courage he looked into his open grave. What blight and ruin met his anguished eyes whose lips may tell! What brilliant broken plans! What baffled high ambitions! What sundering of strong, warm, manhood's friendships. What bitter rending of sweet household ties!

Behind him, a proud expectant nation; a great host of sustaining friends; a cherished and happy mother, wearing the full rich honors of her early toil and tears; the wife of his youth whose whole life lay in his; the little boys not yet emerged from childhood's days of frolic; the fair young daughter; the sturdy sons just springing into closest companionship, claiming every day and every day rewarding a father's love and care; and in his heart the eager, rejoicing power to meet all demands. Before him, desolation and darkness, and his soul was not shaken.

His countrymen were thrilled with instant, profound and universal sympathy. Though masterful in his mortal weakness, enshrined in the prayers of a world, all the love and all the sympathy could not share with him his suffering. He trod the winepress alone. With unfaltering front he faced death. With unfailing tenderness he took leave of life. Above the demoniac hiss of the assassin's bullet he heard the voice of God. With supple resignation he bowed to the Divine Decree.

PAUSE AND THE GATHERING AND CONTROL OF EMOTION.

[Some sentiments, to be effectively expressed, require time for the gathering of the emotion. The following requires an increased pause preceding "before" to enable the speaker to gather the awe, destiny and inspiration that must be exhibited in every word: "Sir, before God I believe the hour is come." Sometimes there is a tendency for an emotion to master the speaker and overwhelm his utterance, as in the lines "I said all well," and, "Ah, Hal, I'll try," in the selection under this head. In such cases increased pause is required in which to control the feeling.]

Our Folks.

ETHEL LYNN.

"Hi! Harry Holly! Halt,—and tell
    A fellow just a thing or two;
You've had a furlough, been to see
    How all the folks in Jersey do.
It's months ago since I was there,—
    I, and a bullet from Fair Oaks.
When you were home,—old comrade, say,
    Did you see any of our folks?

You did? Shake hands,—Oh, ain't I glad;
    For if I do look grim and rough,
I've got some feelin'—People think
    A soldier's heart is mighty tough;
But, Harry, when the bullets fly,

And hot saltpetre flames and smokes,
While whole battalions lie afield,
   One's apt to think about his folks.

And so you saw them—when? and where?
   The old man—is he hearty yet?
And mother—does she fade at all?
   Or does she seem to pine and fret
For me? And Sis?—has she grown tall?
And did you see her friend—you know
   That Annie Moss—(How this pipe chokes!)
Where did you see her?—tell me, Hal,
   A lot of news about our folks.

You saw them in the church, you say;
   It's likely, for they're always there.
Not Sunday? no? A funeral? Who?
   Who, Harry? how you shake and stare!
All well, you say, and all were out.
   What ails you, Hal? Is this a hoax?
Why don't you tell me like a man
   What is the matter with our folks?"

"I said all well, old comrade, true;
   I say all well, for He knows best
Who takes the young ones in His arms
   Before the sun goes to the west.
The axe-man Death deals right and left,
   And flowers fall as well as oaks;
And so—fair Annie blooms no more!
   And that's the matter with your folks.

See, this long curl was kept for you;
   And this white blossom from her breast.

And here—your sister Bessie wrote
  A letter, telling all the rest.
Bear up, old friend." Nobody speaks;
  Only the old camp-raven croaks,
And soldiers whisper: "Boys, be still;
  There's some bad news from Grainger's folks."

He turns his back—the only foe
  That ever saw it—on this grief,
And, as men will, keeps down the tears
  Kind Nature sends to Woe's relief.
Then answers he, "Ah! Hal, I'll try,
  But in my throat there's something chokes,
Because, you see, I've thought so long
  To count her in among our folks.

I s'pose she must be happy now,
  But still I will keep thinking too,
I could have kept all trouble off
  By being tender, kind, and true.
But maybe not. She's safe up there,
  And when His hand deals other strokes,
She'll stand by heaven's gate, I know,
  And wait to welcome in our folks."

Break! Break! Break!

ALFRED TENNYSON.

Break, break, break,
  On thy cold gray stones, O Sea!
And I would that my tongue could utter
  The thoughts that arise in me.

Oh, well for the fisherman's boy,
  That he shouts with his sister at play!

Oh, well for the sailor lad,
    That he sings in his boat on the bay!

And the stately ships go on
    To their haven under the hill;
But O for the touch of a vanished hand,
    And the sound of a voice that is still.

Break, break, break,
    At the foot of thy crags, O Sea!
But the tender grace of a day that is dead
    Will never come back to me.

PAUSE AND THE SUBSIDENCE OF EMOTION.

[The subsidence of emotion manifests itself by increased pause. In the following, increased pause after ''dwelling'' is demanded to give time for the subsidence of the deeply stirred feelings of Spartacus: ''That very night the Romans landed on our coast. I saw the breast that had nourished me trampled by the hoof of the war horse; the bleeding body of my father flung amid the blazing rafters of our dwelling.'']

Spartacus to the Gladiators.

E. KELLOGG.

Today I killed a man in the arena; and, when I broke his helmet clasps, behold! he was my friend. He knew me, smiled faintly, gasped, and died; the same sweet smile upon his lips that I had marked, when, in adventurous boyhood, we scaled the lofty cliff to pluck the first ripe grapes, and bear them home in childish triumph! I told the prætor that the dead man had been my friend, generous and brave, and I begged that I might bear away the body, to burn it on a funeral pile, and mourn over its ashes. Ay, upon my knees, amid the dust and blood of the arena, I begged that poor boon, while all the assembled maids and matrons, and the holy virgins they call Vestals, and the rabble, shouted in derision, deeming it rare sport, forsooth, to see Rome's fiercest gladiator turn pale and tremble at sight of that piece of bleeding clay. And the prætor drew back, as if I were pollution, and sternly said, "Let the carrion rot; there are no noble men but Romans." And so, fellow-gladiators, must you, and so must I, die like dogs. O Rome, Rome, thou hast been a tender nurse to me. Ay, thou hast given to that poor, gentle, timid shepherd lad, who never knew a harsher tone than a flute-note, muscles of iron and a heart of flint; taught him to drive the sword through plaited mail and links of rugged brass, and warm it in the marrow of his foe;—to gaze into the glaring eye-balls of the fierce Numidian lion, even as a boy upon a laughing girl. And he shall pay thee back, until the yellow Tiber is red as frothing wine, and in its deepest ooze thy lifeblood lies curdled.

Ye stand here now like giants, as ye are. The strength of brass is in your toughened sinews; but tomorrow some Roman Adonis, breathing sweet perfume from his curly locks, shall with his lily fingers pat your red brawn, and bet his sesterces upon your blood! Hark! hear ye yon lion roaring in his den? 'Tis three days since he tasted flesh, but tomorrow he shall break his fast upon yours,—and a dainty meal for him ye will be! If ye are *beasts,* then stand here like fat oxen, waiting for the butcher's knife. If ye are *men,* —follow me! Strike down yon guard, gain the mountain passes, and there do bloody work, as did your sires at old Thermopylæ. Is Sparta dead? Is the old Grecian spirit frozen in your veins, that you do crouch and cower like a belabored hound beneath his master's lash? O comrades, warriors, Thracians,—if we must fight, let us fight for *ourselves!* If we must slaughter, let us slaughter our *oppressors!* If we must die, let it be under the clear sky, by the bright waters, in noble, honorable battle!

SELECTIONS

STUDIES IN PROMINENCE

Prominence is the symbol of proportion. It proclaims to the listener the *relative value* of words, groups, clauses, sentences, paragraphs and parts. Its judicious use results in the harmony of the whole.

Prominence is secured mainly by what has been called *emphasis,* that is, by increasing the force or intensity upon a word or group of words. Sometimes Prominence is attained by increase of pause, or again, by a combination of both pause and emphasis, or by pause, emphasis and tone.

Prominence is governed by one's judgment as to what the author intended. That which we believe is vital will receive such prominence as to show that it is vital, that which, comparatively, is unimportant, will receive such relative unimportance in delivery as to make it so valued by the listener.

Analysis of our daily conversation will reveal that those ideas which, to a greater or less extent, are repetitions, are not given prominence, while those which are presented to the listener for the first time are made to stand out. With rare exceptions, we seek prominence for the *new thought*. (See discussion and example in a preceding section.)

Prominence necessarily is associated with *tone*. This will

be perceived in the study of the selections that follow and of those under the Dominant Tones.

WORD PROMINENCE.

[Prominence frequently manifests itself by emphasis upon individual words. In these single terms the speaker finds the main force of his idea, and, therefore, gives them a corresponding importance in delivery. Ex.: "Your government is a government of *manhood.*"]

Liberty.

N. DWIGHT HILLIS.

Society's greatest peril today is the demagogues who teach and the ignorant classes who believe that there is such a thing as liberty. The planets have no liberty; they follow their sun. The seas know no liberty; they follow the moon in tidal waves. When the river refuses to keep within its banks, it becomes a curse and a destruction. It is the stream that is restrained by its banks that turns mill-wheels for men. The clouds, too, have their beauty, in that they are led forth in ranks and columns, generaled by the night winds. And in proportion as things pass from littleness towards largeness, they go toward obedience to law. Because the dead leaf obeys nothing, it flutters down from its bough, giving but tardy recognition to the law of gravity; while our great earth, covered with cities and civilization, is instantly responsive to gravity's law. Indeed, he who disobeys any law of nature flings himself athwart her wheels, to be crushed to powder.

And if disobedience is destruction, obedience is liberty. Obeying the law of steam, man has an engine. Obeying the law of fire, he has warmth. Obeying the law of speech, he has eloquence. Obeying the law of sound thinking, he has leadership. Obeying the law of Christ, he has character. The stone obeys one law, gravity, and is without motion. The worm obeys two laws, and has movement. The bird obeys three laws, and can fly as well as stand or walk. And as man increases the number of laws he obeys, he increases in richness of nature, in wealth, in strength, in influence. Nature loves paradoxes, and this is her chiefest paradox—he who stoops to wear the yoke of law becomes the child of liberty, while he who will be free from God's laws wears a ball and chain through all his years. Philosophy reaches its highest fruition in Christ's principle: "Love is the fulfilment of the law."

On the American War.

LORD CHATHAM.

I cannot, my Lords, I will not, join in congratulation on misfortune and disgrace. This, my Lords, is a perilous and tremendous moment. It is not a time for adulation; the smoothness of flattery cannot save us in this rugged and awful crisis. It is now necessary to instruct the throne in the language of truth. We must, if possible, dispel the delusion and darkness which envelop it; and display, in its full danger and genuine colors, the ruin which is brought to our doors. Can ministers still presume to expect support in their infatuation? Can parliament be so dead to its dignity and duty as to give its support to measures thus obtruded and forced upon it? Measures, my Lords, which have reduced this late flourishing empire to scorn and contempt! "But yesterday and Britain might have stood against the world; now, none so poor as do her reverence!" The people, whom we at first despised as rebels, but whom we now acknowledge as enemies, are abetted against us, supplied with every military store, have their interests consulted, and their ambassadors entertained, by our inveterate enemy; and ministers do not—and dare not—interpose with dignity or effect.

The desperate state of our army abroad is in part known. No man more highly esteems and honors the British troops than I do; I know their virtues and their valor; I know they can achieve anything but impossibilities; and I know that the conquest of British America is an impossibility. You cannot, my Lords, you cannot conquer America. What is your present situation there? We do not know the worst; but we know that in three campaigns we have done nothing, and suffered much. You may swell every expense, accumulate every assistance, and extend your traffic to the shambles of every German despot; your attempts will be forever vain and impotent—doubly so, indeed, from this mercenary aid on which you rely; for it irritates, to an incurable resentment, the minds of your adversaries, to overrun them with the mercenary sons of rapine and plunder, devoting them and their possessions to the rapacity of hireling cruelty. If I were an American, as I am an Englishman, while a foreign troop was landed in my country, I never would lay down my arms; never, never, never!

RECURRENT PROMINENCE.

[At times a speaker seeks again and again to focus the mind of the listener upon a given idea; frequently, in such cases, the speaker uses the same word or group of words at each repetition. Prominence, then, falls upon the repeated word or phrase. Ex. (Adolph Monod): ''God is love. Love is his essense, his substance, his life. Love sums up all his works and explains all his ways. Love inspired him to creation of a holy, and to the redemption of a fallen race. Love prevailed over nothingness to give us existence, and triumphed over sin to give us glory. Love is the object of the admiration of the angels, and will be ours in eternity.'']

Force.

JOHN M. THURSTON.

There are those who say that the affairs of Cuba are not the affairs of the United States; who insist that we can stand idly by and see that island devastated and depopulated, its business interests destroyed, its commercial intercourse with us cut off, its people starved, degraded and enslaved. It may be the naked legal right of the United States to stand thus idly by. I have the legal right to pass along the street and see a helpless dog stamped into the earth under the heels of a ruffian. I can pass by and say, that is not my dog. I can sit in my comfortable parlor, and through my plate-glass window see a fiend outraging a helpless woman near by, and I can legally say, this is no affair of mine— it is not happening on my premises. But if I do, I am a coward and a cur, unfit to live, and, God knows, unfit to die.

And yet I cannot protect the dog nor save the woman without the exercise of force. We cannot intervene and save Cuba without the exercise of force, and force means war; war means blood. The lowly Nazarene on the shores of Galilee preached the divine doctrine of love, "Peace on earth, good will toward men." Not peace on earth at the expense of liberty and humanity. Not good will toward men who despoil, enslave, degrade and starve to death their fellow-men. I believe in the doctrine of Christ. I believe in the doctrine of peace; but men must have liberty before there can come abiding peace. When has a battle for humanity and liberty ever been won except by force? What barricade of wrong, injustice, and oppression has ever been carried except by force?

Force compelled the signature of unwilling royalty to the great Magna Charta; force put life into the Declaration of Independence and made effective the Emancipation Proclamation; force waved the flag of revolution over Bunker Hill and marked the snows of Valley Forge with blood-stained feet; force held the broken line of Shiloh, climbed the flame-swept hill at Chattanooga, and stormed the clouds on Lookout Heights; force marched with Sherman to the sea, rode with Sheridan in the Valley of the Shenandoah, and gave

Grant victory at Appomattox; force saved the Union, kept the stars in the flag, made "niggars" men. The time for God's force has come again. Let the impassioned lips of American patriots once more take up the song:

In the beauty of the lilies Christ was born across the sea,
With a glory in His bosom that transfigured you and me.
As He died to make men holy, let us die to make men free,
For God is marching on.

Others may hesitate, others may procrastinate, others may plead for further diplomatic negotiation, which means delay, but for me, I am ready to act now, and for my action I am ready to answer to my conscience, my country, and my God.

GROUP PROMINENCE.

[Frequently prominence is demanded for a group of words. This occurs when each word of the group forms an essential part of the idea, as, "The usurpation of authority is unwise." Here it is not "usurpation," not "authority," but "usurpation of authority" that is unwise, and, that, therefore, demands prominence.]

The Sources of Poetry.

WILLIAM CULLEN BRYANT.

That there is something in whatever is unknown and inscrutable which strongly excites the imagination and awes the heart, particularly when connected with things of unusual vastness and grandeur, is not to be denied. But I deny that much of this mystery is apparent to an ignorant age, and I maintain that no small degree of inquiry and illumination is necessary to enable the mind to perceive it. He who takes all things to be as they appear, who supposes the earth to be a great plane, the sun a moving ball of fire, the heavens a vault of sapphire, and the stars a multitude of little flames lighted up in its arches—what does he think of mysteries or care for them? But enlighten him a little further. Teach him that the earth is an immense sphere; that the wide land whose bounds he knows so imperfectly is an isle in the great oceans that flow all over it; talk to him of the boundlessness of the skies, and the army of worlds that move through them, and by means of the knowledge that you communicate, you have opened to him a vast field of the unknown and the wonderful. Thus it ever was and ever will be with the human mind; everything which it knows introduces to its observation a greater multitude of things which it does not know; the clearing up of one mystery conducts it to another; all its discoveries are bounded by a circle of doubt and ignorance which is wide in proportion to the knowledge it enfolds. It is a pledge of the immortal destinies of the human intellect that it is forever drawn by a strong attraction to the darker edge of this circle, and forever attempting to penetrate the obscurities beyond. The old world, then, is welcome to its mysteries; we need not envy it on that account; for, in addition to our superior knowledge and as a consequence of it, we have even more of them than it, and they are loftier, deeper and more spiritual.

But the mythologies of antiquity! I cannot but think that human beings, placed among the things of this earth, with their affections and sympathies, their joys and sorrows, and the accident of fortune to which they are liable, are infinitely a better subject for poetry than any imaginary race of creatures whatever. Let the fountain tell me of the flocks that have drank at it; of the village girls that have gathered spring flowers on its margin; the traveler that has slaked his thirst there in the hot noon, and blessed its waters; the schoolboy that has pulled the nuts from the hazels that hang over it as it leaps and sparkles in its cool basin; let it speak of youth and health and purity and gladness, and I care not for the naiad that pours it out. If it must have a religious association, let it murmur of the invisible goodness that fills and feeds its reservoirs in the darkness of the earth. The admirers of poetry, then, may give up the ancient mythology without a sigh. Its departure has left us what is better than all it has taken away; it has left us men and women; it has left us the creatures and the things of God's universe to the simple charm of which the cold splendor of that system blinded men's eyes, and to the magnificence of which the rapid progress of science is every day adding new wonders and glories. It has left us also a more sublime and affecting religion, whose truths are broader, higher, nobler, than any outlook to which its random conjectures ever attained.

PROMINENCE OF PARTS TO WHOLE.

[Besides the prominence of words and groups in relation to the separate ideas, there is also their prominence in relation to the whole composition. Thus, in the line, "Then they rode back" (Charge of the Light Brigade), the "then" requires prominence, not only because of its relation to that group but because it helps to emphasize the story of the whole poem. "Then," that is, after the soldiers had done their duty and not till then, "they rode back." Also (as shown under Pause and Leading Statement), those ideas which are the leading ones of the theme should be given prominence, in order to make clear their relative importance.]

Hamlet's Advice to the Players.

WILLIAM SHAKESPEARE.

Speak the speech, I pray you, as I pronounced it to you, trippingly on the tongue; but if you mouth it, as many of your players do, I had as lief the town crier spoke my lines. Nor do not saw the air too much with your hand, thus; but use all gently; for in the very torrent, tempest, and, as I may say, whirlwind of your passion, you must acquire and beget a temperance that may give it smoothness. O, it offends me to the soul to hear a robustious periwig-pated fellow tear a passion to tatters, to very rags, to split the ears of the

SELECTIONS 321

groundlings, who, for the most part, are capable of nothing but inexplicable dumb-shows and noise. I would have such a fellow whipped for o'erdoing Termagant; it out-herods Herod; pray you, avoid it.

Be not too tame neither, but let your own discretion be your tutor; suit the action to the word, the word to the action; with this special observance, that you o'erstep not the modesty of nature; for anything so overdone is from the purpose of playing, whose end, both at the first and now, was and is, to hold, as 'twere, the mirror up to nature; to show virtue her own feature, scorn her own image, and the very age and body of the time his form and pressure. Now this overdone or come tardy off, though it make the unskilful laugh, cannot but make the judicious grieve; the censure of the which one must in your allowance o'erweigh a whole theatre of others. O, there be players that I have seen play, and heard others praise, and that highly, not to speak it profanely, that neither having the accent of Christians nor the gait of Christian, pagan, nor man, have so strutted and bellowed, that I have thought some of nature's journeymen had made men, and not made them well, they imitated humanity so abominably.

O, reform it altogether. And let those that play your clowns speak no more than is set down for them. For there be of them that will themselves laugh, to set on some quantity of barren spectators to laugh too, though in the meantime some necessary question of the play be then to be considered. That's villainous, and shows a most pitiful ambition in the fool that uses it. Go, make you ready.

The Relative Importance of Activities.

HERBERT SPENCER.

Our first step must obviously be to classify, in the order of their importance, the leading kinds of activity which constitute human life. The actions and precautions by which, from moment to moment, we secure personal safety, must clearly take precedence of others. Could there be a man, ignorant as an infant of all surrounding objects and movements, or how to guide himself among them, he would pretty certainly lose his life the first time he went into the street, notwithstanding any amount of learning he might have on other matters. And as entire ignorance in all other directions would be less promptly fatal than entire ignorance in this direction, it must be admitted that knowledge immediately conducive to self-preservation is of primary importance.

That next after direct self-preservation comes the indirect self-preservation which consists in acquiring the means of living, none will question. That a man's industrial functions must be considered before his parental ones, is manifest from the fact that, speaking generally, the discharge of the parental functions is made possible only by the previous discharge of the industrial ones. The power of self-maintenance necessarily preceding the power of maintaining offspring, it follows that knowledge needful for self-maintenance has stronger claims than knowledge needful for family welfare—is second in value to none save knowledge needful for immediate self-preservation.

As the family comes before the State in order of time—as the bringing up of children is possible before the State exists, or when it has ceased to be, whereas the State is rendered possible only by the bringing up of children; it follows that the duties of the parent demand closer attention than those of the citizen. Or, to use a further argument—since the goodness of a society ultimately depends on the nature of its citizens; and since the nature of its citizens is more modifiable by early training than by anything else; we must conclude that the welfare of the family underlies the welfare of society. And hence, knowledge directly conducing to the first, must take precedence of knowledge directly conducing to the last.

Those various forms of pleasurable occupation which fill up the leisure left by graver occupations—the enjoyments of music, poetry, painting, etc.—manifestly imply a pre-existing society. Not only is a considerable development of them impossible without a long-established social union, but their very subject-matter consists in great part of social sentiments and sympathies. Not only does society supply the conditions to their growth, but also the ideas and sentiments they express. And, consequently, that part of human conduct which constitutes good citizenship is of more moment than that which goes out in accomplishments or exercise of the tastes; and, in education, preparation for the one must rank before preparation for the other.

Such, then, we repeat, is something like the rational order of subordination: that education which prepares for direct self-preservation; that which prepares for indirect self-preservation; that which prepares for parenthood; that which prepares for citizenship; that which prepares for the miscellaneous refinements of life.

PROMINENCE AND INTEREST.

[Prominence is a valuable medium by which there can be aroused in the listener a keener interest. In ''King Robert of Sicily,'' in proportion to the intensity of defiance in the line, ''There is no power can push me from my throne,'' so is the interest increased in the outcome.]

The Jew.

ZEBULON VANCE.

The Jew is beyond doubt the most remarkable man of this world, past or present. Of all the stories of the sons of men

there is none so wild, so wonderful, so full of extreme muta-
tion, so replete with suffering and horror, so abounding in
extraordinary providences, so overflowing with scenic romance.
There is no man who approaches him in the extent and character of the influence which he has exercised over the human
family.   His history is the history of our civilization and
progress in this world, and our faith and hope in that which
is to come.   From him have we derived the form and pattern
of all that is excellent on earth or in heaven.

Though dead as a nation—as we speak of nations—they
yet live.   Their ideas fill the world and move the wheels of
its progress, even as the sun, when he sinks behind the western
hills, yet fills the heavens with the remnants of his glory.   As
the destruction of matter in one form is made necessary to
its resurrection in another, so it would seem that the perish-
ing of the Jewish nationality was necessary to the universal
acceptance and the everlasting establishment of Jewish ideas.
Never before was there an instance of such a general rejection of the person and character, and acceptance of the
doctrines and dogmas of a people.

We admire with unlimited admiration the Greek and
Roman, but reject with contempt their crude and beastly
divinities.   We affect to despise the Jew, but accept and adore
the pure conception of a God which he taught us, and whose
real existence the history of the Jew more than all else
establishes.

The Jews, under most adverse circumstances, made their
mark—a high and noble mark—in every department of human
affairs.   Christian clergymen have sat at the feet of their
rabbis to be taught the mystic learning of the East; Senates
have been enraptured by the eloquence of Jewish orators;
courts have been convinced by the acumen and learning of
Jewish lawyers; vast throngs excited to the wildest enthusi-

asm by Jewish histrionic and aesthetic art; Jewish science has helped to number the stars in their courses, to loose the bands of Orion and to guide Arcturus with his sons.

Jewish literature has delighted and instructed all classes of mankind, and the world has listened with rapture and with tears to Jewish melody and song. For never since its spirit was evoked under the shadow of the vines on the hills of Palestine to soothe the melancholy of her king has Judah's harp, whether in freedom or captivity, in sorrow or joy, ceased to wake the witchery of its tuneful strings.

Time forbids that I should even name the greatest of those who have distinguished themselves and made good their claim to rank with the foremost of earth. No section of the human family can boast a greater list of men and women entitled to be placed among the true children of genius—going to make up the primacy of our race—in every branch of human affairs, in every phase of human civilization. Mr. Draper says that for four hundred years of the Middle Ages—ages more dark and terrible to them than to any others—they took the most philosophical and comprehensive view of all European people.

On the whole, and after due deliberation, I think it may be truthfully said that there is more of average wealth, intelligence and morality among the Jewish people than there is among any other nation of equal numbers in the world! If this be true—if it be half true—when we consider the circumstances under which it has all been brought about, it constitutes in the eyes of thinking men the most remarkable moral phenomenon ever exhibited by any portion of the human family. For not only has the world given the Jew no help, but all that he has ever received, and that but rarely, was to be left alone.

PROMINENCE AND IMITATION.

[Perhaps in no way is a thing made to stand out so prominently as by its imitation, and this fact demands most careful consideration. When and in what degree to imitate is one of the most vital questions in expression. Imitation embraces the reproduction of character, imitating the voice, the dialect, the attitude, the gesture, the appearance, dress, manner, walk; the reproduction of actions such as stumbling, striking, throwing, struggling, and the like; the reproduction of shape, dimensions, direction.

Imitation restricts the listener's imagination. To reproduce a man's exact voice, to show by imitation how a man walked or bowed, to reproduce precise length or shape or size, prevents the listener from using his imagination. Imitation says to the listener: "What you see is a literal reproduction of the thing itself in all detail. Nothing is left for you to do but to use your eyes and ears."

To know when and where to imitate becomes a comparatively easy matter if a student will first determine the author's united aim. What does he wish to make most prominent? In describing Scrooge, Dickens says: "Nobody ever stopped him in the street to say, with gladsome looks, 'My dear Scrooge, how are you? When will you come to see me?'" Here the author is not desirous of making prominent the manner in which these words could be spoken, but the matter. Therefore there is no imitation. On the other hand, in the description of the death of little Joe (Dickens), it is clear the author wishes to make prominent the personality of little Joe, hence imitation of Joe's manner is warranted. The rule that must guide the speaker is: *Leave to the listener's imagination everything which the speaker's imitation would fail to fully convey or would misconvey or overconvey, or which in itself is self-evident, and as a corollary of this—decrease imitation and increase suggestion in proportion to the culture of the listener.*

Throughout each selection under this heading the student should determine carefully whether imitation is demanded, and if so, the kind and degree.]

Dialect and Humor.

MELLVILLE D. LANDON.

All dialects are funny. Why? They are a language deformed. I could tell you a simple story in plain English-

and you wouldn't smile at all, and then I could tell that same story in an Irish, Scotch, Dutch or negro dialect, and you would all burst out laughing.

To illustrate the fun of dialect:

One frosty morning I met a German, shivering with the cold, and remarked:

"Hans, you have frozen your nose."

"Nein, he froze hisself, Mr. Berkins."

"How did it happen, Hans?"

"I no understand dis ting. I haf carry dot nose dese fordy year, unt he nefer freeze hisself before."

A good instance of Irish brogue, or dialect, is instanced in Mrs. Colonel Kelly's cross-examination in the O'Toolihan suit for damages.

"You claim, Mrs. Colonel Kelly," said the Judge, "that Mrs. O'Toolihan gave you that bruised and blackened face?"

"She did, yer Honor—indade she did, or I'm not Irish born."

"And what you want is damages, Mrs. Kelly?"

"It is damages yez says, yer Honor? Damages! No, bad luck ter the O'Toolihan, I have dam-ages enough. I wants sat-is-fac-shun, begorry!"

Again, an Irish judge, who had been over from the old sod but two years, was examining a Corkonian who had just arrived in New York.

"Phat's yer name, yez spalpeen?" he asked.

"Patrick McGoolihan, yer Honor."

"Is it an Irishman yez are? Begorra, yez shows it by yer sthrong wakeness for the Oirish accint."

"Yis, yer Honor; I was born abroad."

"That's what oi thought, sorr. Yer accint is froightful. Yer not in Oirland, mon, and yez should spake our Unighted Shtates toong more dacently and not be givin' uz yer furren brogue."

Scotch dialect is always dry and funny:

"Dae ye ken," said a member of the Newark Caledonian Club, as he walked homeward from church with a fellow-countryman, "dae ye ken, I think oor minister's in the habit o' gemblin'?"

"What gars ye think that?"

"I'll tell ye, Sandy. Ae Sunday no lang ago in his prayer instead o' saying, 'O, Thou who hast the hearts of kings in Thy hands,' he prayed, 'O, Thou, who has the king of hearts in Thy hands.' What dae ye think o' that?"

"It dis'na look richt," commented the other, shaking his head sadly.

The Chinese dialect always amuses.

Mrs. Van Auken, of Fifth avenue, recently employed a Chinese cook—Ah Sin Foo. When the smiling Chinaman came to take his place, Mrs. Van Auken asked him his name.

"What is your name, John?" commenced the lady.

"Oh! my namee, Ah Sin Foo."

"But I can't remember all that lingo, my man. I'll call you Jimmy."

"Velly wellee. Now what chee namee I callee you?" asked Ah Sin, looking up in sweet simplicity.

"Well, my name is Mrs. Van Auken; call me that."

"Oh, me can no 'member Missee Vannee Auken. Too big piecee namee. I callee you Tommy—Missee Tommy."

The Italian dialect is sweet and laughter-provoking. A New York policeman thus accosted an Italian organ-grinder:

"Have you a permit to grind this organ in the street?"

"No. Me no habbe de permit."

"Then, sir, it becomes my duty to request you to accompany me—"

"Alla righta. Vatta you sing?"

The dialect of the dude is very modern, but we recognize it as a deformed language.

"Going widing to-day, Awthaw?" asked one dude of another.

"Naw. Got to work."

"So sawy, deah boy. What is the—aw—job, eh?"

"Maw's written me a lettaw, and I've—aw—got to wead it befaw I can make another dwaft on haw. Did you evaw heah of such a boah?"

"Nevaw, deah boy, nevaw."

The deformed language of the colored preacher always produces laughter among the whites, while the colored auditors, who do not see the deformity, never dream of smiling.

I heard a sermon once from a dear, good old clergyman, who had once been a slave in Maryland. I remember the old man started off with these words:

"I takes my tex' dis maunin', bredrin', from dat po'tion ob de scripter whar de Postol Paul p'ints his pistol to de Fenians."

"Why, bress yer soul, young men," he continued, "I'ze got an' ol' mudder, an' I hab to do fo' her, ye see, an' ef I don't buy her shoes an' stockin's she don't get none. Now, ef I war to get married, young men, I'd hab to buy des fings for my wife, an' dat would be taking de shoes and stockin's *right out o' my mudder's mouf.*"

Dora.

CHARLES DICKENS.

Dora and I were engaged. Being poor, I felt it necessary the next time I went to my darling to expiate on that unfortunate drawback. I soon carried desolation into the bosom of our joys—not that I meant to do it, but that I was so full of the subject—by asking Dora, without the smallest preparation, if she could love a beggar.

"How can you ask me anything so foolish? Love a beggar!"

"Dora, my own dearest, I am a beggar!"

"How can you be such a silly thing," replied Dora, slapping my hand, "as to sit there telling such stories?"

But I looked so serious that Dora began to cry. She did nothing but exclaim, Oh, dear! Oh, dear! And Oh, she was so frightened! And where was Julia Mills? And Oh, take her to Julia Mills, and go away, please! until I was almost beside myself.

I thought I had killed her. I sprinkled water on her face; I went down on my knees; I plucked at my hair; I implored her forgiveness; I besought her to look up; I ravaged Miss Mills' work-box for a smelling-bottle, and in my agony of mind, applied an ivory needle-case, instead, and dropped all the needles over Dora.

At last I got Dora to look at me, with a horrified expression which I gradually soothed until it was only loving, and her soft, pretty cheek was lying against mine.

"Is your heart mine still, dear Dora?"

"Oh yes! Oh yes! it's all yours. Oh don't be dreadful."

"My dearest love, the crust well earned—"

"Oh, yes; but I don't want to hear any more about crusts. And after we are married, Jip must have a mutton chop every day at twelve, or he'll die."

I was charmed with her childish, winning way, and I fondly explained to her that Jip should have his mutton chop with his accustomed regularity.

Time went on, and at last, here in this hand of mine, I held the wedding license.

I doubt whether two young birds could have known less about keeping house than I and my pretty Dora did. We had a servant, of course. *She* kept house for us.

We had an awful time of it with Mary Anne.

"My dearest life," I said one day to Dora, "do you think Mary Anne has any idea of time?"

"Why, Doady?"

"My love, because it's five, and we were to have dined at four."

My little wife came and sat upon my knee, to coax me to be quiet, and drew a line with her pencil down the middle of my nose.

"You know, my love, it is not exactly comfortable to have to go out without one's dinner. Now, is it?"

"N-n-no!" replied Dora, faintly.

"My love, how you tremble?"

"Because I know you're going to scold me."

"My sweet, I am only going to reason. You must remember, I am sure, that I was obliged to go out yesterday when dinner was half over; and that the day before I was made quite unwell by being obliged to eat underdone veal in a hurry; today, I don't dine at all, and I am afraid to say how long we waited for breakfast, and then the water didn't boil. I don't mean to reproach you, my dear, but this is not comfortable."

"Oh, you cruel, cruel boy, to say I am a disagreeable wife. When you know that the other day, when you said you would like a little bit of fish, I went out myself, miles and miles, and ordered it to surprise you."

"And it was very kind of you, my own darling."

"You enjoyed it very much," sobbed Dora. "And you said I was a Mouse?"

"And I'll say so again, my love, a thousand times!"

"I am very sorry for all this, Doady," said Dora. "Will you call me a name I want you to call me?"

"What is it, my dear?"

"It's a stupid name—Child-wife. When you are going to be angry with me, say to yourself, 'It's only my Child-wife.' When I am very disappointing, say, 'I knew a long time ago, that she would make but a Child-wife.' When you miss what you would like me to be, and what I should like to be, and what I think I never can be, say, 'Still my foolish Child-wife loves me.' For indeed I do."

I invoke the innocent figure that I dearly loved to come out of the mists and shadows of the past, and to turn its gentle head towards me once again, and to bear witness that it was made happy by what I answered.

Glaucus.

BULWER LYTTON.

Stunned by his reprieve, doubting that he was awake, Glaucus had been led by the officers of the arena into a small cell within the walls of the theatre. They threw a loose robe over his form, and crowded round in congratulation and wonder. There was an impatient cry without the cell; the throng gave way, and the blind girl flung herself at the feet of Glaucus.

"It is *I* who have saved thee," she sobbed.

"Nydia, my child! my preserver!"

"Oh, let me feel thy touch! Yes, yes, thou livest! We are not too late! That dread door, methought it would never yield! and Calenus, oh it seemed hours ere food and wine restored to him something of strength. But thou livest! thou livest yet! *I* have saved thee!"

"The mountain! the earthquake!" resounded from side to side. The officers fled with the rest; Glaucus and Nydia paced swiftly up the perilous and fearful streets. The Athenian had learned that Ione was yet in the house of Arbaces. Thither he fled, to release—to save her! The few slaves whom the Egyptian had left at his mansion huddled together, stunned and frightened, and Glaucus passed on through the vast hall shouting aloud the name of Ione. At length he heard her voice in wondering reply! To rush forward— to shatter the door—to seize Ione in his arms—to hurry from the mansion—seemed to him the work of an instant!

Which way could they wend? All was rayless to them— a maze without a clew. Wearied, despondent, bewildered, they passed along, the ashes falling upon their heads, the fragmentary stones dashing up in sparkles at their feet.

"Alas! alas!" murmured Ione. "I can go no farther; my steps sink among the scorching cinders."

Advancing, as men grope for escape in a dungeon, Ione and her lover continued their uncertain way. At the moments when the volcanic lightning lingered over the streets they were enabled, by that awful light, to steer and guide their progress; yet, little did the view it presented to them cheer or encourage their path. Cinders and rock lay matted in heaps, from beneath which emerged the half-hid limbs of some crushed and mangled fugitive. The groans of the dying were broken by wild shrieks of women's terror. And ever as the winds swept howling along the street, they bore sharp streams of burning dust, and such sickening and poisonous vapors as took away, for the instant, breath and consciousness.

"Oh, Glaucus! I can go no further!"

"For my sake, for my life—courage, yet, Ione; see—torches —this way!"

The torches flashed full on the eyes of Glaucus and Ione. Several slaves were bearing, by the light, panniers and coffers, heavily laden; in front of them—a drawn sword in his hand—towered the lofty form of Arbaces.

"By my fathers!" cried the Egyptian. "Fate smiles upon me even through these horrors, and, amid the dreadest aspect of woe and death, bodes me happiness and love! Away, Greek! I claim my ward, Ione!"

"Traitor and murderer!" cried Glaucus, glaring upon his foe. "Approach—touch but the hand of Ione, and thy weapon shall be as a reed—I will tear thee limb from limb!"

"Advance slaves!—Athenian, resist me, and thy blood be on thine own head! Thus, then, I regain Ione!"

He advanced one step—it was his last on earth! The ground shook beneath him with a convulsion that cast all round upon its surface. The lightning, as if caught by the metal, lingered an instant on the imperial statue beneath which he stood—then shivered bronze and column! Down fell the ruin, echoing along the street, and riving the solid pavement where it crashed!

Glaucus caught Ione once more in his arms and fled along the street that was yet intensely luminous. But suddenly a duller shade came over the air. Instinctively he turned to the mountain, and behold! one of the two gigantic crests, into which the summit had been divided, rocked and wavered to and fro; and then, with a sound, the mightiness of which no language can describe, it fell from its burning base, and rushed, an avalanche of fire, down the sides of the mountain! At the same instant gushed forth a volume of blackest smoke—rolling on over air, sea and earth.

Glaucus, his bold heart at last quelled and despairing, sank beneath the cover of an arch of the Forum, and resigned himself to die.

Meanwhile Nydia, whose blindness rendered the scene familiar to her, had been searching for Glaucus.

She has gained the Forum—the arch; she stoops down—she feels round—and calls on the name of Glaucus.

A weak voice answers.

"Arise, follow me! Take my hand! Glaucus, thou shalt be saved."

In wonder and sudden hope, Glaucus arose. "Nydia still? Ah! thou, then, art safe!"

Half leading, half carrying Ione, Glaucus followed his guide. With admirable discretion, she sought the shore, and after many pauses and incredible perseverance, they gained the sea. And in the feeling that the worst was past, the overwearied ones turned round, and fell placidly to sleep. And the bark containing the faithful trio drifted calmly onward to safety.

VARIETIES OF PAUSE AND PROMINENCE.

[The selections under this head illustrate most of the varieties of Pause and Prominence.]

The Call to Arms.

PATRICK HENRY.

Mr. President—It is natural to man to indulge in the illusions of hope. We are apt to shut our eyes against a painful truth, and listen to the song of that siren, till she transforms us to beasts. Is this the part of wise men, engaged in a great and arduous struggle for liberty? Are we disposed to be of the number of those who, having eyes, see not, and having ears, hear not, the things which so nearly concern our temporal salvation? For my part, whatever anguish of spirit it may cost, I am willing to know the whole truth; to know the worst, and to provide for it.

I have but one lamp by which my feet are guided; and that is the lamp of experience. I know of no way of judging of the future but by the past. And judging by the past, I wish to know what there has been in the conduct of the British ministry for the last ten years, to justify those hopes with which gentlemen have been pleased to solace themselves and the House? Is it that insidious smile with which our petition has been lately received? Trust it not, sir; it will prove a snare to your feet. Suffer not yourselves to be "betrayed with a kiss!" Ask yourselves, How this gracious reception of our petition comports with those warlike preparations which cover our waters and darken our land? Are fleets and armies necessary to a work of love and reconciliation? Have we shown ourselves so unwilling to be reconciled, that force must be called in to win back our love? Let us not deceive ourselves, sir. These are the implements of war and subjugation; the last arguments to which kings resort.

I ask gentlemen, sir, what means this martial array, if its purpose be not to force us to submission? Can gentlemen assign any other possible motive for it? Has Great Britain any enemy in this quarter of the world, to call for all this accumulation of navies and armies? No, sir, she has none. They are meant for us; they can be meant for no other. They are sent over to bind and to rivet upon us those chains which the British ministry have been so long forging. And what have we to oppose to them? Shall we try argument? Sir, we have been trying that for the last ten years. Have we anything new to offer upon the subject? Nothing. We have held the subject up in every light of which it is capable; but it has been all in vain. Shall we resort to entreaty and humble supplication? What terms shall we find which have not been already exhausted? Let us not, I beseech you, sir, deceive ourselves longer. Sir, we have done everything that could be done, to avert the storm which is now coming on. We have petitioned, we have remonstrated, we have supplicated, we have prostrated ourselves before the throne, and have implored its interposition to arrest the tyrannical hands of the ministry and parliament. Our petitions have been slighted; our remonstrances have produced additional violence and insult; our supplications have been disregarded; and we have been spurned with contempt from the foot of the throne. In vain, after these things, may we indulge the fond hope of peace and reconciliation. There is no longer any room for hope. If we wish to be free, if we mean to preserve inviolate those inestimable privileges for which we have been so long contending; if we mean not basely to abandon the noble struggle in which we have been so long engaged, and which we have pledged ourselves never to abandon until the glorious object of our contest shall be obtained, we must fight; I repeat it, sir, we must fight! An appeal to arms, and to the God of Hosts, is all that is left us!

They tell us, sir, that we are weak—"unable to cope with so formidable an adversary!" But when shall we be stronger? Will it be the next week, or the next year? Will it be when we are totally disarmed, and when a British guard shall be stationed in every house? Shall we gather strength by irresolution and inaction? Shall we acquire the means of effectual resistance, by lying supinely on our backs, and hugging the delusive phantom of hope, until our enemies have bound us hand and foot? Sir, we are not weak, if we make a proper use of those means which the God of Nature hath placed in our power. Three millions of people, armed in the holy cause of Liberty, and in such a country as that which we possess, are invincible by any force which our enemy can send against us. Besides, sir, we shall not fight our battles alone. There is a just Power who presides over the destinies of nations, and who will raise up friends to fight our battles for us. The battle, sir, is not to the strong alone; it is to the vigilant, the active, the brave. Besides, sir, we have no election. If we were base enough to desire it, it is now too late to retire from the contest. There is no retreat, but in submission and slavery. Our chains are forged. Their clanking may be heard on the plains of Boston. The war is inevitable; and let it come! I repeat, sir, let it come! It is in vain, sir, to extenuate the matter. Gentlemen may cry, "Peace, peace!" but there is no peace! The war is actually begun! The next gale that sweeps from the north will bring to our ears the clash of resounding arms! Our brethren are already in the field! Why stand we here idle? What is it that gentle-

men wish? What would they have? Is life so dear, or peace
so sweet, as to be purchased at the price of chains and slavery?
Forbid it, Almighty God!—I know not what course others
may take; but as for me, give me liberty, or give me death!

Cassius Instigating Brutus.

WILLIAM SHAKESPEARE.

Well, honour is the subject of my story.
I cannot tell what you and other men
Think of this life, but, for my single self,
I had as lief not be as live to be
In awe of such a thing as I myself.
I was born free as Cæsar; so were you:
We both have fed as well, and we can both
Endure the winter's cold as well as he:
For once, upon a raw and gusty day,
The troubled Tiber chafing with her shores,
Cæsar said to me, "Darest thou, Cassius, now
Leap in with me into this angry flood,
And swim to yonder point?" Upon the word,
Accoutred as I was, I plunged in
And bade him follow: so indeed he did.
The torrent roar'd, and we did buffet it
With lusty sinews, throwing it aside
And stemming it with hearts of controversy;
But ere we could arrive the point proposed,
Cæsar cried, "Help me, Cassius, or I sink!"
I, as Æneas our great ancestor
Did from the flames of Troy upon his shoulder
The old Anchises bear, so from the waves of Tiber
Did I the tired Cæsar: and this man
Is now become a god, and Cassius is
A wretched creature, and must bend his body
If Cæsar carelessly but nod on him.

He had a fever when he was in Spain,
And when the fit was on him, I did mark
How he did shake: 'tis true, this god did shake;
His coward lips did from their colour fly,
And that same eye whose bend doth awe the world
Did lose his lustre: I did hear him groan:
Ay, and that tongue of his that bade the Romans
Mark him and write his speeches in their books,
Alas, it cried, "Give me some drink, Titinius,"
As a sick girl. Ye gods! it doth amaze me
A man of such a feeble temper should
So get the start of the majestic world
And bear the palm alone.
Why, man, he doth bestride the narrow world
Like a Colossus, and we petty men
Walk under his huge legs and peep about
To find ourselves dishonorable graves.
Men at some time are masters of their fates:
The fault, dear Brutus, is not in our stars,
But in ourselves, that we are underlings.
Brutus, and Cæsar: what should be in that Cæsar?
Why should that name be sounded more than yours?
Write them together, yours is as fair a name;
Sound them, it doth become the mouth as well;
Weigh them, it is as heavy; conjure with 'em,
Brutus will start a spirit as soon as Cæsar.
Now, in the names of all the gods at once,
Upon what meat doth this our Cæsar feed,
That he is grown so great? Age, thou art shamed!
Rome, thou hast lost the breed of noble bloods!
When went there by an age, since the great flood,
But it was famed with more than with one man?
When could they say till now that talk'd of Rome
That her wide walls encompass'd but one man?

Now is it Rome indeed, and room enough,
When there is in it but one only man.
O, you and I have heard our fathers say
There was a Brutus once that would have brook'd
The eternal devil to keep his state in Rome
As easily as a king.

Julius Cæsar, I, 2.

The Dead Heroes.

ROBERT G. INGERSOLL.

As we cover the graves of the heroic dead with flowers the past rises before us like a dream. Again we are in the great struggle. We hear the sounds of preparation—the music of the boisterous drums—the silver voices of heroic bugles. We hear the appeals of orators; we see the pale cheeks of women, and the flushed faces of men; we see all the dead whose dust we have covered with flowers. We lose sight of them no more. We are with them when they enlist in the great army of freedom. We see them part from those they love. Some are walking for the last time in the quiet woody places with the maidens they adore. We hear the whispers and the sweet vows of eternal love as they lingeringly part forever. Others are bending over cradles kissing babies that are asleep. Some are receiving the blessings of old men. Some are parting from mothers who hold them and press them to their hearts again and again, and say nothing; and some are talking with wives, and trying with brave words spoken in the old tones to drive from their hearts the awful fear. We see them part. We see the wife standing in the door with the babe in her arms—standing in the sunlight sobbing; at the turn of the road a hand waves—she answers by holding high in her loving arms the child. He is gone and forever.

We see them all as they march proudly away, under the flaunting flags, keeping time to the wild music of war—

marching down the streets of the great cities, through the towns and across the prairies, to do and to die for the eternal right. We go with them, one and all. We are by their side on all the gory fields, in all the hospitals of pain, on all the weary marches. We stand guard with them in the wild storm and under the quiet stars. We are with them in ravines running with blood, in the furrows of old fields. We are with them between contending hosts, unable to move, wild with thirst, the life ebbing slowly away among the withered leaves. We see them pierced with balls and torn by shells in the trenches by the forts and in the whirlwind of the charge, where men become iron with nerves of steel. We are at home when the news reaches us that they are dead. We see the maiden in the shadow of her first sorrow. We see the silvered head of the old man bowed with the last grief.

Those heroes are dead. They sleep under the solemn pines, the sad hemlocks, the tearful willows, and the embracing vines. They sleep beneath the shadows of the clouds, careless alike of the sunshine or of storm, each in the windowless place of rest. Earth may run red with other wars—they are at peace. In the midst of battle, in the roar of the conflict, they found the serenity of death.

The Ocean.

LORD BYRON.

Roll on, thou deep and dark blue Ocean—roll!
   Ten thousand fleets sweep over thee in vain;
Man marks the earth with ruin—his control
    Stops with the shore;—upon the watery plain
    The wrecks are all thy deed, nor doth remain
A shadow of man's ravage, save his own,
   When, for a moment, like a drop of rain,
He sinks into thy depths with bubbling groan,
Without a grave, unknelled, uncoffined, and unknown.

His steps are not upon thy paths,—thy fields
  Are not a spoil for him,—thou dost arise
And shake him from thee; the vile strength he wields
  For earth's destruction thou dost all despise,
  Spurning him from thy bosom to the skies,
And send'st him, shivering in thy playful spray
  And howling, to his gods, where haply lies
His petty hope in some near port or bay,
And dashest him again to earth:—there let him lay.

The armaments which thunderstrike the walls
  Of rock-built cities, bidding nations quake,
And monarchs tremble in their capitals,
  The oak leviathans, whose huge ribs make
  Their clay creator the vain title take
Of lord of thee, and arbiter of war;
  These are thy toys, and, as the snowy flake,
They melt into thy yeast of waves, which mar
Alike the Armada's pride or spoils of Trafalgar

Thy shores are empires, changed in all save thee—
  Assyria, Greece, Rome, Carthage, what are they?
Thy waters washed them power while they were free,
  And many a tyrant since; their shores obey
  The stranger, slave, or savage; their decay
Has dried up realms to deserts:—not so thou;—
  Unchangeable save to thy wild waves' play—
Time writes no wrinkle on thine azure brow—
Such as creation's dawn beheld, thou rollest now.

Thou glorious mirror, where the Almighty's form
  Glasses itself in tempest; in all time,
Calm or convulsed—in breeze, or gale, or storm,
  Icing the pole, or in the torrid clime

Dark-heaving;—boundless, endless, and sublime—
The image of Eternity—the throne
　Of the Invisible; even from out thy slime
The monsters of the deep are made; each zone
Obeys thee: thou goest forth, dread, fathomless, alone.

And I have loved thee, Ocean! and my joy
　Of youthful sports was on thy breast to be
Borne, like thy bubbles, onward: from a boy
　I wantoned with thy breakers—they to me
　Were a delight; and if the freshening sea
Made them a terror—'twas a pleasing fear,
　For I was as it were a child of thee,
And trusted to thy billows far and near,
And laid my hand upon thy mane—as I do here.

Speech on the Overtures of Bonaparte.

CHARLES JAMES FOX.

Where, then, sir, is this war, which on every side is pregnant with such horrors, to be carried? Where is it to stop?
One campaign is successful to *you;* another to *them;* and,
in this way, animated by the vindictive passions of revenge,
hatred, and rancor, which are infinitely more flagitious, even,
than those of ambition and the thirst of power, you may
go on forever; as, with such black incentives, I see no end
to human misery.

And all this without an intelligible motive. All this
because you may gain a better peace a year or two hence!
So that we are called upon to go on merely, as a *speculation!*
We must keep Bonaparte for some time longer at war, as
a state of *probation!* Gracious God! sir, is *war* a state of
probation? Is peace a rash system? Is it dangerous for
nations to live in amity with each other? Are your vigilance,

your policy, your common powers of observation, to be extinguished by putting an end to the horrors of war? Can not this state of probation be as well undergone without adding to the catalogue of human sufferings?

"But we must *pause!*" What! must the bowels of Great Britain be torn out—her best blood be spilled—her treasure wasted—that you may make an *experiment?* Put yourselves, oh! that you *would* put yourselves in the field of battle, and learn to judge of the sort of horrors that you excite! In former wars, a man might, at least, have some feeling, some interest, that served to balance, in his mind, the impressions which a scene of carnage and of death must inflict.

If a man had been present at the battle of Blenheim, for instance, and had inquired the motive of the battle, there was not a soldier engaged who could not have satisfied his curiosity, and even, perhaps, allayed his feelings. They were fighting, they knew, to repress the uncontrolled ambition of the Grand Monarch.

But, if a man were present now at a field of slaughter, and were to inquire for what they were fighting—*"Fighting!"* would be the answer; "they are not fighting; they are *pausing.*" "Why is that man expiring? Why is the other writhing with agony? What means this implacable fury?" The answer must be,—"You are quite wrong, sir; you deceive yourself—they are not *fighting*—do not disturb them—they are merely *pausing!*

"This man is not expiring with agony—that man is not dead—he is only *pausing!* Lord help you, sir! they are not angry with one another; they have now no cause of quarrel, but their country thinks there should be a *pause!* All that you see, sir, is nothing like fighting—there is no harm, nor bloodshed in it whatever: it is nothing more than a *political pause!* It is merely to try an experiment—to see whether

Bonaparte will not *behave* himself better than heretofore; and, in the meantime, we have agreed to a *pause* in pure friendship!"

And is this the way, sir, that you are to show yourselves the advocates of order? You take up a system calculated to uncivilize the world—to destroy order—to trample on religion—to stifle, in the heart, not merely the generosity of noble sentiment, but the affections of social nature; and, in the prosecution of this system, you spread terror and devastation all around you.

A Tragedy.

T. D. TALMAGE.

How many acts are there in a tragedy? Five, I believe.

Act I.—Young man starting from home. Parents and sisters weeping to see him go. Wagon passing over the hill. Farewell kiss thrown back.

Act II.—Marriage altar. Bright lights. Full organ. White veil trailing through the aisle. Prayer and congratulations, and exclamations of "How well she looks!"

Act III.—Midnight. Woman waiting for staggering steps. Old garments stuck into broken window panes. Many marks of hardship on the face. Biting the nails of bloodless fingers. Neglect, cruelty, disgrace.

Act IV.—Three graves in a very dark place. Grave of a child, who died from want of medicine; grave of husband and father, who died of dissipation; grave of wife and mother, who died of a broken heart. Plenty of weeds but no flowers! Oh! what a blasted heath, with three graves!

Act V.—A destroyed soul's eternity. No light; no music; no hope! Despair coiling around the heart with unutterable anguish. Blackness of darkness forever! Woe! woe! woe! I cannot bear longer to look. I close my eyes at this last act of the tragedy.

Napoleon Bonaparte.

CHARLES PHILLIPS.

He is fallen! We may now pause before that splendid prodigy, which towered amongst us like some ancient ruin, whose frown terrified the glance its magnificence attracted. Grand, gloomy, and peculiar, he sat upon the throne, a sceptered hermit, wrapped in the solitude of his own originality. A mind bold, independent, and decisive—a will, despotic in its dictates—an energy that distanced expedition, and a conscience pliable to every touch of interest, marked the outline of this extraordinary character—the most extraordinary, perhaps, that, in the annals of the world, ever rose, or reigned, or fell.

Flung into life in the midst of a Revolution that quickened every energy of a people who acknowledged no superior, he commenced his course a stranger by birth and a scholar by charity. With no friend but his sword, and no fortune but his talents, he rushed into the lists where rank and genius had arrayed themselves; and competition fled from him as from the glance of destiny. He knew no motive but interest—he acknowledged no criterion but success—he worshiped no God but ambition; and with an Eastern devotion he knelt at the altar of his idolatry. Subsidiary to this, there was no creed that he did not profess—there was no opinion that he did not promulgate. In the hope of a dynasty, he upheld the Crescent; for the sake of a divorce, he bowed before the Cross; the orphan of St. Louis, he became the adopted child of the Republic; and, with a parricidal ingratitude, on the ruins both of the crown and the tribune, he reared the throne of his despotism. A professed Catholic, he imprisoned the Pope; a pretended patriot, he impoverished the country; and under the name of Brutus, he grasped without remorse, and wore without shame, the diadem of the Cæsars!

The gaoler of the press, he affected the patronage of letters; the proscriber of books, he encouraged philosophy; the persecutor of authors, and the murderer of printers, he yet pretended to the patronage of learning. Such a medley of contradictions, and at the same time such an individual consistency, were never united in the same character. A royalist, a republican, and an emperor—a Mahometan, a Catholic, and a patron of the Synagogue—a traitor and a tyrant—a Christian and an Infidel—he was, through all his vicissitudes, the same stern, impatient, inflexible original—the same mysterious, incomprehensible self—the man without a model, and without a shadow. His fall, like his life, baffled all speculation. In short, his whole history was like a dream to the world; and no man can tell how or why he was awakened from the reverie.

Supposed Speech of John Adams.

DANIEL WEBSTER.

"Sink or swim, live or die, survive or perish, I give my hand and my heart to this vote. It is true, indeed, that in the beginning we aimed not at independence. But there's a divinity that shapes our ends. The injustice of England has driven us to arms; and, blinded to her own interest, for our good, she has obstinately persisted, till independence is now within our grasp. We have but to reach forth to it, and it is ours. Why, then, should we defer the declaration? Is any man so weak as now to hope for a reconciliation with England, which shall leave either safety to the country and its liberties, or safety to his own life and his own honor? Are not you, sir, who sit in that chair—is not he, our venerable colleague near you—are you not both already the proscribed and predestined objects of punishment and of vengeance? Cut off from all hope of royal clemency, what are you, what can you be, while the power of England remains, but outlaws? If we postpone independence, do we mean to carry on, or to give up, the war? Do we mean to submit to the measures of Parliament, Boston port bill and all? Do we mean to submit, and consent that we ourselves shall be ground to powder, and our country and its rights trodden down in the dust? I know we do not mean to submit. We never shall submit. Do we intend to violate that most solemn obligation ever entered into by men—that plighting, before God, of our sacred honor to Washington, when, putting him forth to incur the dangers of war, as well as the political hazards of the times, we promised to adhere to him in every extremity with our fortunes and our lives? I know there is not a man here who would not rather see a general conflagration sweep over the land, or an earthquake sink it, than one jot or tittle of that plighted faith fall to the ground. For myself, having, twelve months ago in this place, moved you, that George Washington be appointed commander of the forces, raised or to be raised, for defense of American liberty, may my right hand forget her cunning and my tongue cleave to the roof of my mouth, if I hesitate or waver in the support I give him. The war, then, must go on. We must fight it through. And, if the war must go on, why put off longer the declaration of independence?

"Read this declaration at the head of the army; every sword will be drawn from its scabbard, and the solemn vow uttered, to maintain it, or perish on the bed of honor. Publish it from the pulpit; religion will approve it, and the love of religious liberty will cling round it, resolved to stand with it, or fall with it. Send it to the public halls; proclaim it there; let them hear it, who heard the first roar of the enemy's cannon; let them see it, who saw their brothers and their sons fall on the field of Bunker Hill, and in the streets of Lexington and Concord, and the very walls will cry out in its support.

"Sir, I know the uncertainty of human affairs, but I see, I see clearly, through this day's business. You and I, indeed, may rue it. We may not live to the time when this declaration shall be made good. We may die; die, colonists; die, slaves; die, it may be, ignominiously and on the scaffold. Be it so. Be it so. If it be the pleasure of Heaven that my country shall require the poor offering of my life, the victim shall be ready, at the appointed hour of sacrifice, come when that hour may. But, while I do live, let me have a country, or at least the hope of a country, and that a free country.

"But, whatever may be our fate, be assured, be assured, that this declaration will stand. It may cost treasure, and it may cost blood; but it will stand, and it will richly compensate for both. Through the thick gloom of the present I see the brightness of the future as the sun in heaven. We shall make this a glorious, an immortal day. When we are in our graves, our children will honor it. They will celebrate it with thanksgiving, with festivity, with bonfires and illuminations. On its annual return they will shed tears, copious, gushing tears, not of subjection and slavery, not of agony and distress, but of exultation, of gratitude, and of joy. Sir, before God, I believe the hour has come. My judgment approves this measure, and my whole heart is in it. All that I have, and all that I am, and all that I hope, in this life, I am now ready here to stake upon it; and I leave off, as I began, that, live or die, survive or perish, I am for the declaration. It is my living sentiment, and, by the blessing of God, it shall be my dying sentiment; independence now, and independence forever."

EXPRESSION AND THE GENERAL ENDS OF SPEECH.

In speech there are five General Ends. We talk to have something seen—Clearness, or felt—Impressiveness, or accepted—Belief, or done—Action, or enjoyed—Entertainment, or we have in view a combination of these Ends.

Expression is influenced by these Ends. If the General End is Clearness, the delivery should be intellectual, avoiding the emotional. If the General End is Impressiveness the delivery should aim to convey feeling. When the General End is Belief the delivery should be characterized by sincerity and earnestness. If the End is Action there not only should be earnestness, but, at times, a pleading or urging. If Entertainment is the General End stress should be laid upon variety in delivery. The following selections illustrate the General Ends:

CLEARNESS.
The Barometer.

NEIL ARNOTT.

Galileo had found that water would rise under the piston of a pump to a height only of about thirty-four feet. His pupil, Torricelli, conceiving the happy thought, that the weight of the atmosphere might be the cause of the ascent, concluded that mercury, which is about thirteen times heavier than water, should only rise, under the same influence, to a thirteenth of the elevation:—he tried, and found that this was so, and the mercurial barometer was invented. To afford further evidence that the weight of the atmosphere was the cause of the phenomenon, he afterwards carried the tube of mercury to the tops of buildings and of mountains, and found that it fell away in exact proportion to the portion of the atmosphere left below it; and he found that water-pumps in different situations varied as to sucking power, according to the same law.

It was soon afterwards discovered, by careful observation of the mercurial barometer, that even when remaining in the same place, it did not always stand at the same elevation; in other words, that the weight of atmosphere over any particular part of the earth was constantly fluctuating; a truth which, without the barometer, could never have been suspected. The observation of the instrument being carried still further, it was found that in serene, dry weather, the mercury generally stood high, and that before and during storms and rain it fell; the instrument, therefore, might serve as a prophet of the weather, becoming a precious monitor to the husbandman or the sailor.

The reason why the barometer falls before wind and rain is that when water which has been suspended in the atmosphere, and has formed a part of it, separates as rain, the weight and bulk of the mass are diminished; and that wind must occur when a sudden condensation of aeriform matter, in any situation, disturbs the equilibrium of the air, for the air around will rush towards the situation of diminished pressure.

IMPRESSIVENESS.

Doom of the Indians.

JOSEPH STORY.

There is in the fate of these unfortunate beings, much to awaken our sympathy, and much to disturb the sobriety of our judgment; much which may be urged to excuse their own atrocities; much in their characters, which betrays us into an involuntary admiration. What can be more melancholy than their history? By a law of their nature, they seem destined to a slow, but sure extinction. Everywhere, at the approach of the white man, they fade away. We hear the rustling of their footsteps, like that of the withered leaves of autumn, and they are gone forever. They pass mournfully by us, and they return no more. Two centuries ago, the smoke of their wigwams and the fires of their councils rose in every valley, from Hudson's Bay to the farthest Florida, from the ocean to the Mississippi and the lakes. The shouts of victory and the war dance rang through the mountains and the glades. The thick arrows and the deadly tomahawk whistled through the forests; and the hunter's trace and dark encampment startled the wild beasts in their lairs. The warriors stood forth in their glory. The young listened to the songs of other days. The mothers played with their infants, and gazed on the scene with warm hopes of the future. The aged sat down; but they wept not. They should soon be at rest in fairer regions, where the Great Spirit dwelt, in a home prepared for the brave, beyond the western skies. Braver men never lived; truer men never drew the bow. They had courage, and fortitude, and sagacity, and perseverance, beyond most of the human race. They shrank from no dangers, and they feared no hardships. If they had the vices of savage life, they had the virtues also. They were true to their country, their friends, and their homes. If they forgave not injury, neither did they forget kindness. If their vengeance was terrible, their fidelity and generosity were unconquerable also. Their love, like their hate, stopped not on this side of the grave.

But where are they? Where are the villagers, and warriors, and youth; the Sachems and their tribes; the hunters and their families? They have perished. They are consumed. The wasting pestilence has not alone done the mighty work. No,—nor famine, nor war. There has been a mighty power, a moral canker, which has eaten into their heart-cores—a plague, which the touch of the white man communicated—a poison, which betrayed them into a lingering ruin. The winds of the Atlantic fan not a single region, which they may now call their own. Already the last feeble remnants of the race are preparing for their journey beyond the Mississippi. I see them leave their miserable homes, the aged, the helpless, the women, and the warriors, "few and faint, yet fearless still." The ashes are cold on their native hearths. The smoke no longer curls round their lowly cabins. They move on with a slow, unsteady step. The white man is upon their heels, for terror, or despatch, but they heed him not. They turn to take a last look of their deserted villages. They cast a last glance upon the graves of their fathers. They shed no tears; they utter no cries; they heave no groans. There is something in their hearts which passes speech. There is something in their looks, not of vengeance or submission; but of hard necessity, which stifles both; which chokes all utterance; which has no aim or method. It is courage absorbed in despair. They linger but for a moment. Their look is onward. They have passed the fatal stream. It shall never be repassed by them,—no, never. Yet there lies not between us and them an impassable gulf. They know and feel that there is for them still one remove further, not distant, nor unseen. It is the general burial-ground of their race.

BELIEF.
The Sword.

T. S. GRIMKE.

To the question, "what have the people ever gained but by revolution?" I answer, boldly, If by revolution be understood the law of the Sword, Liberty has lost far more than she has ever gained by it. The Sword was the destroyer of the Lycian Confederacy and the Achæan league. The Sword alternately enslaved and disenthralled Thebes and Athens, Sparta, Syracuse and Corinth. The Sword of Rome conquered every other free State, and finished the murder of liberty in the ancient world, by destroying herself. What but the Sword, in modern times, annihilated the Republics of Italy, the Hanseatic towns, and the primitive independence of Ireland, Wales and Scotland? What but the Sword partitioned Poland, assassinated the rising liberty of Spain, banished the Huguenots from France, and made Cromwell the master, not the servant, of the people? And what but the Sword of Republican France destroyed the independence of half of Europe, deluged the continent with tears, devoured its millions upon millions, and closed the long catalogue of guilt, by founding and defending to the last the most powerful, selfish, and insatiable of military despotisms?

The Sword, indeed, delivered Greece from the Persian invaders, expelled the Tarquins from Rome, emancipated Switzerland and Holland, restored the Bruce to his throne, and brought Charles to the scaffold. And the Sword redeemed the pledge of the Congress of '76, when they plighted to each other "their lives, their fortunes, and their sacred honor." And yet, what would the redemption of that pledge have availed towards the establishment of our present government, if the spirit of American institutions had not been both the birthright and the birth-blessing of the colonies? The Indians, the French, the Spaniards, and even England herself, warred in vain against a people, born and bred in the household, at the domestic altar, of Liberty herself. They had never been slaves, for they were born free. The Sword was a herald to proclaim their freedom, but it neither created nor preserved it. A century and a half had already beheld them free in infancy, free in youth, free in early manhood. Theirs was already the spirit of American institutions; the spirit of Christian freedom, of a temperate, regulated freedom, of a rational civil obedience. For such a people, the Sword, the law of violence, did and could do nothing, but sever the bonds which bound her colonial wards to their unnatural guardian. They redeemed their pledge, Sword in hand; but the Sword left them as it found them, unchanged in character,—freemen in thought and in deed, instinct with the immortal spirit of American institutions!

ACTION.

To the Young Men of Italy.

GUISEPPE MAZZINI.

Could Attilio and Emilio Bandiéra, and their fellow-martyrs, now arise from the grave and speak to you, they would, believe me, address you, though with a power very different from that given to me, in counsel not unlike that which now I utter.

Love! Love is the flight of the soul towards God; towards the great, the sublime, and the beautiful, which are the shadow of God upon earth. Love your family; the partner of your life; those around you, ready to share your joys and sorrows; the dead, who were dear to you, and to whom you were dear. Love your country. It is your name, your glory, your sign among the people. Give to it your thought, your counsel, your blood. You are twenty-four millions of men, endowed with active, splendid faculties; with a tradition of glory, the envy of the nations of Europe; an immense future is before you,—your eyes are raised to the loveliest Heaven, and around you smiles the loveliest land in Europe; you are encircled by the Alps and the sea, boundaries marked out by the finger of God for a people of giants. And you must be such, or nothing. Let not a man of that twenty-four millions remain excluded from the fraternal bond which shall join you together; let not a look be raised to that Heaven, which is not that of a free man. Love humanity. You can only ascertain your own mission from the aim placed by God before humanity at large. Beyond the Alps, beyond the sea, are other peoples, now fighting, or preparing to fight, the holy fight of independence, of nationality, of liberty; other peoples striving by different routes to reach the same goal. Unite with them,—they will unite with you.

And love, young men, love and reverence the Ideal; it is the country of the spirit, the city of the soul, in which all are brethren who believe in the inviolability of thought, and in the dignity of our immortal natures. From that high sphere spring the *principles* which alone can redeem the peoples. Love enthusiasm,—the pure dreams of the virgin soul, and the lofty visions of early youth; for they are the perfume of Paradise, which the soul preserves in issuing from the hands of its Creator. Respect, above all things, your conscience; have upon your lips the truth that God has placed in your hearts; and, while working together in harmony in all that tends to the emancipation of our soil, even with those who differ from you, yet ever bear erect your own banner, and boldly promulgate your faith.

Such words, young men, would the martyrs of Cosenza have spoken, had they been living amongst you. And here, where, perhaps, invoked by our love, their holy spirits hover near us, I call upon you to gather them up in your hearts, and to make of them a treasure amid the storms that yet threaten you; but which, with the name of our martyrs on your lips, and their faith in your hearts, you will overcome.

ENTERTAINMENT.

Supposing.

HELEN WAITHMAN.

They met beneath a tree and lingered talking,
   Her eyes were very sweet and clear and blue;
He said, "Supposing we continue walking,
   For I should like so much to talk to you."
She answered with a blush and softly smiling,
   "Supposing—we—supposing that we do."

He said, "If I should tell you that I love you,
   Have loved you long and tenderly and true,
Supposing—I am only just supposing—
   That you for answer said, 'I love you too?'"
The answer came softly through the twilight,
   "Supposing—ah—supposing that I do?"

He said, "If I should ask you for a kiss dear,
   And were not quite content with one or two,
I wonder, would you take it much amiss, dear—
   Supposing, pretty sweetheart, that I do?"
The answer, like echo of a whisper—
   "Supposing—oh—supposing that you do."

INDEX OF SELECTIONS

INDEX OF AUTHORS

INDEX OF SELECTIONS FROM SHAKESPEARE

EFFECTIVE SPEAKING

BY ARTHUR EDWARD PHILLIPS, Author of "Natural Drills in Expression,"
etc., Director, Department of Public Speaking, the Theological Seminary of the Evangelical
Lutheran Church at Chicago ; Principal, Phillips School of Oratory, Chicago

---

THIS WORK IS AN EXPOSITION OF THE LAWS OF EFFECTIVENESS IN THE
CHOICE OF MATERIAL IN SPEECH WITH EXAMPLES AND EXERCISES. IT HAS
BEEN ADOPTED BY REPRESENTATIVE SCHOOLS AND COLLEGES THROUGHOUT
THE NATION

"In 'Effective Speaking,' a practical classroom textbook by Arthur Edward Phillips, the problem of a book that will meet the demands of the student has been solved.

" 'Effective Speaking' presents practically the essentials of effectiveness in all departments of speaking, whether it be impressiveness, entertainment, convincingness, or persuasion. The training of the judgment in the use of the psychological principles that govern success in speech has been the aim of Mr. Phillips. The book is in no way experimental, since all the principles advanced have been applied by the author in his professional work and by the student and man of affairs. Even for those not directly interested in the work of public speaking, the reading of the volume, aside from the exercises, is of interest.''—*Chicago Journal.*

" 'Effective Speaking' is the first practical classroom textbook on how to prepare and make an effective address. Mr. Phillips' work is destined to replace every other textbook on the subject in every progressive teacher's classroom.—*S. H. Clark, Professor of Public Speaking, University of Chicago.*

" 'Effective Speaking' is a real contribution to the literature of the subject. It is, I think, the most unique analysis of Public Speaking since the time of Quintilian.—*H. B. Gislason, Instructor in Debate and Oratory, University of Minnesota.*

" 'Effective Speaking' is an admirable book in every way.''— *E. W. Smith, Department of Rhetoric and Public Speaking, Colgate University.*

THE NEWTON COMPANY
CHICAGO